THE GREAT TERROR WAR

THE GREAT TERROR WAR

RICHARD FALK

OLIVE
BRANCH
PRESS

An imprint of Interlink Publishing Group, Inc.
New York • Northampton

This edition first published in 2003 by

OLIVE BRANCH PRESS
An imprint of Interlink Publishing Group, Inc.
99 Seventh Avenue • Brooklyn, New York 11215 and
46 Crosby Street • Northampton, Massachusetts 01060
www.interlinkbooks.com

Library of Congress Cataloging-in-Publication Data

Falk, Richard A.
  The great terror war / by Richard Falk.
    p. cm.
Includes bibliographical references and index.
  ISBN 1-56656-460-3
  1. Terrorism—Prevention—Government policy—United States.
  2. September 11 Terrorist Attacks, 2001. 3. War on Terrorism, 2001-
  4. War (International law) 5. Intervention (International law) I. Title.
  HV6432 .F34 2002
  973.931--dc21

                                                    2002008389

To request our complete 40-page full-color catalog,
please call us toll free at **1-800-238-LINK**, visit our
website at **www.interlinkbooks.com**, or write to
Interlink Publishing
46 Crosby Street, Northampton, MA 01060
e-mail: info@interlinkbooks.com

FOR HILAL

This moon
that criss crosses
my heart
never never
wanes and never
chooses the obscurity
of clouds

CONTENTS

Acknowledgements viii
Introduction xi

1.	Winning and Losing the War Against Global Terror	1
2.	The Dimensions of Megaterrorism	38
3.	Appraising the Afghanistan War	61
4.	The US Government's World-Order Argument	73
5.	Wrecking World Order	82
6.	Challenging the New Patriotism	129
7.	The Eclipse of Human Rights	147
8.	Facing the Future	173

Notes 191
Index 197

ACKNOWLEDGEMENTS

A book of this sort is particularly dependent on the historical and human contexts of its composition. Rarely has an event exerted such leverage on the collective imagination of a society as did the attacks of September 11. The mere fact that we can find no better descriptive language for their occurrence than the date is itself an expression of our mental unpreparedness for what in this book I call "megaterrorism," to diffentiate it sharply from prior experiences of terrorism.

This whole project owes its reality to the energy, wit, and persistence of my friend and colleague, Phyllis Bennis, who long before September 11 had exhibited heroic patience in waiting for my delivery of a manuscript devoted to terrorism, which was originally intended as a sequel to my 1988 book, *Revolutionaries and Functionaries: The Dual Face of Terrorism.* The main argument of that book was an insistence on depolemicizing the use of the term terrorism that arose from its exclusive application by the US government, and some other important states, to taint with utter criminality anti-state political violence. To align the idea of terrorism with the facts of political life meant to me that first and foremost one had to conceive of terrorism as also encompassing state violence that was deliberately directed at civilians and their basic life-support systems, and was often the provocation and efficient cause of anti-state violence. After September 11, I finally felt ready to resume the thread of the earlier argument under the greatly altered world conditions of the early twenty-first century. At this point, despite my years of resistance, I am finally ready to thank Phyllis profusely for leading me in these directions, hoping that she is not disappointed, and certainly not holding her responsible for what I have managed to write in these pages.

My thinking about terrorism, religion, and Islam were very much shaped by two extraordinary visits to Iran in the midst of its revolutionary turmoil in 1979–1980, and the opportunity to meet many of the new leaders, as well as to observe the rapid transition from revolutionary promise to disillusionment. On the first of these trips, during which the Shah went into dramatic exile and we met with Ayatollah Khomeini on his last day in Paris before his triumphal return to Iran, I was accompanied by two exceptional individuals who enriched and illuminated the experience in many ways: Ramsey Clark and Don Luce. On the second trip, in the midst of the hostage crisis, I traveled with Eqbal Ahmad, a dear friend and a brilliant interpreter of the themes in this book, from whom I learned much over the course of more than three decades. His death in 1999 was an agonizing personal loss, as well as a great setback for all of us who are trying to understand the bewildering course of recent world history.

My views on these matters were also shaped by the experience of serving on two international commissions in recent years that touched on terrorism in fundamental respects: the Independent International Commission on Kosovo (1999–2001) and the Human Rights Inquiry Commission (of the UN Human Rights Commission) on the Palestinian Territories (2001). I learned much from my colleagues in both of these experiences, and worked especially closely with John Dugard and Kamal Hussein in our attempt to come to terms with the tormented relationship between the second intifada and international humanitarian law.

In this period, through discussion and friendship, I have clarified my thinking about this unexpectedly traumatic sequel to the cold war, with many wonderful persons. I name a few who were especially influential: Asli Bali, Michael Doyle, Robert Gilpin, David Griffin, Abdullah Hammoudi, Mary Kaldor, David Krieger, Maivan Clêch Lam, Stephen Macedo, Saul Mendlovitz, Zia Mian, Chandra Muzaffar, Eric Rouleau, Edward Said, Peter Singer, Andrew Strauss, Carl Tham, Burns Weston, and Susan Wright.

I also want to thank Katrina vanden Heuvel and her colleagues at *The Nation* for inviting my commentary on the evolving American response to September 11. I believe this magazine more than any other I knew sustained its integrity and enhanced its relevance in a difficult time, neither succumbing to ultra-nationalism nor indulging diversionary exercises in America-bashing.

I owe a big debt of gratitude to Pam Thompson for being such a talented and supportive editor, saving me from many lapses in judgment, while being unfailingly warm-spirited.

And finally, I thank my wife, Hilal Elver, who has been a constant and loving presence throughout this process, enduring with a smile the inevitable sense of preoccupation that arises in such an undertaking.

In the end, of course, I have no one to blame but myself for the pages that follow.

INTRODUCTION

I t was inevitable that a tidal wave of interpretations of September 11, and of the unfolding American response, would find their way into print. This one comes from a progressive generally opposed to the foreign policy of the US government—to the wide political spectrum that stretches from initiatives of liberal Democrats to iron-fisted approaches of reactionary Republicans. My opposition is practically without exception when it comes to the overseas use of force by the United States during the last half-century, including this country's reliance on the threat of using nuclear weaponry and our interventionary diplomacy throughout the decades of the cold war. I consistently favored the view that phased and negotiated total nuclear disarmament, preceded by a renunciation of nuclear first use, should have been the goal of national security policy during the years of rivalry with the Soviet Union. Similarly, from the early 1950s I opposed both CIA-led and direct US military interventions in Third World countries that imposed brutal dictatorships denying various peoples seeking national independence and the exercise of their right of self-determination. This opposition was based on my understanding of the converging perspectives of international law, basic morality, and the decolonizing drift of international history and politics since the end of World War II. In retrospect, I have no second thoughts about such a critical outlook.

The Vietnam War, which generated such intense controversy during the 1960s and early 1970s, clarified my worldview on the fundamental issues of building global security and interpreting America's role in the world. It provided a defining benchmark for where and how one fit into foreign policy debates raging in the country, especially after the pro-war domestic consensus was shattered in February 1968 by the Tet Offensive, encouraging mainstream political figures (such as Robert Kennedy, George McGovern, and Eugene McCarthy) and the national media to question for the first time the wisdom of persisting with the war effort and to advocate ways of rapidly ending the involvement without weakening America's wider global commitments. But the moral and legal case against such interventionism was never made to the American people. Even the so-called anti-war doves in the mainstream built their argument around pragmatic considerations of prudence and self-interest, the high costs and ineffectuality of the intervention, with almost no expression of support for respecting the nationalist aspirations of the Vietnamese peoples or of regret arising from the massive suffering inflicted for more than a decade on the peoples of Indochina. The United States and its citizens have yet to learn the *real* lessons of Vietnam! And indeed every president since the Vietnam War has tried to unlearn the inhibiting impact of the defeat on the willingness of Americans to support projections of its military force around the world. The elder George Bush's first, telling comment after the US success in the 1991 Gulf War was to proclaim, "we have finally kicked the Vietnam syndrome."

It was at that time, after the ending of the cold war, that a new era in world politics emerged. Again I found myself deeply disappointed by the approach taken by Washington. There were incredible historical opportunities to create a safer and fairer world order by exercising American leadership in a bold, reformist, and self-interested spirit: proposing a comprehensive regime for the prohibition of all weaponry of mass destruction, including nuclear weapons; providing the United Nations with the authority and capabilities to engage in law enforcement and peacekeeping roles, including humanitarian intervention to prevent genocide and crimes against humanity; using its extensive diplomatic leverage to insist upon a fair (that is, based on legal rights more than on power and facts on the ground) solution of the Israel/Palestine encounter; and other long-festering regional conflicts. But none of this happened. Instead, the energies of US governing elites were directed toward globalizing the world economy and subordinating foreign policy to the pressures exerted at home by ethnic politics. Not to mention basking in the triumphalist glow of the cold-war outcome, with its implicit global endorsement of the American models of capitalism and political democracy, euphemistically described as "market-oriented constitutionalism." The first Bush administration briefly invoked the prospect of "a new world order," consisting of collective security under United Nations auspices, but only opportunistically, to mobilize support for confronting Iraq in the Gulf War of 1991. The Clinton presidency in its early years emphasized "enlargement" as the prime goal of its foreign policy, namely, promoting change in other countries that moved toward electoral democracy and a strong free market. Here, too, the real thrust of Clinton's foreign policy was to achieve rapid economic growth through overseas trade and investment—in effect, an unreserved embrace of predatory globalization, with its adoption of a neoliberal version of minimally regulated capitalism known as the "Washington consensus."

As earlier, I was a consistent, harsh critic of this capital-driven focus on economic growth, and its tendency to widen income gaps between North and South, as well as to ignore persisting poverty and longer-term environmental decay. In the Clinton years, no effort was made to get rid of nuclear weaponry or to create the sort of United Nations that could be genuinely responsive to the uneven needs of peoples throughout the world. There was also no attempt to soften the distortions in Middle East policy arising from US military assistance and unconditional diplomatic support of Israel, including its defiance of almost unanimous calls in the world community to withdraw from occupied Palestine and to stop building the settlements on Palestinian land whose very existence flagrantly violates the Fourth Geneva Convention and stymies hopes for a tenable peace process.

The first important occasion for questioning US world leadership in the aftermath of the cold war was, of course, the Gulf War and its aftermath. This war was undertaken in response to the Iraqi conquest and annexation of Kuwait in mid-1990. The White House led the march to war without explaining the necessity, and exhibiting little disposition to allow time for economic sanctions and diplomatic pressure to achieve the important goal of restoring Kuwaiti sovereignty and producing an Iraqi withdrawal *without war*. Other issues seemed at the time to be high on the policy agenda of Washington, including the strategic benefits of undertaking a preventive war against an Iraq that was alleged to be capable in the future of posing a regional threat, especially to Israel and the oil reserves of the Gulf, on the basis of its supposedly growing arsenal of weapons of mass destruction. The Gulf War exhibited total American military predominance in a desert setting, but it also reinforced the impression of indifference to the human well-being of the Iraqi people: leaving Saddam Hussein in control of Iraq, exposing the Kurds to a Baghdad backlash, and compensating at the expense of the Iraqi people for such a failure to achieve a regime change in Baghdad by maintaining under the mantle of the UN for more than a decade a cruel regime of comprehensive sanctions. According to reliable and objective estimates, these sanctions have by now been responsible for almost a million civilian deaths and widespread societal suffering, all without shaking to any degree Hussein's hold on the reins of government. Unable to acknowledge the failure of US policy toward Iraq in the 1990s, successive US presidents have sustained or escalated the policy, despite its unpopularity with the countries in the region and most of America's closest allies. US behavior toward Iraq suggests a lethal replay of the latter stages of the Vietnam War, when policymakers understood that the war was lost but continued nonetheless. This time the stakes are higher, and the United States is no longer restrained, as it was during the cold-war period, by anxieties about Soviet and Chinese military responses that might well have produced an escalating scale of violence that could easily have ended in nuclear war. At present, there is no country, or even combination of countries, that possesses the will and capability to deter the United States. This is a profoundly unsettling circumstance for others, and unhealthy for ourselves, especially so, given the seeming imprudence of America's current leadership, and its disregard for adverse world opinion.

If opposing the Gulf War and subsequent US policy toward Iraq was a clear matter, the several Balkan wars of the 1990s arising from the breakup of former Yugoslavia divided the left's opposition to US foreign policy. Unlike many friends on the left, I was initially wary of encouraging anti-Serb intervention in Bosnia under UN American-led auspices because I felt that there was an unwillingness by leading states, especially the United States, to commit the resources needed to enable the United Nations to succeed in carrying out a campaign of humanitarian intervention that might have lessened the violence and suffering on all sides. My anti-interventionism was shaken to the core by the bloody spectacle of ethnic cleansing in Bosnia, culminating in the 1995 Serb massacre of 7,000 Muslim males at Srebrenica within the confines of a UN "safe haven," which discredited the UN as impotent or worse, and amounted to a scandal of passivity on the part of the international community. Such a scandal was magnified by the UN's disgraceful failure to lift a finger to prevent or minimize the massive genocide (some 800,000 victims) in Rwanda a year earlier, despite strong indications from its own field officers that a small effort might have achieved dramatic humanitarian results, saving perhaps hundreds of thousands of lives.

It needs to be understood, and was not, of course, that the UN failure was directly a result of the lack of political will on the part of the permanent members of the Security Council, above all the United States, to accept the burden and responsibility for protecting peoples vulnerable to such catastrophes by making available the needed capabilities (funds and peacekeeping forces), or better for the long term, augmenting UN capabilities (with a Tobin Tax[1] and UN peacekeeping forces) to take more autonomous action (that is, without needing to wait for a geopolitical green light) in response to imminent or ongoing humanitarian catastrophes.

In short, I continued to oppose the main directions of American foreign policy in the 1990s, despite the changing global agenda relating to security, although my opposition wavered in a couple of key instances. For instance, I did in the end, on balance, and reluctantly, support the 1999 NATO war in Kosovo as a necessary step to emancipate the Albanian Kosovars from the fate endured by the Bosnian Muslims a few years earlier, although I distrusted American motives and disapproved of the means used to achieve beneficial goals.

The Kosovo War was confusing because of its mixed motives and effects. It seemed a disturbing replay of the Gulf War in its essential expression of American militarism, though worse in a procedural sense because American policy engendered geopolitical resistance and lacked UN approval. This time, due to the assured expectation of opposition by Russia and China, the United States bypassed the UN altogether; pre-war diplomatic negotiations with Belgrade seemed half-hearted, if not disingenuous, and were quite likely intended to fail, so as to clear the path to war. The American approach gave short shrift to the most basic undertaking of international law during the twentieth century— to make war a defensive instrument of last resort or a collective undertaking of the world community given legitimacy by the UN Security Council.

At the same time, the NATO intervention, followed by a UN role in administering Kosovo as an independent entity, has given the Kosovars a taste of normalcy, helped move their political life in the hopeful direction of self-determination, even induced democratizing changes in Belgrade's governing process, and so qualified as a flawed, yet genuine, case of humanitarian intervention. Without such forcible external action, Serb oppression would have certainly persisted in Kosovo and, given the depth of Albanian resistance and demographic dominance, a process of ethnic cleansing abetted by Serb crimes against humanity would have undoubtedly gone forward, and likely gained in severity as it proceeded. Having served on the Independent International Commission on Kosovo established in late 1999, I came slowly to the conclusion, reflecting the overall view of the commission members, that the NATO War, while technically illegal, was politically and morally legitimate, given its overall beneficial effect. Such an endorsement was intended to be extremely limited; it did not extend to an acceptance of US claims of humanitarian motivation, and it did not overlook such concealed intentions of Washington to ensure the viability of NATO in a Europe unmolested by a potential aggressor or of shaking once and for all "the Vietnam syndrome" that had supposedly inhibited American interventionary diplomacy since the fall of Saigon in 1975.

Indeed, the Kosovo dilemma disclosed an undesirable gap between legitimacy and legality that needed to be closed at the earliest possible time to avoid allowing sovereign states to take the regressive step of abandoning altogether the charter prohibition on non-defensive force. To close the gap by political consensus might have proved to be impossible due to principled disagreements among permanent members of the Security Council, pitting governments advocating respect for territorial sovereignty against those favoring increasing responsibility at global and regional levels for protecting peoples vulnerable to genocide and crimes against humanity. The best solution would be a formal UN acknowledgement of the lawfulness of collective action undertaken by regional organizations outside the UN in circumstances where the Security Council was blocked *by the veto* from fulfilling its charter role of upholding global peace and security. If this were impossible to achieve, the effort to do so would clarify the exceptional and limited character of the legitimacy claim, and thus implicitly reaffirm the general applicability of the UN Charter, especially its prohibition on non-defensive force.

For various reasons, the alternative approaches to this challenge to the relevance of international law seem less satisfactory. Some international law experts, for instance, proposed that it would be preferable to acknowledge violations of existing law rather than adapt law to new circumstances. I find that such an approach rests on the ad hoc and subjective judgment of the state that breaks the old rules, thereby avoiding debate on the principled reform of the rules so as to meet the requirements of action in situations where security imperatives and values change. The claims of intervention in the Balkan Wars arose from a change in the global climate of opinion associated with the upgrading of human rights, and the acceptance of their integral relationship to a revised sense of security that stressed the security of peoples as well as that of governments.

This book argues that a different approach is also needed in response to the challenge of megaterrorism, partly because the September 11 attacks disclosed a structural modification in the character of power and security and the need for a reformulation of applicable limits on the use of force. The argument rests on the idea that the demonstrated potency of non-state actors calls for the acceptance of a postmodern framework of restraint that acknowledges the inapplicability of the former, modern template of international law. That template had evolved over the course of several centuries, gradually establishing restraints on recourse to force in a world order based on the interaction of sovereign states exercising formal rights of territorial supremacy, but itself often a disappointment to the extent that larger states, especially, refused to accept the discipline of international law when their strategic interests were at stake.

US Foreign Policy and Terrorism

Even before the cold war came to an end, the US government had started to be concerned about terrorism, especially as targeted against Americans and the American overseas presence. Such a concern reached its first early peak in 1983 when 241 US marines were killed in the Beirut barracks by a giant truck bomb, an event that led the Reagan White House to end abruptly the American military presence in Lebanon. Although an attack on military installations and personnel is not properly understood as "terrorism," which is most usefully associated with violence deliberately targeting civilians and civilian society, the scale of the damage inflicted first disclosed the seriousness of the threat to the US grand strategy in the world, and specifically the Middle East, posed by non-state militant political actors. The Iranian Revolution of 1978–79, followed some months later by the US embassy seizure, was a further reminder of intense anti-Americanism and of a new willingness of Middle East forces to challenge American regional dominance by relying on tactics that could not be addressed within a statist matrix, and were not susceptible to traditional diplomatic resolution. Such unconventional challenges to the established order and to the regulatory capabilities of leading states was from the outset portrayed as terrorism even if it did not at the outset seem to fall within the dictionary definition of terrorism. The political idea behind this one-sided conception of terrorism was to mobilize a sense of outrage in the face of anti-American violence. The political cost of such a manipulation of the idea of terrorism is to cause intellectual and moral confusion and controversy that works against the formulation of a needed anti-terrorist consensus.

In the background, but not very much so, were Israeli efforts to portray their Palestinian opposition as terrorists, while obfuscating their own illegal and brutal occupation, including state terrorism against an array of Palestinian civilian targets. By most objective international law accounts, as a result of Israel's prolonged refusal to heed UN directives to withdraw from territories occupied during the 1967 Six Day War and persistent failure to comply with the Geneva Conventions governing military occupation, there exists a Palestinian right of resistance (although not the right to strike at Israeli civilian targets deliberately.) "Terrorism" as a word and concept became associated in US and Israeli political discourse with anti-state forms of violence that were so criminal that any method of enforcement and retaliation was viewed as acceptable, and not subject to criticism. By so appropriating the meaning of this inflammatory term in such a self-serving manner, terrorism became detached from its primary historical association dating back to the French Revolution. In that formative setting, the state's own political violence against its citizens, violence calculated to induce widespread fear and achieve political goals, was labeled as terrorism, most famously by Edmund Burke in his diatribe against the French Revolution. With the help of the influential media, the state over time has waged and largely won the battle of definitions by exempting its own violence against civilians from being treated and perceived as "terrorism." Instead, such violence was generally discussed as "uses of force," "retaliation," "self-defense," and "security measures."

This deformation of political language must be kept in mind to understand later developments, including September 11. The over-generalized US response to a very specific kind of extremist transnational violence has had the unfortunate effect of sending a green light to governments around the world to intensify their own violence against opposition and resistance activity branded as terrorism, and even to wage war against neighboring states that allegedly support anti-state forces. The United States government, partly to enlist support for its response to September 11, blurred the important distinction between the scope of response to the megaterrorist attacks on the World Trade Center and Pentagon and the myriad struggles for self-determination going on around the world, many of which seek goals consistent with international law.

In the latter stages of the cold war, this labeling of political violence had been given a further twist. During the flourishing of the Reagan Doctrine in the 1980s, the United States gave various kinds of support to those who violently opposed governments or interventions that were seen as leftist or favorable to the Soviet Union. Two of the most notorious recipients of such support were the Contras, who were seeking by terroristic means to overthrow the Sandinista government in Nicaragua, and the mujahedeen resistance movement, which was formed among Afghan warlords and Islamic extremists to oppose the Soviet attempt to control Afghanistan by installing a government responsive to Moscow's wishes. An ideological facet of the Reagan Doctrine was to carry the labeling of violence to hypocritical extremes: these "terrorists" were called "freedom fighters," while at the same time the US lectured the Palestinians and others that there can never be "a good terrorist," whatever the cause. These political mind games were in many respects as vicious as the violent tactics, and with as serious deadly and daily consequences that are still with us, seemingly more than ever.

Building on the Carter legacy of identifying lawless states, the Reagan presidency put forward the delegitimizing idea of "outlaw" or "rogue" states that were either alleged to be sponsors of terrorism or to be illicitly seeking to obtain weaponry of mass destruction. Such a unilateral and highly publicized delegitimation of states deemed hostile to the United States was connected with policies that were designed to stigmatize and punish such actors and to take steps to deny them beneficial participation in the world economic system. The states on this list included Iran, Iraq, Libya, Sudan, Cuba, and North Korea. Geopolitical considerations were always paramount in shaping such a list, which in its final analysis served to justify the imposition of sanctions, and even the use of force and recourse to covert, CIA-directed operations, in violation of the normal restraints on interventionary diplomacy associated with international law and morality. Increasingly, the White House has passed judgment on the acceptability of the leaders of this class of states, even initiating discussions as to whether political assassination should be adopted as an explicit and official tool of foreign policy.

It is now widely accepted that Osama bin Laden's role and experience during the 1980s in the Afghan resistance effort generated a new reality in world politics. His power arose directly from his control of financial resources and his organizational effectiveness in the recruitment and training of volunteers from around the Islamic world to engage in armed struggle against outsiders who encroach upon the Muslim world, above all the sacred territory associated with Mecca and Medina and, according to some views, the surrounding territories in Saudi Arabia. Bin Laden's success in Afghanistan may have come as a surprise to him that lent plausibility to future projects relying on similar tactics. It did not require much of a leap of imagination for Islamic militants, especially from Arab countries, to switch adversaries from Moscow to Washington, and to adopt the view that the biggest threat to the Muslim world and its holy places was posed by the United States. Looking back, it has become clear that some of the forces the US mobilized in a cold war setting to play anti-Soviet roles have generated the most monstrous blowback in all of history. The first major success of political Islam in Iran in the late 1970s was certainly facilitated by the American tactical belief throughout the cold war that traditional religions were the best counter to the ideological appeal of Marxist and leftist politics, which was viewed as the main threat to American interests in Iran and the region generally at the time.

Some scholars who specialize in Islam have been receiving widespread attention of late for the view that the September 11 attacks on the United States was mainly motivated by the desire to initiate an intra-civilizational war in the Arab world that would finally overthrow secular and Western-oriented regimes and bring to power genuine Islamic leadership embodying traditional values.[2] It is presumed on the basis of bin Laden's statements and experience, that a principal grievance against the United States was its crucial support given to the monarchy in Saudi Arabia, and that by targeting the United States, the prospects of regime change in Riyadh would increase. This line of interpretation is highly speculative, and to the extent correct, suggests a deep misunderstanding of how Washington would respond to an attack of this magnitude. Promoting regime change in the Arab world, especially on the Arabian peninsula, as far as we can tell, seems to have been high on the al-Qaeda agenda, but it still seems more plausible to suppose that Osama bin Laden's principal intention was to initiate an inter-civilizational war against the United States and, to a degree, the infidel West. The visionary character of bin Laden's worldview suggests the primacy of non-specific goals such as the mobilization of the Islamic world in general. The terrorist pedagogy of al-Qaeda and its practice up through September 11 add weight to an interpretation that stresses the goal of pushing the US out of the region as a prelude to stepping up the pressures mounted on the established order in the Arab world, especially toppling the monarchy in Saudi Arabia. But this interpretative line of shifting Islamic grievances to issues internal to the region, although attractive for hawks in Washington, is deceptively dangerous to the extent that it relieves the United States from any need to rethink its own Middle East policies, which have given rise to legitimate grievances and rabid anti-Americanism throughout the Islamic world—especially the US relationship with the Israel/Palestine encounter over the course of decades, as well as Washington's implacable hostility to the Islamic government in Iran and its harsh policies toward Iraq since 1991.

After September 11

It is against such a background that I approach the September attacks, reacting with shock and bewilderment to the magnitude of what happened, and of course, with grief given the familiarity of the scene and the tragic loss of innocent life. Such an unprovoked assault on the peace and security of the most powerful and richest country in the world was immediately, and correctly, perceived as a transformative event. I believed then, and continue to do so, that no government, let alone the widely acknowledged world leader, could have ignored the challenge, or treated it as one more terrorist incident. And more than this, I agreed this time with the US government that meeting the challenge probably implied waging war against the Taliban regime in Afghanistan. It is here, of course, that my views diverge from those of many in the progressive community; without intending to reignite the early debate,[3] I write this book to clarify what I believe to have been an appropriate response to September 11.

Our response as a country should have been situated in between recourse to war (specifically delineated with utmost care because of its unprecedented character and its necessary departure from prior understandings of the constraints of international law) and reliance on peaceful methods of conflict resolution. Saying this is not, in any sense, intended to give a stamp of approval to what President Bush has done up to now, and is doing. But it is to accept the main rhetorical and tactical thrust of the initial policy of American response, although even that only partially, and to challenge directly the post-Afghanistan reliance by the United States on the modalities of war. The book is written to suggest what "winning" such a war would entail, and why the current course is not so oriented, and hence makes losing likely.

My assessment of the American international response breaks down into three parts: (1) dealing with the Afghanistan headquarters base of al-Qaeda, and destroying and superseding the Taliban regime; (2) minimizing the effectiveness of al-Qaeda as a global network dispersed in more than 60 countries; and (3) addressing the root causes of global terrorism, and our duty and capacity to address them. Now that, for better and worse, the United States has seemingly dealt to a significant extent with the first part of this admittedly daunting undertaking, I would contend that any eventual success vis-à-vis global terrorism depends almost exclusively upon non-military police and intelligence tactics, as well as a credible willingness to address the root causes of political extremism, at least to the appropriate extent of American responsibility, as it has emerged in the Islamic world.

As the American homeland experience with indigenous terrorism demonstrates, the terrorist virus can flourish in a constitutional and affluent democracy even under conditions of political and economic moderation, and may under certain circumstances represent a reactionary backlash against precisely those efforts to establish a more humane society. Bombing black churches, mosques, abortion clinics, and government buildings are examples of right-wing paranoia and militia terrorism here in America, so let us not deceive ourselves that a turn toward justice in American foreign policy would make global terrorism go away overnight. But what does seem convincing is that the message of extremism is not nearly as likely to resonate as broadly and nearly as menacingly if its animating grievances are not widely shared in the broader affected community. As it stands, official US behavior before and since the attacks has shown little evidence of the political disposition to address the concerns of the Arab world; in fact, the US has exhibited extreme insensitivity to legitimate grievances, especially in the Palestine context, with the probable effect of intensifying frustrations with and hostility toward the United States.

The book proceeds from an attempt to show why September 11 was of such a distinctive character that the response needed to be *initially* guided by the framework of war, rather than better policing or other methods. But war against al-Qaeda, with its "sleeper cells" and networked dispersion, should have meant something dramatically new and different than any past war. This indeed is "a new war." Such a war could itself degenerate into another form of terrorism unless the use of force is subject to a revision of meaningful limits as formerly established by international law to regulate conflict among sovereign states, so as to take account of large-scale violent conflict involving a dispersed network in opposition to a territorial state. I believe that rethinking the just-war framework provides the most acceptable and accessible basis for discovering these limits, and of resisting the patrioteering and militarist temptations to act on the sheer basis of "effectiveness," or worse, vindictively, with no boundaries on goals or methods. Worst of all is the manipulation of the public mood of fear and anger as a *pretext* for enlarging and accelerating a US global empire-building project. It is of particular importance to maintain an awareness that September 11 does not provide a mandate to wage, or even to threaten, preemptive war against hostile states or to deal with unresolved territorial struggles that involve reliance on terrorist tactics by either states or political movements, or more likely, both. Pre-September 11 restraints on force contained in international law and the UN Charter should be reaffirmed as applicable to both warfare between states and in relation to self-determination struggles. As well, the inapplicability of the state-oriented international law to the al-Qaeda challenge does not mean that all restraints are suspended, but rather that appropriate restraints needs to be revised and selectively loosened in light of the values at stake, as well as balancing considerations of effectiveness against efforts to minimize the scope and intensity of warfare.

In order to imagine what victory might be in this war our government has declared, I will consider ways this war might be lost, too. The American side will not prevail in the war against global terrorism if its leadership and citizenry exempt American policies, including its regional role in the Middle East and global leadership position, from self-criticism. Up until now the ultra-nationalistic mood that has emerged dysfunctionally celebrates America as it is, an atmosphere incessantly orchestrated by a flag-waving media and the White House.

This resistance to any scrutiny of past and present American responsibility for injustices and suffering may turn out to be a fatal flaw in the response strategy undertaken by the US government. To reinforce this tendency, the only policy advice that receives a serious hearing emanates from the hawkish voices of retired generals and think-tank "war thinkers," as well as from such conservative specialists on the Arab world as Bernard Lewis or Fouad Ajami, who do not hesitate to cheerlead an expanding American-led war from the sidelines of power, insisting that only by following "the good work" in

Afghanistan elsewhere can the challenge of global terrorism be met. Ajami invokes his credentials as a knowledgeable Arab to convey the message to Washington that only toughness works in the Arab world, dismissing as deluded the anti-terrorism of the Clinton presidency on these grounds. In Ajami's words, "[t]here was a pattern of half-hearted responses to terrorist attacks, pinpricks that fooled no one."[4] Note that these pinpricks included raining Tomahawk missiles on al-Qaeda training camps in Afghanistan and destroying the main pharmaceutical factory in the Sudan, killing many civilians and eliminating the source of 40 percent of a poor country's medical drugs, on the basis of highly dubious allegations that the facility was being used to produce biological and chemical weapons, and was linked to al-Qaeda. When these thin allegations were strongly challenged by the government of the Sudan, and a UN inspection invited to verify their contentions, the US government used its formidable influence to block a UN fact-finding mission. Blunter still in his bellicosity is the counsel of Daniel Pipes, who offers the following advice certain to be well-received in Washington: "The only way to defeat militant Islam is through a willingness to fight it, and the sooner it is confronted, the less bloody the fight will be."[5] Such reassuring and essentially militarist whispers in the ears of the White House and Pentagon princes are extremely dangerous, pushing the world toward an ever wider conflagration that could in time come to merit the now still hyperbolic appellation of World War III.

The jihadist ethos of al-Qaeda's approach to violence has unfortunately seemed to set the tone for the American response. Deploying the idiom of counterterrorism and war against global terror, goals are enunciated in an unconditional language of good and evil that acknowledges no limits. Respect for the sovereignty of others is subordinated or altogether suspended, both at home and abroad. At home, the values associated with a vibrant political democracy, in which citizenship and residence is not qualified by racial, religious, and ethnic identities, are being gratuitously undermined far beyond what is justified by the genuine and serious security threats that persist.

Abroad, the relevance of international law and the United Nations is situated at, or beyond, the outer margins of an American response. Osama bin Laden and his cadres are demonized, and when held captive are transported to the distant and primitive prison facilities hastily constructed at Guantanamo Bay, held in cages that have offended the sensibilities of human rights groups around the world, eliciting objections even from the normally deferential International Committee of the Red Cross and America's closest allies. Other governments are warned by President Bush that if they do not join the American global effort, they are on the side of the terrorists. Not even during the ideological height of the cold war, with its bipolar geopolitics, was the political space for detachment and neutralism by independent foreign countries so narrowly circumscribed.

In this mood of extreme self-righteousness, the code name initially chosen by the Pentagon to describe the American response was Operation Infinite Justice. Revealingly, such a label did not raise eyebrows in the US. When it was replaced a few days later, it was not because of its hubris, but because the language chosen happened to be a Quranic phrase, making its use for a military undertaking blasphemous. And this was seen in Washington as interfering with coalition-building efforts. In its place, Washington adopted Operation Enduring Freedom, a rather bland substitute that does not capture the holy war fervor that has so far dominated the American reaction to September 11. The Great Terror War has been so far conducted as a collision of absolutes, a meeting-ground of opposed fundamentalisms, and reenactment of a cosmic struggle between good and evil.

And in this spirit, all inhibitions relating to the oppressiveness of foreign governments are cast aside, and once more unsavory regimes are embraced as allies, recalling the geopolitical opportunism of the cold war. Considerations of human rights have no role at all in such an atmosphere. Deals have been struck with central Asian states that before September 11 were shunned because of their authoritarian and corrupt ways. Not only are the Faustian bargains troublesome, but so is the accumulating evidence that the geopolitics of energy is a part of the counterterrorist scenario purged from the public script. The establishing of an American presence in Central Asia certainly cannot be divorced from the latest phase of the great game of oil and gas. Indeed, the degree to which the Taliban regime was replaced by a leadership seen as receptive to American investors may help to explain the willingness of the Bush administration to abandon its nation-building phobia, and carry its response well beyond goals associated with eliminating the presence of al-Qaeda and capturing or killing Osama bin Laden and his principal associates.

Still further behind the smokescreen of global terrorism exists an earlier and even more fundamental American project of global domination associated with the weaponization of space, of which the so-called defensive shield of missile defense is but one aspect. The real undertaking is to extend the sort of military predominance now exercised from the earth's atmosphere through airpower and from the oceans through naval power to space-based military weapons and communication systems and unmanned attack aircraft. As in Iraq, Kosovo, and Afghanistan, a military encounter in these circumstances would mean American casualties as near zero as possible, combined with an unlimited capability to destroy at a moment's notice a point of resistance or hostility anywhere on the planet. The empire-building quest for such awesome power is an unprecedented exhibition of geopolitical greed at its worst, and needs to be exposed and abandoned before it is too late. If this project aiming at global domination is consummated, or nearly so, it threatens the entire world with a kind of subjugation, and risks encouraging frightening new cycles of megaterrorism as the only available and credible strategy of resistance. Another possibility, of course, would be for states to behave as they have in the past, forming a countervailing alliance that would seek to deter and contain the United States—a prospect that would at the very least likely spark a high-risk and expensive arms race that would divert attentions from the needs and hopes of most of the peoples of the world. Also, given Europe's increasing identity as a region as well as a collection of states, the possibility of a new type of geopolitics based on an encounter between a region and an aspiring global empire looms as a still remote, yet not entirely implausible, sequel to the present period of tension and discomfort.

The idea of prevailing in the war against global terrorism that is put forward here is one that acknowledges an appropriate and necessary role for military force in the first phase of response, but relies on transnational law enforcement in the second phase, and places a deciding emphasis on successfully addressing the root causes of political extremism in the third phase. Prevailing against terrorism necessarily involves engaging in the wider struggle to establish humane global governance, eliminate poverty, achieve human rights, build regional and global democracy, and overcome the grievances that arise in reaction to the oppressive structures of repression and occupation. Prevailing in this sense depends more on moral, and even spiritual, resources than it does on military capabilities. Whether we as a people and political culture will have the humility, wisdom, vision, and courage to pursue such a course is the greatest test ever of the robustness of the democratic ethos so proudly affirmed throughout the entire course of American history. This positive alternative requires, first of all, a vigorous public debate on all dimensions of the American response to September 11 and, beyond this, a political engagement by Americans on a scale greater even than that of the golden days of the civil rights movement or the height of the grassroots movement opposing the Vietnam War.

I. WINNING AND LOSING THE WAR AGAINST GLOBAL TERROR

The traumatic surprise of September 11 caused an initial interpretative panic due to the nature of the attack, and its seeming success in flying under the radar of America's vast power. Now that such an enemy had launched this devastating attack, could it ever be defeated? Was the United States exposed on September 11 as a geopolitical dinosaur?

TV commentators were desperately searching in the immediate aftermath for explanatory tools. They naturally turned to history, and the still vivid collective memory of Pearl Harbor to assess the similarities and differences. Government voices tried to fit the attacks into the framework of prior wars, casting Afghanistan in the role of the enemy, while acknowledging what was self-evident: that waging such a war could not itself end the threat posed by al-Qaeda. This chapter makes a preliminary effort to deal with the originality of this challenge, and to evaluate the first phases of response, by exploring what winning and losing such a war means, given current levels of understanding.

Echoes of Pearl Harbor?

The Japanese attack on Pearl Harbor on December 7, 1941 is the most important historical memory that was activated by September 11. What Franklin Roosevelt called "a day of infamy" has inscribed itself on the American political consciousness with poignant immediacy. And like the reactions to September 11, the strong public emotions aroused by Pearl Harbor reversed overnight the earlier "isolationist" reluctance to engage in the wider European and Asian wars against fascism and militarism, and a blank check was issued to the White House to wage unlimited war. The American public has never looked back to examine the evidence that has raised serious doubts among respected historians about the surprise nature of the attack, suggesting that the pro-war forces gathered around FDR had convincing advance knowledge that a Japanese attack on Pearl Harbor was in the offing, but chose to ignore such warnings. Historians continue to quarrel over whether this dynamic was part of a deliberate plan to lure the country into World War II or whether it represented some sort of bureaucratic snafu at higher levels of government of such gigantic proportions as to be barely credible. There were certain scare tactics used to ensure maximal public support for security priorities at home and in relation to the reallocation of resources from peace to war. One expression of this support was to herd Japanese-Americans on the West Coast into concentration camps called "relocation centers" for the duration of the war, refusing to accord individual treatment or due process of any kind, and accompanied by the confiscation of substantial property interests. This reaction of ethnic paranoia and political paranoia has been viewed during the past twenty years with increasing expressions of shame and remorse by most Americans, but in the wartime atmosphere of the 1940s this policy was upheld by the US Supreme Court, despite its frontal assault on the basic liberties of American citizens and permanent residents.

This Pearl Harbor precedent is chastening because for the duration of the war, and for some years subsequently, critical judgment and the normal restraints on the exercise of government power and authority were virtually suspended. In many ways, the mandate of September 11 is even more unrestricted and menacing, both in relation to foreign policy and domestic liberties. At least in the 1940s there was a certain ambivalence about recourse to war associated with strong isolationist sentiments that enjoyed significant backing in the Congress and at the grassroots, especially in the Midwest.

There is nothing comparable in relation to this Great Terror War. Beyond this, the degree to which the September 11 attacks penetrated the American mainland was a further reminder, far more persuasive than Pearl Harbor, that the United States was no longer insulated by oceans and distance from its foreign enemies. And here, the targets being purely civilian and directly impinging on the mainsprings of American identity, there was a sense of helplessness that instantly morphed into patriotic fervor never before seen in America, with flags waving everywhere and public events framed by nationalist songs and music as well as rituals of mourning and remembrance. Such a martial atmosphere was continuously nurtured by a president who was in any event an old-fashioned patriot and by a media that saw its role as one of nationalist reinforcement. Patriotic enthusiasm was largely substituted for analysis and understanding.

One final aspect here is notable and was missing from the Pearl Harbor precursor. The attackers were persuasively portrayed as religious extremists inspired by the demonic figure of Osama bin Laden, who became the embodiment of evil, although his iconic TV presence gave him an appearance uncannily similar to many artistic representations of Jesus. As such, bin Laden was treated, without saying so, as an anti-Christ despite his Muslim identity, and George W. Bush, himself a devout Christian of conservative stripe, immediately presented the conflict as one of good against evil, defining an approach to the conflict for the country that further removed American conduct from any form of critical scrutiny.

Fashioning an American Response

September 11 gave reactionary and pro-military forces a greatly strengthened hand in their pre-existing bid to shape American foreign policy in more hawkish directions. Advocates of an even more militarist approach by the US government to Middle Eastern politics, took full advantage of the anti-terrorist mobilization to press their case on quite unrelated issues such as regime change in Iraq, Saudi Arabia, and even Iran.

As argued, then, any possible challenge to the Bush approach on global issues was utterly and immediately cast into outer darkness by September 11. The White House skills in managing the response were so effective that virtually every American citizen felt that creating an impression of unity was a patriotic duty of the highest order. The immediate result was to insulate the Bush administration from any serious criticism. Such an affirmation has given the president a free hand across a wide range of issues in the months after September 11, a discretionary authority further reinforced by presidential popularity as registered by public opinion polls, giving Bush approval ratings above 90 percent in this early period. These approval ratings have dropped off gradually, but not as much as might have been expected considering the continuing doubts about the economy, corporate scandals, and the failure to capture the main megaterrorists, especially Osama bin Laden.

As a result, the whole outlook of American foreign policy changed drastically overnight, and instead of the Bush administration being viewed with suspicion and as a troublesome international annoyance (mainly because of its unilateralist and obstructive approach to problems of worldwide concern), a new global anti-terrorist consensus emerged that was centered in Western Europe but now, significantly, included Russia and China. As in the cold war, other governments deferred almost unconditionally to Washington's leadership, at least with respect to the campaign against Afghanistan. What was new here was that all the important states in the world lined up behind the United States, treating September 11 as an attack on the states system as a whole, which is what Bush in his speeches presumably meant by referring to "civilization." This was truly a coalition without precedent in the history of international relations. Given American military dominance, especially in relation to nuclear weaponry, this meant that the United States was, for the first time in its history, neither "balanced," nor "deterred."

It is notable that the administration's post-Afghanistan emphasis on the war against al-Qaeda has turned from terrorism to the alleged dangers of hostile states acquiring weaponry of mass destruction. As for Osama bin Laden, he risks the fate of not only losing his notoriety as the most wanted criminal in the world, but what is worse, becoming a forgotten man. This strange twist is only partly a reflection of the awkwardness of not even knowing whether or not he is alive. It is mainly a realization that the new wars being contemplated by the White House and Pentagon would have made as much sense before September 11! This shift in American priorities also diverts attention from the inherent inability to assess the degree to which the al-Qaeda threat persists, and what to do about it in the absence of a state that can serve, as Afghanistan did, as a target area.

Nuclear Threats

The claim being made by Washington is that weapons of mass destruction (WMD) in the hands of hostile states now pose intolerable dangers because such weaponry could be transferred to terrorist groups, enabling the launch of a devastating megaterrorist attack. But the more likely explanation of this aspect of the American response is a concern that the proliferation of this weaponry might deter the United States in the pursuit of its global strategy. Especially in the Middle East, the US government seems determined to remain undeterred with respect to its use of power, including even nuclear weaponry, and therefore wants to deny potential adversaries any deterrent capability. In this context, terrorism functions mainly as a surrogate enemy, disguising the main goal of geopolitical intimidation. It should be clear to objective observers that states such as Iraq, Iran, and North Korea are at this point far more threatened than threatening, and that their efforts to have some deterrent capability is fully consistent with the sort of security arguments that have been treated as valid for states throughout the entire history of modern international relations. If the dominant states had themselves renounced WMD, or had lived up to their promises and obligations to seek nuclear disarmament, then the denial of such a deterrent to such subordinate states would seem far more reasonable. As it is, without commenting on whether these states pose risks of expansion in relation to their neighbors, it seems obvious that the United States, under the cover of September 11, is seeking to impose a geopolitical regime of nonproliferation that arbitrarily sets and interprets the rules governing the acquisition, and even the threat or use, of WMD, especially nuclear weaponry. By so doing, Washington is substantially rewriting the security rules that have governed the behavior of sovereign states for centuries, which are based on an acceptance of the self-help nature of the system, without the existence of external restraints, absent specific treaties of prohibiton, relating to the acquisition and possession of weaponry. What the United States is imposing is a two-tier structure in which WMD are retained for potential use by a small number of large states (and Israel), while being denied to specific others.

The US response to September 11 also seized the moment to alter its own policy bearing on the use of nuclear weapons in disturbing ways. The Pentagon's leaked Defense Posture Statement that was adopted as policy in late 2001 clearly reconsidered the military benefits to the United States of threatening and using nuclear weapons in a global setting where the US government was no longer deterred, as had been the case throughout the cold war. What seems to be taking shape in the minds of American military planners is what might be called the Hiroshima temptation, a normalization of nuclear weaponry with their role newly determined by a primary reference to battlefield advantages that might derive from their threat, and even their use. Such a move is of potentially epic magnitude, as it means that the most powerful country in the world is neither deterred nor self-deterred, and is working toward a policy that abandons the formal and informal inhibitions that have evolved since 1945 based on the illegality and immorality of nuclear weapons and all weapons of mass destruction.

These inhibitions were given a sweeping, although not absolute, endorsement by a majority of the judges in the 1996 Advisory Opinion of the International Court of Justice. The most important conclusion of the UN's judicial arm was that nuclear weapons were illegal, except possibly, and only, in circumstances where the ultimate survival of a state was at issue. By this legal reasoning, the case for development, possession, and deterrence is ironically much stronger for the "rogue" states, given the threats directed at their regimes, than it is for the current members of the nuclear weapons club.

Terrorist Networks

As suggested earlier, the unique character of the September 11 attacks shaped the initial pattern of response, lending plausibility and virtually uncontested support to US counterterrorist claims outside of the Islamic world. The magnitude and implications of September 11, together with a string of major attacks in recent years, the globally dispersed terrorist network, and the credible prospect of further severe attacks lent urgency to fashioning an American response that would be effective. Unlike most past radical movements that were embedded in a specific society whose ruling structure was being challenged, al-Qaeda exemplified the organizational form of the current era of globalization: a network that could operate anywhere and everywhere, and yet was definitively situated nowhere. The network was and remains without an address, and its very existence is a matter of conjecture and heaps of indirect evidence. What if we discover decades hence that al-Qaeda was an imaginary network conjured up by intelligence agencies unable to otherwise explain their own failures to anticipate and thwart such an attack? This remains unlikely, but it cannot be entirely ruled out, nor can the possibility of al-Qaeda fading into oblivion.

When the forces of al-Qaeda struck so decisively, they strangely posted no demands and made no claims, and did not even leave behind a signature, although the bin Laden interviews after the events partly filled this latter gap. This anonymity was also an aspect of the main earlier lethal attacks officially attributed to al-Qaeda, including the 1996 Khobar Towers bombing in Dhahran, Saudi Arabia, the bombings of the American Embassies in Kenya and Tanzania in 1998, and the 2000 Yemen harbor attack on the USS Cole. The animus was unmistakably anti-American in each instance, and it certainly seemed to be the work of this far-flung network that had operating capabilities in many countries, estimated to be anywhere between 40 and possibly as many as 80. Al-Qaeda also had an inspirational leader with seemingly exceptional organizational and business talents in Osama bin Laden, whose demonization lent an immediate, yet temporary and misleading, concreteness to the goals of a response—bringing to justice the leadership of al-Qaeda, especially delivering bin Laden, in the unforgettable phrasing of President Bush, "dead or alive." In this respect, the degree to which the bin Laden operation had been centered in and associated with Afghanistan, with the indulgence of an extremist and repressive Taliban regime headed by another demonized figure, Mullah Mohammed Omar, dominated the early approach adopted by military planners and political leaders in Washington, and was generally supported around the world.

As time has passed, and these prominent figures have eluded capture or confirmed death, the goals of the military campaign have become less and less focused on these individuals, and more and more on what is even more elusive, the complete annihilation of "terrorism" everywhere. The scope of this undertaking was expanded still further, and more controversially, by the Bush doctrine of preemptive war against Iraq (and potentially others) based on the rationale that the United States could not wait to be attacked, which in effect became "the lesson of September 11," at least as learned by the Bush administration. But even more amorphous, yet no less significant, were the interweavings of this unfolding American war against terrorism with plans to impose regime changes on foreign countries and to accelerate the completion of a global empire-building project.

The Distinctive Challenge of Megaterrorism
Megaterrorism is violence against civilian targets that achieves significant levels of substantive as well as symbolic harm, causing

damage on a scale once associated with large-scale military attacks under state auspices, and thus threatening the target society in a warlike manner that gives rise to a defensive urgency to strike back as effectively as possible. But how to strike back against a nearly invisible enemy? We must clarify who this war is against and what exactly this war is about. Such a clarification is both difficult and controversial. It is difficult first because the megaterrorism of al-Qaeda does not fit neatly within the global political and legal framework based on the interaction of sovereign states. Winning and losing wars within the established framework of states can be assessed clearly, but when the framework does not hold, evaluative standards need to be reconstituted. This framework is based on authority being distributed among sovereign states as the only full members of international society, and alone entitled to use international force as an instrument of national policy, and then only to the extent allowed by international law. This extent has narrowed over time as states have tried to protect the general welfare by legally restricting uses of force to circumstances of self-defense. With no government to admit defeat, no territory to occupy, there is no reliable way to have confidence that the threat giving rise to the war has ended, or that it is sufficient to rely on enhanced defensive and reactive capabilities to offset the prospect of further megaterrorism directed at US targets. But neither is there any way to validate the disappearance of the threat, removing the domestic and international measures undertaken on assumptions of wartime jeopardy.

Clarifying what this war means is controversial because of the specific way the US government has chosen to define the threat associated with the September 11 attacks, which is to extend it beyond the al-Qaeda challenge to encompass what Washington calls "terrorism" in general. This generalizing of terrorism misdirects the American-led response, weakening the commitment of the coalition formed to struggle specifically against the al-Qaeda network, while at the same time distracting needed energies from the appropriately conceived "war," as well as ignoring international law and pervasively violating the sovereign rights of other countries. It also compounds the difficulty of identifying the war's end.

The effort to delineate the proper scope of the war against megaterrorism is difficult to reconcile with most interpretations of international law restraints on the use of force. There is little doubt that a literal reading of international law does not help us very much in clarifying what limits should govern a response to the challenge of megaterrorism. It is necessary to adapt the limits on the use of force so as to enable an effective response, which may involve some subordination of sovereign rights and the norm of non-intervention in internal affairs in certain specific settings. It may be helpful to realize that international law, throughout its entire history, has evolved mainly by such a dynamic of adaptation to the special demands of new circumstances, with world community reactions of acceptance or rejection shaping whether the contested action should be treated as "a legal precedent" rather than as "a violation of international law."

Unlike many anti-war activists who extended their condemnation of the Bush administration policies to include the Afghanistan military campaign,[1] the limited war unleashed against the Taliban regime and the al-Qaeda forces in Afghanistan seemed to me to be a reasonable extension of the right of self-defense in the context of a megaterrorist attack, and was so accepted by the Security Council, although less specifically and circumspectly than seems desirable, which would have included the identification of an applicable set of limits on these novel defensive claims. There was a rather casual and mechanical acceptance at the UN of the American claims, reflecting partly the sense that the al-Qaeda attacks made all states vulnerable and sharing an interest in reducing the danger as quickly and effectively possible. There was no reasoned discussion, much less debate, about why the charter should be interpreted as allowing reasonable measures of self-defense even in the absence of an armed attack as generally understood, or about the overall problem of dealing with threats posed by extremist political networks that operate transnationally. International law, which historically evolved and developed over time to cope with relations among sovereign states, needs to be stretched to deal with megaterrorism, if it is to remain at all relevant.

Nevertheless, I believe that the over-generalized US approach to the megaterrorist challenge is dangerously serving to exempt state violence and policies from being regarded as terrorism—even when their violence is deliberately directed at civilian society. This purported exemption allows governments around the world to rely on large-scale violence against their civilian populations, and avoid the stigma of terrorism, while at the same time tending to taint all reactive violence from oppressed peoples, even in resistance to foreign occupation, as terrorism. This "anti-terrorist" bias weights the outcome of civic struggles in favor of the state and the status quo, depriving many peoples of the world of their fundamental right of self-determination.

In effect, the US approach to the war on global terror has made the undertaking at once too large (terrorism in general) and too small (excluding state terrorism). This failure to calibrate the response to the distinctive character of the challenge further complicates any assessment of winning and losing. An analogous failure of calibration is also present in many anti-war denunciations of the US approach, which also over-generalize by repudiating altogether any recourse to "war," and not acknowledging the need to take the initiative in combating the threat, establishing the reasonableness of incapacitating the al-Qaeda forces in Afghanistan as a logical and essential first step. Both sides in this debate, which in any case has never been properly joined, seem insensitive to the depth of the challenge arising from this new reality of extremist *networks* being able to rival or surpass sovereign states in their capacity to inflict harm and exploit the vulnerabilities of traditional forms of territorial defense, while rendering themselves virtually immune to retaliation. It is this encounter between the new and the old that partially disables international law and the United Nations from providing authoritative guidelines, on the basis of the UN Charter and prior state practice, as to defensive rights and limits on the use of force. In view of these conditions, it is necessary to articulate a new normative (law and morality) template appropriate to the parameters of the megaterrorist phenomenon as so far enacted by the organizational reality, ideology, and tactics of al-Qaeda.

I take the position that the war can be won only by a narrowing process that refocuses the defensive undertaking of the US government on al-Qaeda. To the extent that global terrorism, as distinct from megaterrorism, is a legitimate concern on the part of target states, and it often is, then terrorism needs to be understood as political violence that is deliberately aimed at civilians and civilian society, whether perpetrated by political movements or by states. And even with such refocusing, a further process of clarification is necessary—namely, the limited role of military force in the war on global terror. Here again the Bush administration has been vague and indefinite, refusing to acknowledge any limitations on their recourse to force, unwilling to admit the relevance of international law or to allow a supervisory role for the United Nations. The US government has fashioned its policies on an ad hoc basis as it proceeds, treating the goals and scope of its military campaign as matters purely to be determined by its own, non-accountable policymaking. The impact of this approach is intensified by other related unilateralist moves: the rejection of widely endorsed international treaties on global problems, the refusal to transfer needed authority to international institutions, the insistence on its right to administer selectively the nonproliferation regime on the basis of its strategic interests, and the maintenance of cruel international sanctions on Iraq for years, despite the opposition of the great majority of members of the United Nations.

Already, it is obvious that this American pattern has resulted in considerable damage to the normative dimensions of global governance—that is, to international law, morality, and collective procedures (see Chapter 5 for more on these norms). It is difficult for the international public not to think that power politics is what counts, at least for the strongest and most imperial of sovereign states. And to "normal" members of international society intent on promoting more humane and practical patterns of global governance (normal meaning here states that seek their own survival and development, as well as the establishment of institutions and procedures to address global problems, but are neither expansionist nor revisionist in their pursuit of national goals), the challenge for the future seems more and more likely to be centered around the containment of and resistance to American geopolitical designs, at least through diplomatic means. For these latter dissatisfied states, or for revolutionary movements, the option of resistance and struggle seems likely to rely on more radical means, both violent and nonviolent.

As I will discuss further in the next chapter, al-Qaeda arguably undermines global governance by way of its organizational resilience, its concealed multi-state presence, its avowal of genocidal tactics and goals, and its reliance on suicidal warriors to carry out megaterrorist missions. To reiterate, megaterrorism needs to be understood as a new genre of war, but with the assailant being a global network rather than a territorially based sovereign state. This network mode of organizational reality can neither be ignored, nor can it be addressed by diplomacy or traditional notions of territorial self-defense. So much is granted to Washington. But the US government has seized the occasion to make extravagant claims about the use of force that cannot be persuasively justified by reference to megaterrorism. The United States appears to be itself undermining global governance by claiming this *unrestricted* right to decide unilaterally upon the use of international force, by ignoring sovereign rights of third states, by marginalizing international institutions, and by setting a precedent that authorizes state violence without restriction against civilian targets, provided only that it be done in the name of counterterrorism.

It is against this complex and evolving background that the distinction between winning and losing in war needs to be reformulated. Any proper evaluation of the US government's response to the September 11 attacks needs to consider both their effectiveness and proportionality, and additionally, their legitimacy. By overreaching, the US has not only eroded the effectiveness of its response, but is also setting a dangerous example for others to claim similar rights to react disproportionately in circumstances where megaterrorism is absent and where the opposition is seeking to achieve rights recognized by international law. Furthermore, the United States has been making "illegal" threats directed at the "axis of evil" countries, especially Iraq, states that lack the links to al-Qaeda that Afghanistan possessed. The US is thereby flouting international law and the UN by fashioning this wider reach of its response to September 11. In effect, the US government is substituting its unilateralist doctrine of preemption for the modern rules of international law governing permissible uses of force, which should remain applicable where the territorial template of conflict and regulation remains fully applicable. If upheld, these norms in international law make a seemingly beneficial contribution to world order.

Winning: Minimizing the al-Qaeda Threat
After September 11, the immediate priority of the American response was to act with urgency and effectiveness to disable or destroy the al-

Qaeda network, minimizing its capacity to the extent possible to mount further megaterrorist operations. It should be understood that the essence of the post-September 11 al-Qaeda challenge was the appreciation that the global network had the will and capacity to launch such attacks against its enemies in the future. The US government seemed alert to this disturbing prospect, although at first the White House grossly over-personalized its goals, by seeming to suggest that killing or capturing Osama bin Laden was the primary task. With the passing of weeks, that misleading demonization was tempered, and downgraded to the point that by just a half a year later, bin Laden was only occasionally mentioned in official language describing the progress and goals of the war.

The actual nature of the al-Qaeda threat is not fully known, probably not even in internal sources that possess the sort of intelligence information that would give such an interpretation somewhat greater weight. Certainly within the public domain, the actuality of the level and extent of a continuing megaterrorist threat is currently impossible to assess reliably. So far, despite the periodic and feverish governmental warnings, further attacks and continuing dangers have not materialized, except possibly for the lone "shoe bomber" whose apparent mission of setting off a highly explosive substance packed into the soles of his shoes was successfully foiled by suspicious passengers. There are intimations of "sleeper cells" of operatives situated in various countries around the world, including quite likely within the United States. At this point, their existence can neither be validated nor entirely discounted, which complicates further an assessment of the extent to which the threat persists, and exceptional protective measures are justified. Seemingly farfetched high alerts have been declared by high government officials based on alleged threats to the bridges in New York City and San Francisco, to seaports in various cities, and to Texas oil refineries, but without the release of evidence that might help us understand whether this was a responsible warning about an uncertain risk, a misreading of random low-level intelligence data on a huge variety of supposed threats, or even a manipulative effort to sustain the public anxiety level of Americans so as to ensure that the patriotic moment would be extended indefinitely and criticism of government action would continue to be off-limits. As the fallout from the corporate scandals has increased in mid-2002 and come closer to implicating the political leadership, a wag-the-dog incentive for the White House to put the war back on the front pages of American newspapers has been growing by the day.

There seems at this point to be provisional indications that the strategy of attacking Afghanistan has been a tactical success in many respects, seemingly destroying, disabling, and dispersing the al-Qaeda leadership, including Osama bin Laden, and its Afghan nerve center. Again, there is a need to acknowledge a high degree of uncertainty as to the impact of the war on al-Qaeda's capabilities and future plans. Who and how many escaped the military operations to fight another day is unclear. How to assess reports that the al-Qaeda leadership has regrouped in remote regions of Western Pakistan is also highly speculative. The ferocity of the American attacks on suspected al-Qaeda outposts in Afghanistan may have dissuaded some of the surviving members from continuing with their struggle, at least in the current atmosphere and by military means. But perhaps not. What does seems to have been achieved beyond reasonable doubt is the annihilation and replacement of the Taliban regime. Further, military operations throughout Afghanistan, which are continuing months later, appear to have effectively destroyed this primary base of al-Qaeda operations that had been providing training, planning, leadership, and organizational direction for the network as a whole. Whether al-Qaeda has discovered or is searching for alternative sites for regrouping and planning future megaterrorist undertakings of spectacular scope is not known at this point. Whether or not the fury and scale of the American response has undermined the morale of whatever remnants of al-Qaeda survive will only become apparent in the months and years ahead. Part of the difficulty associated with fighting against a transnational network is that its state of mind and capabilities are almost impossible to evaluate reliably, which is a piece of the larger puzzle of when, if ever, it will be possible to pronounce that the threat has receded to the point that the war can be considered won, and over.

The Afghanistan war was not, of course, the only first-stage effort made in response to the September attack. The US government from the outset recognized the distinctive nature of its adversary, and the need to supplement a military, territorially conceived "war" with a variety of non-military and quasi-military undertakings. In this regard, it summoned the UN to support its response, at least to the extent of demanding that all states take steps within their capacity to deal with the presence of segments of the al-Qaeda network situated within their territory. Security Council Resolution 1373 is especially important in this regard, as it regards the attacks as posing a Chapter VII "enforcement" challenge, by adopting the language of obligatory participation in the campaign against transnational megaterrorism, and through its specification of the duties of UN members to cooperate in the global struggle against terrorism. The UN resolution "decides" that all states ensure that persons participating in "the financing, planning, preparation or perpetration" of terrorism are "brought to justice," and that their domestic legal order establishes terrorism as a serious criminal offense and enacts the laws and regulations that recognize this conclusion. In this spirit, also, states are obliged to offer "one another the greatest measure of assistance in connection with criminal proceedings and investigations" relating to terrorist activities, "including assistance in obtaining evidence in their possession."

Beyond this, Resolution 1373 in its third paragraph "calls upon all states" to "exchange information... to cooperate, particularly through bilateral and multilateral arrangements and agreements, to prevent and suppress terrorist attacks and to take action against the perpetrators of such acts." It also seeks to oblige states to become parties to relevant anti-terrorist international treaties, and to implement earlier Security Council resolutions, especially Resolution 1368, framed in terms of the charter affirmation of "the inherent right of individual or collective self-defense" (Article 51) that supports indirectly the US on recourse to force against Afghanistan, as well as the more comprehensive non-military dimensions of response. In this fundamental regard, there exists a basic endorsement of US claims and retaliatory strikes by a UN consensus of states, without any formal dissent. Such an endorsement of the general response in its initial phases does not, of course, mean approval for the manner in which force was used or the political goals being implemented in Afghanistan and elsewhere. Also, the UN approach finessed the issue as to the scope of "terrorism," neither particularizing its resolutions in relation to al-Qaeda and megaterrorism, nor resolving the issue as to whether terrorism should be understood to include state terrorism. The UN unfortunately also left ambiguous whether its legitimation of counterterrorism extends to various struggles and political violence not directly related to September 11.

There is a gray sector associated with military operations in foreign countries undertaken with the consent of the territorial government, and hence in accordance with sovereign rights. Some argue that such action is necessary to deal with anti-state groups in other countries that have strong positive links with al-Qaeda. In this regard, the US has sent troops and military assistance to a wide range of countries (including Pakistan, the Philippines, Somalia, Georgia, and several central Asian republics), which has raised empirical, political, and legal issues. First of all, are the links to al-Qaeda of a nature that is plausibly connected with the September 11 attacks or with al-Qaeda's ongoing global campaign against the United States? It seems that the anti-state armed movements that are being targeted are by and large preoccupied with their own territorial struggles of a political character against a particular government in power, and their al-Qaeda links are not significantly related to the sort of megaterrorist vision of Osama bin Laden, but are designed to facilitate their local struggles. If this is correct, then it becomes an analytical mistake with serious policy consequences to conclude that because a certain movement contains elements that received training and funding from al-Qaeda, it is part of the megaterrorist threat. From this perspective, evidence of training or financing under al-Qaeda auspices is far from conclusive that any meaningful connection exists to megaterrorism. To presuppose the connection based on some element of linkage is to widen the challenge of megaterrorism unnecessarily, making any prospect of ending or winning the war on global terror more and more improbable. These issues need to be considered if we are to determine how "winning" should be understood.

Such consideration is ever more important in settings where covert operations are being undertaken with either only the tacit consent of the territorial sovereign or without consent. Here again, it is possible that such undertakings have a real connection with the persisting al-Qaeda threat, but there is no way of knowing, given their inherently secret character. It would be impossible to tell whether the targets of such operations were obstructive of US foreign policy goals unrelated to its encounter with megaterrorism. In Central Asia, US motivations are viewed with great suspicion in many non-American settings because they seem to have more to do with the geopolitics of energy, with oil and gas resources and pipelines, than with megaterrorism. Obviously, the pursuit of such goals is outside the scope of what has been authorized by the UN, and tends to violate both sovereign rights, the rights of self-determination, and the generalized prohibition against recourse to international force, especially to achieve economic and non-defensive strategic goals. Without good faith adherence to limits by Washington it is nearly impossible to draw a line between what is impermissible and what is not in this new global setting.

In these respects, the ambiguities and silences of the UN on these crucial issues reflect two unfortunate realities in international life: the absence of consensus about the nature of international terrorism and the weight of US geopolitical influence, which has been used to oppose a more restrictive definition of a legitimate response to September 11. As a result, the UN role in clarifying the nature of "winning" is not nearly as helpful as it could and should have been. The UN, as the main institutional expression of the widespread societal desire "to save succeeding generations from the scourge of war" (as the preamble to the UN Charter puts it), needed to express more strongly its commitments to minimizing reliance on force and war in world politics, at the same time acknowledging the authority of the US to take necessary defensive action to address the novel and frightening threat posed by al-Qaeda (its ideas, as well as its capabilities). Unfortunately, this failure by the UN leaves international society without an authoritative conception of the war against global terror, and no way to establish conclusively that the authority to use force is specific and limited by considerations of international law and the application of the just-war doctrine, as modified by the underlying novelty of the megaterrorist challenge. Given this deficiency, it is to be expected that geopolitics will fill the normative vacuum, and this is particularly dangerous because the UN has provided the United States with a cover for its wider ambitions associated with regional dominance in the Middle East and more generally with global empire-building. It must be understood that these secondary US goals lack legitimacy from the perspectives of law and morality as evolved to sustain stability and civility in a society of sovereign states, and that this concern should have been so indicated, at least indirectly, in the UN anti-terrorist resolutions discussed above. Such limitations could have been achieved by formulating the authorization to use force in specific, bounded language, and explicitly excluding more generalized interpretations of the right to use force in foreign countries.

At this first level of evaluation, it is clear that there are such great difficulties even defining the war that is to be won that it is almost impossible to imagine what "winning" might be. But I would argue that if legitimate war aims are narrowly conceived, then the war in its literal and immediate sense of dismantling and disabling the al-Qaeda network seems to be succeeding, if at an exceedingly uncertain pace. Such a judgment is necessarily tentative, and is subject to reversal, should subsequent megaterrorist attacks by al-Qaeda succeed in inflicting harm comparable to or greater than what occurred on September 11. While such prospects seem quite unlikely, they cannot be ruled out. But because the White House has stated its war goals in much more grandiose terms, the very concept of winning remains obscure, and would depend on a more or less arbitrary claim of victory by the US government that, in a sense, could be made at any stage, but always at the risk that future events would reveal the claim to have been premature. If indeed an attack on Iraq occurs, the issue will be more clouded than ever. For even if the US should succeed in achieving its goals in such a war, it would be an essentially different war than the one waged against al-Qaeda, and in all likelihood it would lack any convincing rationale by way of international law or UN authority, or by way of an appeal to special circumstances that called for some degree of adaptation of existing rules and restraining policies.

Addressing Legitimate Grievances

The arguments about the disabling of al-Qaeda are only the tip of the iceberg in deciding what winning the war against global terror is about. It is necessary to look beyond this network dedicated to conducting a megaterrorist war, and to understand the relevance of the political and moral climate that generates such extremes of attitude and behavior. Those Pentagon warriors who maximize the terrorist threat tend overwhelmingly to support the argument that terrorism is a cancer that should be removed from the global body politic, and that this can and should be done without worrying about antecedent causes such as conditions of injustice and oppression. For them, a main purpose of winning is to demonstrate resolve and toughness, principally by waging war against those political forces that resist the American presence in any place of strategic importance. In this hawkish view, the extension of the military response to Iraq, and possibly elsewhere, is the litmus test of whether the war will be won or lost. The war thinkers who articulate these views have close ties to the military sector of government and the economy, tend to be fervently pro-Israeli, are keen to promote the militarization of space, and confuse national security with empire-building.

With respect to the role of force in addressing the threat of September 11, the minimalists (as distinguished from opponents of any recourse to war) oppose the extension of the war to Iraq and favor varied attention to the roots of terrorism, as well as encouraging an empathetic understanding of anti-Americanism. Whereas the militarists ask, "Why don't they fear us?" those who seek peace and justice are seeking to understand and address the question "Why do they hate us?" And, of course, this latter question needs refinement. The "us" is not the American people or Jews and Christians in general except at the extremes of opinion in the Arab world, but it is rather the US government, its policies and ties with oppressive forces in the region, its decade-long sanctions (not to mention periodic military attacks) imposed on the Iraqi people, its refusal to normalize relations with Iran, and, above all, its underwriting of the Israeli occupation of Palestinian territories and support for Israeli brutality directed against the Palestinians.

Those who understand the war against terrorism in this way view it as essential to address the *legitimate* grievances in the Arab/Islamic world with as much seriousness and objectivity as is devoted to fashioning a response to al-Qaeda. Such an approach to "winning" presents a bigger challenge than megaterrorism itself, because it requires a sea change in the manner by which the US government conceives of security in the Middle East, at home, and globally.

This sea change must start with the Palestinian issue, but should move on to address related problems associated with Jerusalem, sanctions against Iraq, relations with Iran, and weaponry of mass destruction in the Middle East. There is little doubt throughout the Muslim world, especially in Arab countries, but also in other parts of the world, increasingly including Europe and Asia, that the American role in supporting an unjust and illegal Israeli policy with respect to the Palestinian struggle is a fundamental and legitimate grievance directed against US policy. This grievance has been aggravated by the inability and limited willingness of the Arab governments to help the Palestinians, creating a sense of humiliation and Arab guilt associated with Israel's success in a series of wars that now stretches back for more than half a century. The United States has not only been Israel's financial and diplomatic backer par excellence, but it has managed to dominate the political space taken up by peacemaking diplomacy, marginalizing the UN, Europe, and more genuinely neutral and balanced alternatives.

Israel's strength has been partly exhibited in its refusal to consider any source of intermediation other than that provided by their staunchest ally and the only superpower. Similarly, the Palestinian weakness is expressed by their acceptance of such a framework for conflict-resolving diplomacy, which, if examined closely, is not a negotiation, but as illustrated by the Barak/Clinton proposals of 2000, an Israeli offer that is put on the table for the Palestinians to accept or reject. The Palestinians have not helped themselves, either in response to Israeli proposals or with regard to public relations, by failing to explain their reasons for rejecting proposals as presented, and by their seeming unwillingness to indicate clearly what sort of "peace" would be acceptable and why Israeli security could be best achieved by a result that gave both sides truly independent, sovereign states.

This failure of explanation became particularly important in the aftermath of the Camp David II/Taba phase of the Oslo Peace Process in the Fall of 2000, especially after President Clinton blamed the Palestinians for the breakdown of the move toward peace and the Barak proposals were being touted as "generous," "unprecedented," supposedly giving the Palestinians 95% or more of what they wanted. Such an assessment of Israeli generosity has been seriously contested from any number of sources, Palestinian and non-Palestinian. Arafat's silence, followed by the outbreak of the second intifada, was a big public relations setback for the Palestinians, leading to a tightening of Israeli oppression, a softening of international criticism of Israeli moves, and much bloodshed and suffering on both sides, but particularly for the Palestinians.

Yet, the underlying situation remains the same. The Palestinian ordeal, as it evolves and worsens, continues to feed and intensify anti-American resentments and indirectly contributes to the emergence of political extremism, which in certain configurations can produce violent resistance and even lead to megaterrorism. A fair solution for the Palestinians should have been the goal of a responsible American foreign policy for decades, and stands on its own as a beneficial and stabilizing goal. September 11 adds a pragmatic dimension, the extent of which cannot be accurately calculated or officially acknowledged, but is related to the relevance of an anti-American societal climate and a popular receptivity to violent and vicious attacks against Americans and US interests. Resolving the Palestinian issue at this stage carries no assurances, but since it seems worth pursuing for its own sake, there are strong reasons to break with the partisanship of the past and provide leadership for a fair process and outcome. If such a step has a moderating impact on the relationship between the West and its Islamist adversaries, so much the better.

What such a diplomatic sea change would entail in concrete behavior is difficult to identify with precision. It could be a matter partly of stepping to one side in the diplomatic dynamic, supporting real negotiations between the two sides, and thereby contributing to an atmosphere of mutual respect and equality. Arguably, a few tentative baby and inconclusive steps in this direction have been taken by the Bush administration: supporting the establishment of a Palestinian state prior to final-status negotiations; improving the diplomatic balance by naming the UN, the EU, and Russia, along with the US, as conveners of a conference to address the Middle East crisis, a new configuration dubbed "the Quartet." It remains to be seen whether such initiatives presage anything more than a cosmetic shift. It is difficult to evaluate the importance of such action, as it has been accompanied by unjustified support for Sharon's brutality toward the Palestinian population as a whole, which currently includes the military re-occupation of the seven leading West Bank cities, coupled with cruel curfews maintained on a 24-hour basis, accelerated house demolitions, and threatened deportations. This iron fist of Sharon has been coupled with an unwarranted, one-sided US/Israel insistence that Arafat stop the cycle of violence against civilians, reinforced by a White House willingness to meet frequently and sympathetically with Sharon, while avoiding any direct contact with Arafat, and indeed having Bush arrogantly calling in public for his replacement as Palestinian leader as a precondition for the resumption of a peace process. At this point, every policy initiative undertaken by either side appears to be a dead end, but the desperation of the situation is likely to generate growing pressure to find a solution acceptable to both sides or to impose a settlement that seems fair to both peoples.

The outcome of a genuine peace process for the two peoples needs to be guided to a far greater extent than in the past by reference to international law and to UN authority. The ritualistic invocation of SC Resolutions 242 and 338 does identify the common ground of Israeli withdrawal in rather clear language, but so abstractly that it allows Israel to put forward implausible self-serving interpretations of the clear intention of the drafters on such key issues as redrawn boundaries, settlements, water rights, the status of Jerusalem, and the rights of refugees.[2] If international law were seen as relevant for the identification of the contours of a fair solution, then the Palestinian position would prevail on all of these substantive issues, and a truly viable and equal Palestinian state would be the result of a new peace process, which would probably produce a gigantic peace dividend favorable to Israel and its long besieged society. There is room for adjustment and compromise to be responsive to understandable and reasonable Israeli anxieties, especially on the issue of refugees. The Palestinian claims of a right of return is supported by the generality of GA Resolution 194 and by international law and practice, but there is a widespread, although far from unanimous, Palestinian indication of a willingness to exercise these rights in a self-denying manner that does not threaten the Jewish or Zionist character of the Jewish state. For this to happen, Israel must reciprocate with reconciling initiatives of its own. While searching for a formula of accommodating compromise, it is not politically or morally feasible, or legally appropriate, to put to one side the rights of Palestinian refugees who have endured decades of privation and are arguably the most victimized constituency arising from the underlying conflict. There must be found a blend of symbolic and substantive moves that will give Israelis as much reassurance as possible about the durability of their state and Palestinians some sense that justice, under the circumstances, is being rendered. Some formula of Israeli symbolic acknowledgement of responsibility for the 1948 expulsion, combined with mechanisms for compensation and procedures for family unification and limited returns, needs to be discussed with an eye toward a compromise that would be acceptable to the overwhelming majority on both sides, but equally sure to be resisted by the opposed extremist minorities. International law offers a starting-point, but given the historical and ideological realities, it should be applied flexibly, in such a manner that seems reasonable in light of the political realities of the situation as it has evolved. It should be appreciated that the Palestinian mainstream, although without the backing of some important political factions, has already endorsed huge baseline concessions: limiting their claims for a state and right of self-determination to 22 percent of historic Palestine, thereby conceding 78 percent to pre-1967 Israel; accepting the existence of Israel *as a Jewish state*, despite the presence of more than one million Arabs (about 20 percent of the total population) within its borders who as Israeli citizens do not enjoy anything approaching equality of status or rights to that of their Jewish counterparts.

There are other regional grievances that should also be addressed with more of an eye toward accommodation and reconciliation than on the basis of interventionary threats and coercion. One starting point would be to seek a full normalization of relations between the US and Iran. There is every reason to suppose that such diplomatic initiatives, especially if followed by economic gains, would strengthen the hands of moderate and liberal forces associated with President Mohammad Khatami, and ease one source of tension in the region. It could also signify an American acceptance of democratically organized Islamic states on the same level of legitimacy as the Jewish state of Israel. This, too, might radiate defusing effects that would improve the inter-civilizational climate quite dramatically. It would be reasonable to anticipate in response that Iran might cease its support for Islamic extremist movements in the region, especially if moves toward normalization were taking place in the context of an acceptable resolution of the Israel/Palestine conflict.[3]

Closely related would be a drastic revision of the approach taken toward Saddam Hussein, Iraq, and the regional question of weaponry of mass destruction. As a start, it is long past time to end the sanctions regime, possibly in conjunction with and under the cover of some resumption of inspection under UN control.[4] This resumption should be coordinated with plans to institute some greater degree of inspection relating to weapons of mass destruction throughout the region, and to organize a regional conference including Israel that would seek agreement on the Middle East as a zone without weapons of mass destruction in any category, including nuclear weaponry. American leadership in such an endeavor of peace, justice, development, and reconciliation, if genuine, could achieve a substantial revision in the perception of the United States as a sinister presence in the life of the region and its peoples. This sea change, it should be stressed, is directed toward the redress of legitimate grievances, an improvement in overall regional conditions that should have been undertaken long *before* September 11. It should be understood and presented not as appeasement in the face of threats, nor as moves to accommodate illegitimate demands, such as the destruction of Israel, an indulgence of oppressive practices or terrorism associated with either secular or Islamic rule, or with revolutionary opposition, or indifference to violations of human rights.

The Deeper Roots
Beyond the resentments associated with the widely shared regional perception of the West as an abusive and domineering presence, there remain strong collective memories of exploitation as well as feelings that Arab disempowerment during the colonial and post-colonial period is a result of manipulation by Europe and the United States. Also relevant is the grassroots sentiment in the Middle East that the extraordinary concentration of oil reserves in the region has disproportionately benefited the West, and not the peoples of the countries and region where the oil is found. Such feelings of exploitation are primarily associated with the realities of the oil-producing countries, both those with large poor populations and oppressive governments that use

revenues largely to meet their annual budgetary needs, and those with small populations that invest a large proportion of their oil revenues overseas in the world economy. Somehow, such wealth has not been used to produce either an experience of human well-being and civic satisfaction or to create modern societies that flourish in the manner of the more successful East Asian countries. The explanation for this failure is contested. Most commentators attribute this disappointing pattern of development in the Middle East to the play of indigenous forces, the legacy of Ottoman and colonial rule, and also the inability of indigenous elites to surmount such disempowering legacies by avoiding corrupt and autocratic forms of rulership. How to move forward to a better future is a matter for appropriate debate, and finally of politics, in each of these countries.

There are influential enthusiasts for modernity who argue that the whole problem of the Arab world is associated with the reluctance and inability of its elites to embrace globalization as a positive opportunity of extraordinary promise, a position argued repeatedly and with arrogant self-assurance by Thomas Friedman, who couples journalism with ultra-materialist punditry. There are others who seek to combine an affirmation of tradition, which means essentially Islam, with participation in the modern world, a position being pursued on the borders of the Arab world with great dignity and political courage, given difficult internal and global conditions, by Iran's President Khatami. The choices of how to move forward, given present actualities, need to be made by the peoples of the various countries in the region, exercising more fully and creatively their rights of self-determination. The most that can be done by way of positive forms of external influence is to push hard for adherence to human rights, the practice of democracy, and a readiness of outsiders to provide development assistance where it can be used constructively, and to engage in the give-and-take of dialogue.

A secondary and closely related explanation of despair, futility, and the rise of extremism is associated with the manner in which globalization is being enacted worldwide.[5] The causal relationship between the world economy and regional distress is not manifest, and is being challenged by some recent widely noticed social science studies that question the linking of poverty and social deprivation with recourse to terrorism.[6] It is true that on a class basis the empirical foundation for claiming a connection between social injustice and political extremism does not exist. Those most deprived are often less capable of acting and less disposed to do so, being caught up in the struggle for survival on a daily basis, and they often tend to have less focused anger and less analytic clarity about societal failures, although the so-called "Arab street" is a reminder of the militancy of the masses as compared with the willingness of several governing elites in the Arab world to subordinate their national goals to Western interests. Those who are educated in these countries, especially if lacking promising career prospects, seem more readily attracted to and persuaded by extremist and conspiratorial explanations of their circumstances and are recruited to serve history in distorted ways. Osama bin Laden and the leadership of al-Qaeda seem to exemplify this pattern of deformed and deforming backlash.

Even so, the societies that give rise to significant terrorist movements are those with a combination of deep historic grievances and those that appear victimized to various degrees by the contemporary reality afflicting their country and region. True, there are small extremist groups and sociopathic individuals that have emerged in the most democratic and prosperous societies, but their conduct is at the outer margins of socially acceptable conduct. Police methods, perhaps stepping across a few constitutional lines, have been able to isolate and eliminate the wider threats posed to the established order by such extremism, mainly relying on democratic procedures to achieve change. Such was the fate of the Red Army Faction, also known as the Baader-Meinhof Gang, in Germany, the Red Brigades in Italy, and Aum Shinrikyo in Japan. Domestic law enforcement dealt with Timothy McVeigh, who was found by an American court to have been responsible for the 1995 Oklahoma City terrorist attack on a federal office building that killed 168 persons. A society as complex, competitive, diverse, and as riven by social tensions as the United States is bound to be faced with bizarre violent behavior associated with the sociopathic fantasies and destructive impulses of disturbed and alienated individuals. The horrendous school shootings of recent years by adolescents and likely the dissemination through the mails of anthrax in late 2001 are illustrative of such behavior. It seems likely that the incidence of domestic terrorism in the United States would be reduced by the elimination of guns from civil society and greater efforts to nurture a non-violent political culture, but even in a country such as Germany with tight gun control and great deference to government, terrible incidents of anarchic violence have been directed against completely innocent members of society. What is notable, however, is that societies that handle grievances peacefully, that enjoy the benefits of democracy and human rights, and that are not humbled and disadvantaged by globalization never give rise to terrorist activity that is societally sustained and incapable of being controlled by normal policing methods. In effect, *there is no sea that sustains terrorists swimming in such essentially legitimate societal waters.*

The most elusive dimension of winning the war against global terror is to engage in the process of overcoming the global democratic deficit, seeking to establish for the world a humane form of global governance to supplant the present geopolitical and hegemonic structures. There are a variety of transition steps that might have been taken at the end of the cold war a decade ago, but American leadership failed to seize the initiative, moving instead to consolidate its geostrategic gains in purely conventional ways associated with a world of distinct, yet unequal, sovereign states. The most notable of these steps would have been a determined effort to achieve total nuclear disarmament by way of a phased treaty process that included adequate verification mechanisms, as well as, and coordinated with, the establishment of a strong UN peacekeeping capability to address humanitarian catastrophes throughout the world and to deal with the implementation and enforcement of treaties dealing with weaponry. Such developments could have proceeded with greater confidence had there also been good progress in addressing legitimate grievances throughout the world in the spirit discussed in the prior section, as well as with an engagement with a more equitable approach to global economic policy, including development assistance by the rich to the poor.

More ambitious innovations were being promoted during the 1990s by new coalitions of moderate governments and civil society actors that led to such notable outcomes as the Anti-Personnel Landmines Treaty and the Rome Treaty of 1998 to establish a permanent International Criminal Court. Both of these initiatives went forward despite obstructive resistance by the United States. Whether US obstructionism can be overcome in these settings of attempted global reform remains to be seen.

There are other initiatives that would help give tangible expression to the quest for humane global governance. One of the most notable, both symbolically and potentially substantively, would be the establishment of a global parliament or global peoples assembly, either free-standing or within the United Nations, possibly as a second chamber of the General Assembly. The experience of the European Parliament is suggestive, both by its early obscurity and seeming irrelevance, and through its growth over time into a respected, influential, and integral part of the European Union.

Even more central to the aspirations and perceptions of the peoples of the world, especially those in the South, would be the negotiation of a more socially equitable framework for the world economy, starting with the mandate of such prominent institutions as the IMF, World Bank, and above all, the WTO, as well as with regional embodiments such as NAFTA. There were a variety of reactions generated by the Asian Financial Crisis of 1997, the continuing problems of heavily indebted countries and financially troubled countries (for instance, Argentina and Turkey), and the anti-globalization movement that challenged the ideological dominance of neoliberalism, sometimes known as "the Washington consensus." Also challenged by transnational civic action were the decidedly undemocratic operating procedures of international institutions relating to trade and finance.

The World Economic Forum that was associated with annual meetings in Davos until 2002 when it met in New York City, apparently as an act of solidarity with the city victimized by the September 11 attacks, has itself moved slowly and hesitantly away from an unconditional endorsement of capital-driven globalization. The need for the regulation of financial markets has been widely recognized, along with a greater emphasis on anti-poverty initiatives, corporate codes of conduct relating to environmental, labor, and human rights standards, and a renunciation of an anti-regulatory ethos associated with "market fundamentalism." Reinforcing this greater receptivity to global economic reform have been encouraging initiatives in global civil society reflecting alternative values and ideas, including the counterpart annual forum held annually at Puerto Allegre, Brazil under the banner of the World Social Forum.

A dramatic innovation, advocated by such prominent figures as Jacques Delors, would be the establishment within the United Nations of an Economic Security Council, with balanced North/South representation and a mandate to achieve *humane globalization.* September 11, especially in the United States, has had a devastating regressive effect on these encouraging developments of the 1990s by diverting energies and fears to the dangers posed by megaterrorism and the retaliatory ethos associated with punishing those associated with the harm done. We have yet to see how long the trauma of that day will throw the US off course in adjusting to the postmodern challenge of heightened interdependence, the digitalization of information, and the rise of networked, transnational organizational structures. If moves toward humane global governance can be resumed with sufficient impact on societal awareness around the world to foster hope in the future, then the prospects of political moderation, peaceful resolution of conflicts, and a generalized repudiation of violence as the necessary agency of change could alter our understanding of security. A decisive conceptual and behavioral shift in the direction of *human* security would definitely constitute a final victory in the war against global terror!

Losing the War

My understanding of "losing" is implicit in what I mean by "winning." Essentially, losing comes from treating the attacks in isolation from their social and political and cultural contexts, and reasserting as unambiguously as possible American hegemonic control over the Middle East, relying on direct and indirect means (that is, subordinated regimes, allies) and on military and non-military instruments of power, and pushing the world into a new phase of strategic rivalry by inducing reactions to an empire-building project undertaken behind the smokescreen of the war on global terror. Losing also means refusing to acknowledge the relevance of legitimate grievances, especially in the Arab world, but with respect to Islam generally, and even more broadly with respect to how the leadership role of the United States is exercised in world affairs. The targeting of the US and Americans generally has not arisen in a political and moral vacuum, but against a background of perceived and actual abuse. Losing, in the sense intended here, would also be a consequence of expanding the defensive goals beyond the al-Qaeda threat, especially to address a variety of loosely linked concerns, such as the continued leadership of Saddam Hussein in Iraq, a variety of violent anti-state movements engaged in a variety of nationalist struggles, and, most of all, the spread of weapons of mass destruction to the category of states self-servingly labeled by Washington "rogue," re-packaged by President Bush as "axis of evil" countries.

Losing is primarily understood in this analysis to mean a willful or negligent loss of focus on the September 11 threat, thereby embarking on a wider war than is legally and morally justifiable or necessary, with a reliance on much more controversial benchmarks of effectiveness, and with the increased likeliness of a backlash effect arising from provoking both additional manifestations of extremism directed at the US and its interests, and the stimulation of a drive by other countries to join together to contain what is regarded, with reason, as a US bid for global dominance. This kind of defeat is almost certain to result from the prevailing American effort to restore its security by an almost total reliance on geopolitical influence and coercive means, with a minimal or non-existent attention to moral, political, and legal dimensions.

Secondarily—though this seems politically irrelevant given the prevailing climate of opinion in the United States—losing could conceivably mean seeking to acknowledge *illegitimate* grievances or failing to heed legitimate American rights and interests. This sort of defeat in the global war would have resulted, in my view, from heeding the counsel of those critics of American imperialism who argued against adopting even a minimal defensive war mode of response, insisting instead that the US government rely exclusively on law-enforcement techniques combined with actions under the direct authority of the United Nations and strict adherence to pre-existing rules of international law. Specifically, such a perspective opposed recourse to war against Afghanistan, even with a UN mandate, and opposed the displacement of the Taliban regime. As such, it opposed the reasonableness, legality, and necessity for the US government to act in self-defense. In my view, the exercise of such a US right of self-defense seemed valid and necessary despite the existence of the legitimate grievances in the Arab world as discussed above. No government with the capabilities to reduce the threat of megaterrorism could be expected under the circumstances to refrain from a coercive response based on the need for anticipatory action and forward defense. If a government had somehow been so inclined to respond in a timid manner, its citizenry would have repudiated such passivity.

To call the preference for such non-violent initiatives "losing" is a position susceptible to misunderstanding, for generally the promotion of non-violence is an essential element in any wider effort to overcome war, which is, after all, along with economic disparities, the decisive obstacle to achieving humane governance on a global scale. But in addressing the al-Qaeda network under present world conditions, given its past behavior and proclaimed future mission, the rationale for *limited* war seems to me persuasive, provided the focus on al-Qaeda is not superseded by more expanded war aims, which lamentably seems to be happening as a matter of deliberate choice by American political leaders.

Another way of understanding this policy and security dilemma is to acknowledge the deficiencies of global governance that do not make it currently reasonable to rely on non-violent instruments to restore security and address the threat of megaterrorism, and to propose the sort of reforms at the United Nations and elsewhere that would make the avoidance of the war mode feasible in these circumstances because alternative response capabilities existed. But such an assessment identifies a project for global reformers; it does not provide guidance for those who needed to fashion a response on September 12.

A New Statist Twist

Tariq Ali writes in somewhat exaggerated prose that "[r]eligious fundamentalists do not single out the United States for special treatment for any other reason than its hegemonic power."[7] Even prior to September 11 there were good reasons to believe that the United States was seeking to achieve an imperial grip on the *new* geopolitics of globalization: by controlling the technological frontiers of information technology; by shaping the world economy along neoliberal lines as articulated through the medium of such subordinate actors as the IMF, World Bank, and the WTO; by presiding over an innovative "humanitarian" diplomacy of selective intervention; by aspiring to and demonstrating military dominance, exhibited in "zero-casualty warfare" (NATO War in Kosovo); and by pursuing new generations of nuclear weaponry and quietly moving ahead with plans to militarize space. Whether this empire-building was state-centric, ultimately controlled from Washington rather than Davos, was open to question before September 11, with political leaders, even in the United States, seeming to take their cues from the views prevailing among the managers of financial markets and global corporations rather than from their own citizenry or bureaucracy. Such capital-driven empire-building seemed essentially consistent with a long-term trend toward the de-territorialization of power and authority, and the new distribution of power giving structure in the form of global governance appropriate for the emergent era of globalization had yet to gel fully.[8] It is this trend that has been reversed, at least temporarily, in the aftermath of September 11. The nerve center of empire-building has been, for the time being, decisively shifted back to the state, with the political discourse moving from "globalization," an economistic framing of the new reality, to "war" and "security," a revived and altered statist framing that is being articulated by the White House and Pentagon, and their think-tank intellectuals. As Eliot Cohen, long an intelligent commentator and supporter of such an American posture writes in the new context:

> ... [T]he US military plays an extraordinary and inimitable role. It has become, whether Americans or others like it or not, the ultimate guarantor of international order—something quite different from what it was only a few years ago as the leader of a coalition of free states against the well-defined threats of the Cold War.[9]

Imagine the impact of such unvarnished sentiments of global power projection by the United States on a security planner in Paris or Beijing, or a vigilant citizen in New York or Chicago. Or imagine the hysterical responses in the Washington bureaucracy and American media if a comparable Chinese vision of global dominance were being set forth by officials making policy in Beijing. Eliot Cohen's idea that the country is pursuing a global mission "whether Americans or others like it or not" is a step beyond "the arrogance of power" and a large retreat from accountable government, especially considering the spread of destructive weaponry around the world, and the presumed unwillingness of many societies to stay passive in the face of such American geopolitical pretensions.

This new deep structure of geopolitics requires us to restate "losing" with a significantly new (really the renewal of what had been superseded in the 1990s) statist twist: as almost certainly giving rise over time to a new phase of geopolitical rivalry organized primarily along statist lines, with coalitions of resistance involving quite possibly China, Japan, Russia, and Europe in various combinations now impossible to predict. Prior to September 11, the patterns of resistance to capital-driven empire-building were primarily undertakings of global civil society (the anti-globalization movement) as reinforced in some settings by "a new globalism" (collaboration between moderate, democratic governments and civil society actors to promote reforms animated by the values and goals of humane global governance). At this point, these forms of resistance seem difficult to mobilize effectively to oppose on their own the new statist, militarist phase of empire-building, but such populist resistance that is almost certain to materialize if, as now seems a virtual certainty, a war is launched against Iraq, may galvanize a variety of governments to move toward a posture of geopolitical resistance. It would seem, then, that "losing" scenarios are being shaped from two sides: to the extent the American empire-builders succeed, the peoples of the world lose out on their freedom and forfeit prospects for the emergence of humane global governance; to the extent that the empire-builders generate strong forms of resistance, the likelihood of catastrophic war casts its dark, dark shadow across the future. Basically, no scenario for winning exists except through the voluntary abandonment of the project for a global empire, which presupposes its rejection by the American people, which is not likely given the degree to which both political parties appear to endorse the project and no political alternative has been clearly articulated and given political expression by a clear-eyed mass movement.

A less spectacular way of losing seems on its way to happening: the embrace of secular fundamentalism in the form of hyper-nationalism and the portrayal of adversaries as "evil." President Bush has shaped the American response to September 11 in these absolutist terms of good versus evil, extending such an understanding beyond al-Qaeda to include "the axis of evil" countries and to encompass indirectly many political movements of resistance and self-determination around the world, some of which have been struggling for decades against oppressive conditions. Such ideological mimicry of megaterrorism poisons the well of public debate in the United States, thereby undermining one of the central strengths of liberal democracy: its reliance on the marketplace of ideas. This dynamic is led by the US government, but the media has fallen into line with hardly a whimper of protest, providing one-sided nightly presentations often by retired military officers or right-wing think-tank operatives, marginalizing critics and dissenters, portraying controversial moves of policy as patriotic in a manner that locates them beyond argument, and pretending as if there is no occasion to regard major choices as subject to reasonable debate except on issues of tactics. The merger of this closed intellectual atmosphere with the one-sided treatment of the Israel/Palestine conflict contributes further to the fundamentalist climate of opinion in the United States. The one-sided vote (94–2 in the Senate, 352–21 in the House) by the US Congress on May 2, 2002 to reaffirm unconditional US support of Israel in the wake of its offensive against the Palestinian territories and re-occupation of Palestinian cities confirms the impression of a fundamentalist turn of political mind in American political institutions (as well as disclosing a craven expression of ethnic politics), oblivious to equities, to the legal status of what was done by Israel, and to the opinions of others around the world evoked by the images of death and destruction at Jenin, and Israeli reliance on inflicting collective punishments of great severity throughout the West Bank and Gaza. This American governmental response, accentuated in its one-sidedness during the period of Sharon's leadership, represents ethnic politics and American grand strategy at its extremist, opportunistic worst.

Losing also relates to human rights and international humanitarian law. To the extent that the US government moves to over-regulate the entry and movements of immigrants, it creates an atmosphere of fear and intimidation within the country, and discourages individuals from studying and working here, especially those of Muslim background. Whole countries are branded as sponsors of terrorism whose nationals will be denied US visas. As of 2002, these include Iraq, North Korea, Iran, Sudan, Cuba, Libya, and Syria. New legislation also involves close monitoring of all foreign students, moves toward a surveillance society that are facilitated by new technologies of observation and snooping.

Again the threats to democracy mount as the government claims the need for greater regulatory discretion, less judicial supervision and constitutional restraint, and ever greater secrecy. Instead of opening the government to scrutiny in the interests of accountability, there is an opening up of previously autonomous domains of civil society to authorized governmental spying and control, including a likely reliance on informers and expanded authority for police and intelligence operations that impinge upon domains of behavior previously regarded as out of bounds. The expected result of implementation is to dampen the democratic spirit.

Of comparable concern is the treatment of al-Qaeda and Taliban detainees, particularly those being held at Camp X-Ray, Guantanamo Bay. The exaggerated security precautions involving humiliating and cruel confinement, the movement of these prisoners far from their homelands, and the disregard of public criticism of such treatment, works to undermine the protection of all individuals, especially unconventional combatants, captured in wartime condition that is embodied in the Third Geneva Convention on the Treatment of Prisoners of War, as supplemented by the 1977 Protocols. There is no plausible basis for denying Taliban detainees full protection under international humanitarian law, and to the extent that low-ranking al-Qaeda members are involved, they too should receive the benefits of the Geneva framework. Also, the proposed reliance on special military commissions operating in secret to press charges against non-Americans, with no right of appeal, is an unnecessary abridgement of due process for individuals accused of serious criminality. Also deeply troubling is the claimed capacity of the government to label anyone, including American citizens, as "unlawful combatants," and then hold them in detention indefinitely, denying due process rights without even making charges.

There might have been an argument for some downward adjustment of these rights of individuals in the early days after September 11 when there were genuine concerns about additional plans for megaterrorist follow-up attacks being in the al-Qaeda pipeline. Under such circumstances, expanded rights of interrogation would have seemed reasonable, taking into account the reality that the old template of security and rights seemed quite inapplicable to this new kind of threat.

But this time has passed, and the general goal of international humanitarian law to maintain standards of protection for vulnerable individuals deserves respect as a high priority. We will surely lose this war if we betray the values of democracy, including the rule of law, which includes human rights and the humane treatment of prisoners taken in the course of warfare.

A Concluding Observation

These ideas of winning and losing are crude, yet revealing, simplifications that overlook nuances and the degree to which the issues are intertwined, and beset by uncertainties, and alteration due to new and unforeseen developments. Two of these are worth mentioning: first, will the al-Qaeda threat continue to wane in the months and years ahead? And not be replaced by some similar kind of danger? Secondly, will market forces seek to preempt a new cycle of statist rivalry generated by US empire-building? Will the anti-globalization and pro-global democracy movements mount a challenge to both predatory globalization and American empire-building?

As of now, the American geopolitical project seems to be imposing its will on the world and its peoples, but history in turbulent times has a cunning that often eludes the most informed interpreters. Most of our hopes about the future depend on such cunning at the moment, as more ordinary sources of inspiration and hope seem either intimidated by brute force or rendered mute by failures of political and moral imagination. Yet recent history has been so full of surprises (the end of the cold war, the collapse of the Soviet Union, the peaceful dismantling of apartheid in South Africa) that it would be a grave mistake of appraisal to suppose that we understand the future well enough to be pessimistic. In the face of such uncertainty, and in a regressive political atmosphere, the rationale for the progressive engagement of the citizenry has never seemed greater: we must rescue shipwrecked democracy here at home and find the path that leads away from American empire-building toward humane global governance.

To pursue this line of inquiry, I shall begin in Chapter 2 with the crisis posed by the events of September 11, and seek to depict the particular challenge that megaterrorism and al-Qaeda presented to the US and to the world order that emerged from the twentieth century. In

Chapter 3, I examine the case for an American response that began by waging war against the al-Qaeda presence and the Taliban regime in Afghanistan, discussing the various dimensions of the debate relating to the necessity, effectiveness, and legality of the military campaign. Perhaps from the outset, and certainly in the weeks after September 11, the White House and the Department of Defense launched the Great War on Terror, a mandate expanded well beyond the megaterrorist challenge and a cover for American empire building. In Chapter 5, "Wrecking World Order," I consider the costs, risks, and inappropriateness of this magnification of the rationale for war.

Chapter 6, "Challenging the New Patriotism," offers a critique of the orchestration of support for this governmental agenda by way of an unprecedented mobilization of patriotic fervor, shaped by a jingoistic and xenophobic nationalism, especially inappropriate for the globalizing world of the twenty-first century. This assessment is then followed by a chapter, "The Eclipse of Human Rights," that assesses the domestic costs of the official American response to September 11, stressing the longer term impingement on traditional American liberties, as well as acknowledging the genuine security requirements arising from the likelihood that al-Qaeda operatives are physically present in the United States and available to carry our terrorist missions in the future. And finally, the book ends with a discussion, "Facing the Future," that speculates about where these Great Terror War policies are leading us as a people and nation, and the urgency of mounting opposition to the Washington scenarios of empire-building and perpetual war.

2. THE DIMENSIONS OF MEGATERRORISM

B efore turning to the question of how the US should best wage its proclaimed war on terror, it is essential to understand how the September 11 attacks were different from earlier instances of terrorism. Though this chapter outlines the crucial difference between this new form and earlier forms of terrorism, it should be read knowing that the terrorism of that sunny Tuesday morning was not entirely without precedent, for the 1993 bombing of the World Trade Center and the 1995 Oklahoma City bombing of the Murrah Federal Office Building were also undertakings designed to strike major symbolic centers of national power and to inflict maximum substantive harm on ordinary civilians.

What most generally distinguishes the September 11 attacks was their perpetrators' daring method, their selection of prime targets of power and wealth, their astonishing degree of success in carrying out the deadly mission, and the extraordinary shock effects of the overall spectacle of death and destruction, as well as the acute sense of continuing danger and vulnerability along with a grudging acknowledgement of the ingenuity and resolve displayed by the attack. These immediate effects were magnified by continuous TV coverage, permanently inscribing the unforgettable imagery of human tragedy and the evil perpetrators in the political consciousness of the world, and especially the American viewing audience. Within such an inflamed atmosphere of grief and anger, recourse to an extreme response by the political leadership of the country was inevitable: "September 11 has changed everything, forever!" It remains common to hear people divide their interpretation of the world into two categories: Before September 11/After September 11. It is still too early to tell whether this recent fault-line is a temporary phenomenon or does point to a historical rupture of lasting significance for both the United States and the world. Nor do we yet know whether the changes made in American foreign and domestic policy were well-adapted to the originality of the challenge, or rather represented outmoded patterns of response ill-suited to cope with the present dangers.

Megaterrorism is a unique challenge, differing from earlier expressions of global terrorism, by magnitude, scope, and ideology, representing a serious effort to transform world order as a whole, and not merely change the power structure of one or more sovereign states. To evaluate the response that is unfolding around the world under the sole proprietorship of American geopolitical leadership, let us first depict the unprecedented nature of these megaterrorist attacks by outlining their defining elements.

Substantive and Symbolic Harm

The magnitude of the attacks, the loss of life of thousands of persons from all walks of life, from all backgrounds, immediately conveyed to the world the depth of tragedy. The sheer numbers involved, although scaled back from over 6,000 at one point close to the time of impact to slightly fewer than 3,000 a few months later, were given greater weight by the loss of life on the part of several hundred New York City firefighters and police officers who sacrificed their own lives in what turned out in many instances to be futile attempts to rescue those trapped inside the Trade Center, and also by the plight of the passengers on the four airliners that crashed leaving no survivors. Many were rescued from the buildings or managed to escape, or the death toll would have been even higher. The psychological impact of this human dimension was also dramatized by cell phone conversations between family members in their last moments of life, along with the testimony of those who escaped, giving an anguishing concreteness to the personal pain of the survivors, which prevented the experience of loss from being reduced to a statistical, impersonal body count. Such a close encounter with this human dimension was further reinforced by published individual profiles, complete with family pictures and often complemented by TV biographical narratives of many of those who lost their lives on September 11, in dramatic juxtaposition with the grief of surviving family members, depicted at funerals and in public events dedicated to mourning and remembering those who gave their lives on September 11. The feelings aroused were further heightened by frequent images on TV screens of Osama bin Laden giving interviews from terrorist training camps and hideouts in Afghanistan and by pictures and accounts of the lives of those who hijacked the four planes on the morning of September 11.

Beyond this, the symbolic effects were initially shattering: the World Trade Center, the prime expression of American economic dominance in an era of globalization, had been obliterated, almost simultaneously with a major hit on the Pentagon, the core embodiment of American military power. To aim at such targets was itself a wildly ambitious project for a non-state terrorist group to embark upon, but to carry out the mission with such significant destructive results, conveyed, as never before, the reality and depth of America's vulnerability to al-Qaeda, now its most dedicated and credible enemy. And there was an immediate public realization that what had happened on September 11 could be repeated in the future with even worse consequences. This interpretation of danger was endorsed by President Bush and other national leaders, and given a certain added fearsomeness by the anthrax sequel (even if the latter events now seem in reality disconnected). Periodic and highly publicized warnings of the near-certainty of megaterrorist incidents in the future reinforced the public fear. What had been done to the United States could be done to any modern or semi-modern society, creating some plausibility to the contention that what was at stake was "civilization" or, in some lines of interpretation, "modernity." What was threatened beyond American viability were the underlying capabilities of territorial states to continue to provide tolerable levels of security for their inhabitants in the face of cleverly concealed and devoutly dedicated networked adversaries.

Terrorism could no longer be treated as an unpleasant nuisance that inflicted tragedy on the unlucky victims and their families: it had become a challenge to the fundamental ideas of security underlying world order. The strongest state in the history of the world was paradoxically emerging as the most menaced, although friends and allies shared much of the danger, and the far-flung global presence of the United States distributed potential "American" targets globally. Under these circumstances, there could be no resumption of societal normalcy until such security had been restored, or at least there was the appearance of a maximum effort being made to achieve such results. It was not possible to accommodate megaterrorism of the September 11 variety in the manner of earlier high profile terrorist incidents that captured the public imagination for a few days, but then gave way to new national and world developments. Here, as the special daily section of the *New York Times* expressed the persisting crisis for the remaining days of 2001—"The Nation Challenged"—there could be no return to normalcy until the sense of threat had subsided and some measure of revenge exacted, or at least punishment inflicted. Although not so interpreted by political leaders and mainstream commentators, megaterrorism posed a structural challenge, that is, one that could not be met by the tried and true methods of the past, and, indeed, relying on such methods could end up compounding the threat being posed.

At the same time, the situation was complicated by an awareness that the economic well-being of the country, already then on the brink of a serious economic recession as a result of the bursting of the dot-com bubble, required as much normalcy and reassurance as possible. This general interest was at its height in New York City, which had sustained heavy economic damage from the attacks, leading its newly charismatic mayor, Rudy Giuliani, to plead for tourists to visit the city and spend money. Hence, mixed messages were sent to the American people by their leaders: mobilize energies and resources for all-out war, but remain avid consumers! Little doubt exists that considerable economic damage was done by the attacks—property damage and stock market losses alone have been estimated to be in the many billions, a million jobs were said to be lost at least temporarily—although it is not easy to disentangle the impact of a preexisting declining economy from the aggravating effects of September 11. Of course, the established order would like to shift as much blame for the economic woes as possible to economic reverberations stemming from the attacks. President George W. Bush added his weight to the effort to revive the economy, and yet keep the connection to September 11 alive, by appearing in airline commercials to convince the public of the renewed safety of commercial air travel.

Without doubt the combined severity of effects, the actual losses together with the traumatizing realization that the inner core of the American colossus was severely vulnerable, did shatter once and for all the earlier attitude of complacency about the visionary challenges posed by non-state foreign enemies of the United States prepared to rely on terrorism in pursuit of their goals. But until September 11 the American public and the media, while giving lip service to such warnings, never seemed convinced. Perhaps because the leaders, despite their words of warning, themselves seemed not particularly worried, devoting most of their energies to promoting globalization. Certainly the public was not sufficiently impressed before September 11 to support a return to the security-oriented preoccupations of the cold war. It was the economy, stupid, as the first Bush president learned in the 1992 elections, despite his popularity just months earlier in the afterglow of an easy and decisive American military victory in the Gulf War. Globalization displaced traditional security concerns in the aftermath of the cold war, emphasizing a shift of attention from strategic rivalries among sovereign states to a world order dominated by markets instead of states. To the extent that this image was challenged, it was from a different direction entirely, by the insistence that the future would witness a "clash of civilizations," a view that also held that states were being superseded as the primary political actors on the global stage, but now by civilizations rather than by market forces. These ideas of Samuel Huntington's attracted a surprising amount of attention and concern—as well as criticism and denial—around the world. But whether global markets or civilizations were viewed as the waves of the future, megaterrorism did not figure prominently in the political imagination of either citizens or governments prior to September 11.

In retrospect, we now realize that the apocalyptical musings of bin Laden should not have been dismissed merely as the reprehensible, but essentially unthreatening, sentiments of a demented and still obscure underground leader, even before September 11. After all, bin Laden and al-Qaeda had already demonstrated their ability to attack successfully well-defended manifestations of the American presence in the Islamic world. They were widely believed to be responsible for the Khobar Tower attacks in Saudi Arabia, the 1998 Embassy bombings in Nairobi and Dar es Salaam, and the attack on the USS Cole in 2000, each of which had been boldly carried out, inflicting significant loss of life and directed at symbolic embodiments of the American military and diplomatic presence and power in the Arab world. But such incidents, spectacular though they were as terrorist events, were not treated as paradigm-shattering. As such, these incidents seemed to call only for better intelligence, greater police cooperation, and strengthened vigilance at official American overseas sites—they were not then widely appreciated as forming the sort of challenge that called for either a new genre of warfare or for extraordinary measures of prevention and protection within the territorial limits of the United States.

Genocidal Intent

The character of Osama bin Laden's megaterrorism was further distinguished by his chilling acknowledgement that it was the duty of Muslims to kill indiscriminately anyone who was an American, a Jew, or in some formulations "a Crusader," which could be understood as anyone of Christian or Judeo-Christian background. Such an embrace of genocidal intent and tactics—that is, targeting individuals for lethal attack solely on the basis of their ethnic, religious, national, and civilizational identities—was reinforced by bin Laden's statements on frequent occasions, including his taped interviews after September 11 that cheerfully acknowledged the commission of megaterrorism as a morally acceptable means of struggle, which was further validated with a rhetoric of religious justification and political destiny. To deliver a genocidal message to the Muslim masses must be taken seriously in view of the degree of despair and resentment that exists toward the United States, especially in Arab countries. The context is such that genocidal undertakings must be repudiated as clearly and unconditionally as possible, and not allowed to develop further. How to do this is, of course, among the most contested aspects of the counterterrorist global policy that has taken shape in the months since September 11, raising directly the core question as to whether legitimate grievances exist with respect to the American role in the Muslim world, and, if so, how to rectify them so as to discourage racial and ethnic hatred without rewarding terrorism.

The genocidal character of this terrorism adds to and intensifies the dangers posed, and makes the attacks of September 11 take on a depraved character that aggravates the crime of international terrorism. Whether the attacks are an instance of the crime of genocide, as distinct from having a "genocidal" dimension, is far from legally clear. Certainly, such a deliberate attack aimed at civilians qualifies as a Crime Against Humanity, subjecting perpetrators to indictment and punishment on a basis that parallels and even exceeds the gravity of charges of international terrorism. But on the basis of currently available evidence, the struggle waged by al-Qaeda, as articulated by bin Laden, lacks the programmatic implementation associated with ethnic killing to qualify as "genocide." The genocidal dimension seems incidental to the political goals associated primarily with "evicting" the Americans, or alternatively, "Crusaders," from Muslim lands, serving primarily pragmatic ends rather than representing an intrinsic goal of its own. But this is a thin line, especially if the megaterrorist campaign continues to mobilize support by disseminating a genocidal message, inspiring incidents of gratuitous violence against Jewish and American civilian targets around the world, including places of religious worship and centers of learning.

Visionary Goals

Osama bin Laden's declaration of war on the United States in 1996 conveys the visionary and purportedly religious nature of his project. Though he lacks the credentials to speak with any widely recognized religious authority, he clearly serves as the inspirational foundation for the political extremism of al-Qaeda's tactics. Bin Laden's declaration was expressed in the form of *jihad*, or holy struggle, claiming sanctification from Islam and the Koran. In bin Laden's words, "… we have declared *jihad* against the US, because in our religion it is our duty to make *jihad* so that God's word is the only one exalted to the heights and so that we drive the Americans away from all Muslim countries."[1] The immediate goals of bin Laden are primarily political rather than cultural or social, although perhaps such a distinction should not be so sharply drawn. The emphasis in his statements, and certainly in the tactics of his movement, is to focus on the expulsion of the American presence from the Arab world, especially from its holiest places on the Arabian peninsula, and not on the social policies of the Arab regimes. This point should not be overstated. Bin Laden's praise for the Taliban administration of Afghanistan as having been the finest embodiment of Islamic values visible in the contemporary world leaves no doubt about his sense that what Islam implies is a heartless and male-dominated purification process of the most severe character, with the longer-range objective of uniting the entire Muslim world, and from there converting the rest of the world to Islam. But al-Qaeda likely conceived of its role as doing the political and military job that needed to be completed before the serious social and cultural work could be undertaken.

Goals like bin Laden's, which are of an essentially visionary nature, are off the radar screen of plausible diplomatic demands that could at some point be partially accommodated. It would not be plausible for the United States to satisfy, or even entertain discussion of these goals by negotiation as an alternative response to war, given either the grandiosity of challenging the way security has been organized by existing governments in the Arab world, by denying the validity of Israel's existence, and by challenging the rights of the West to dominate the region, including arrangements relating to the pricing and supply of oil. Past challenges directed at an oppressive established order even if based on terrorist tactics by non-state actors have on occasion led to "peace processes" that amount to political compromises over a governing process in a particular sovereign state or in response to specific claims of self-determination. The recent examples of the Good Friday Agreement seeking an end to civil strife in Northern Ireland and the Oslo Peace Process unsuccessfully seeking to settle the long Israel/Palestine struggle indicate that groups treated as terrorists at one stage of a conflict may be accepted as the legitimate representatives of an aggrieved people or nation at another stage, and accepted as negotiating partners in the search for peaceful resolution.

An additional difficulty is conceptual—and political. Bin Laden claims by self-appointment to represent and speak on behalf of Islam as a whole; he says he is not tied to the viewpoint or authority of a specific state or nation. He has treated Islamic identity as the proper unit for participation in global arrangements, which in effect is contending that the world is constituted by "civilizations" or "religions," rather than territorial "states" enjoying sovereign rights, or even regions encompassing contiguous states. Existing Arab governments, even those with a religious orientation, do not support the supra-nationalism associated with the claims being made by bin Laden and are themselves, as leaders of sovereign states, threatened by the worldview, modes of struggle, and underlying vision he advocates. Indeed, it is the alleged corruption and complicity of these governments in the Arab world, their refusal to uphold the integrity of the wider Islamic world and their unwillingness to oppose the

American role, that bin Laden cites as his main reasons for issuing a declaration of *jihad* against Western domination. But more than this, such governments are a major part of the problem, according to bin Laden, for he seeks (and they obstruct) the reestablishment of a caliphate for the widest embrace of Islamic adherents within the *umma*, or community of Islam. Such a reconstituted caliphate would essentially eliminate, or at least subordinate, the state structure of governance that operates in the regions and countries where Islam is the dominant religion. And the image of rulership that would accompany the realization of this vision has been prefigured, according to bin Laden, by the Taliban rule in Afghanistan, but also by the original polity established in the seventh century by Mohammed.

Osama bin Laden appears to have fashioned his vision in the crucible of armed struggle, his initial holy war experience in Afghanistan during the 1980s. Such a struggle was of a relatively conventional character, opposing Soviet aggression, liberating a people and an Islamic country from foreign domination and domestic oppression, fighting against occupying military forces, and supporting subsequently the establishment of a governing process in a particular country that possessed an Islamic character. Such an undertaking enjoyed the backing of the United States and was not seen as posing any kind of challenge to the geopolitical dynamics of world politics. It also did not extend the field of struggle on an ethnic or religious basis to include "Russians" and all those of "Orthodox" or "Communist" persuasion, nor did it engage in transnational terrorism directed at the Soviet Union. In these respects, bin Laden's operations fit within the familiar categories of the statist politics that had come to define the modern era of world politics.

Bin Laden appears to have grossly misinterpreted the success and nature of his sponsorship of an Islamic contribution to the outcome in Afghanistan by moving toward a new *jihad* against the United States' role in the Arab world. His own words, uttered during a 1999 interview, are revealing. When speaking of the experience in Afghanistan, bin Laden says that *jihad* there had

> managed to crush the greatest empire known to mankind. They crushed the greatest military machine. The so-called superpower vanished into the air. We think that the United States is very much weaker than Russia. Based on the reports we received from our brothers who participated in *jihad* in

Somalia, we learned that they saw the weakness, frailty, and cowardice of US troops. Only 18 US troops were killed. Nonetheless they fled in the heart of darkness, frustrated, after they had caused the greatest commotion about the new world order.[2]

There are several important confusions present in this account. First of all, the idea that the Soviet Union was the stronger superpower seems fanciful in the extreme, particularly in view of its total collapse only a few years later, with the Afghanistan failure a symptom more than a cause. Secondly, bin Laden totally misinterprets the American impotence in Afghanistan and elsewhere, confusing its shallow commitment to humanitarian diplomacy as in Somalia with its unwillingness to defend its strategic interests. True, even where strategic interests are strongly involved, as they were in the Gulf War, the US aversion to accepting casualties feeds an impression of an unwillingness to engage deeply, but it is obviously a misimpression. As the response to September 11 vividly demonstrates, the US is fully prepared to pay whatever price is involved to destroy attackers and reestablish its security, upholding fully its strategic interests, which often possess global reach of their own. Once aroused, the United States has consistently demonstrated throughout its history that it ignores the human and other costs of war in its resolve to achieve total victory. Of course, in the midst of war, it seeks to use its technological superiority to shift the human costs of war away, to the extent possible, from its military personnel.

Revealingly, Bernard Lewis and others urging maximal responses to September 11 share bin Laden's reasoning, spinning their interpretations in militarist directions of their own. In articulating "what went wrong" with American policy in the Arab world, Lewis, relying on the same and similar statements by bin Laden, suggests that it was indeed the soft American policies in Somalia and elsewhere that emboldened the terrorists to entertain the idea that they could realistically challenge the United States. Lewis gives great weight to bin Laden's frequent assertions that America was a paper tiger, and he himself suggests that if the United States does not respond with sufficient force to do the job, then Islam will in the future be crushed by another more robust secular state. Lewis names India, Russia, and China as candidates for this role, asserting somewhat mournfully and disingenuously that they "may prove less squeamish than the Americans in using their power against Muslims and their sanctities."[3] Such a statement is incredible for a scholar to make given the actualities of the American role in the Middle East over the course of the last decade or so, which has included the Gulf War, a decade of punitive sanctions against Iraq, massive economic assistance to the Israeli military, as well as unwavering support of Israel's brutal and relentless occupation of Palestine. Nevertheless, Lewis polemicizes on behalf of a diplomacy of force and intimidation by selectively invoking past incidents in such a way as to argue that Arabs consistently back down when threatened and do the opposite when encouraged by American "retreats."

Generalizing on these views, Lewis, writing in the *National Review* of American prospects in the Middle East, insists that "[t]he range of American policy options in the region is being reduced to two alternatives, both disagreeable: Get tough or get out."[4] When asked to explain on TV what he was proposing by insisting on such stark alternatives, Lewis replied, "Well, by get tough I mean continue the good work that was started in Afghanistan and deal with other countries or groups, terrorists… The alternative, get out, is find a substitute for oil so that the Middle East no longer matters."[5] To so structure the American policy choice, given the dependence of the world economy on affordable and ample oil supplies, is to issue a chilling call for a civilizational war, and to do so on a simplistic and misleading basis.

To devote attention to such views is important, as Lewis is clearly regarded by much of the world media and the US government as the reigning expert on the Islamic world. His views carry great weight in the debates as to whether to alter those American policies that enrage the Arab world in general or to send a primary message of force that would result from expanding the war beyond Afghanistan to Iraq and elsewhere. The point here is that the Lewis interpretation of past behavior feeds a visionary counterterrorism under US auspices as surely as bin Laden's rather complementary interpretation encourages visionary terrorism from his direction. Lewis reinforces the White House view that the past US role in the Middle East should not be critically scrutinized (except for its supposed weakness when it comes to the use of military power to enforce its will) and that there are no legitimate Arab grievances that should be addressed either on their own merits, or even simply pragmatically, to stem the current high tide of anti-Americanism that has swept across the region.

Osama bin Laden, in his own statements and interpretations, discloses himself as a dedicated, unwavering visionary, but also as a deeply confused thinker when it comes to geopolitical reasoning and calculations. Despite these confusions as to the nature of an American response to mounting megaterrorist challenges, bin Laden can only be comprehended as a visionary leader. As Edward W. Said observed in the course of an interview not long after the attacks:

> ... it was not meant to be argued with. No message was intended with it... It transcended the political and moved into the metaphysical. There was a kind of cosmic, demonic quality of mind at work here, which refused to have any interest in dialogue and political organization and persuasion.[6]

Mark Juergensmeyer, writing before September 11, makes a similar assessment without specific reference to bin Laden, suggesting that "[r]eligious concepts of cosmic war, however, are ultimately beyond historical control, even though they are identified with this-worldly struggle. A satanic enemy cannot be transformed; it can only be destroyed."[7] Eric Rouleau seeks to extend the distance separating Osama bin Laden and his extremism from authentic Islamic thought by arguing that

> [r]ather than focusing on Islam and its alleged relationship with fanaticism and terrorism, it may be wiser to question the sanity of the killers of September 11, as well as bin Laden's emerging cult of death, which parallels various infamous sects in Europe and the US.[8]

Of course, it is important to treat the al-Qaeda threat as being separate from the central tenets of Islam so as to avoid the trap of engaging in a civilizational war, but at the same time it needs to be recognized that there exists a wider appeal of bin Laden's message to the Islamic world in light of Western policies and practices. Bin Laden can be conceived as essentially a leader of a deviant religious cult that purports to respresent Islam as a whole, but achieves its political potency by tapping into grievances intensely felt throughout the Islamic world.

This visionary or pathological component of the attacks was not independently influential in explaining the American recourse to war, but it did make it seem irresponsible for peace forces to insist that a diplomatic alternative to war existed. In this respect it is useful to contrast the situation that existed after the Iraqi conquest and annexation of Kuwait in 1990, or later in connection with Serb oppressive tactics in Kosovo. In both instances it was possible to argue credibly that the stated and only legitimate objectives of response could be achieved by a combination of sanctions and diplomatic initiatives, and that war could and should have been avoided, lessening the human suffering associated with restoring Kuwaiti sovereignty and keeping faith with the core idea of relying on the United Nations to solve international conflicts without recourse to war.[9] That failure of diplomacy in the 1990s seemed partly deliberate, as there were secondary reasons for the United States and Britain to undertake a preventive war to eliminate Iraq as a regional threat in relation to Israel, gulf oil reserves, regional stability, and the spread of weaponry of mass destruction as well as to mount a punitive war against Serbia both to protect the Kosovars, but also to give NATO a life after the cold war.

It is of great importance to interpret efforts to rely on non-military approaches such as sanctions in this period. The alleged failure of these approaches is part of what has contributed to such a strong consensus, especially in the United States, favoring military solutions. It is also crucial to distinguish those efforts that were pursuing constructive political goals, such as the peaceful restoration of Kuwaiti sovereign rights in the aftermath of the Iraqi invasion, and those instruments of coercion used to punish and humble a country. In this regard the sanctions policies used against Iraq ever since 1990 are instructive, yet disturbing. It is crucial to distinguish and contrast, particularly with respect to Iraq, those sanctions imposed before the Gulf War, used supposedly as a means of reinforcing diplomatic demands and threats of force associated with achieving the "peaceful" withdrawal of Iraqi forces from Kuwait from those sanctions imposed after a destructive war that are maintained for vague political objectives, and operate in a manner that inflicts severe suffering on the most vulnerable civilian sectors of an already devastated society. Arguably, the pre-war sanctions were not meant to achieve their stated goal, as Iraq was given no diplomatic space to withdraw in a manner that respected its sovereign status, and thus even these sanctions should be seen mainly as a prelude to war. This line of evaluation suggests that even in the presidencies of Bush, Sr. and Clinton, there was an American rejection of peacemaking diplomacy and a preference for warmaking. September 11 and the presidency of Bush, Jr. can thus be understood as carrying forward, with mass backing in the United States, this emergent American militarism. This tendency can in turn be understood as arising in a global setting where American assertiveness is no longer deterred by the Soviet presence and where innovations in military technology reduced wartime American casualties to near zero. A further part of this picture is the disillusionment of Washington with the role of the United Nations, either as instrument of foreign policy or as an effective actor on its own.

The Iraq situation has resurfaced in relation to the war against terror as a central drama, but again its shape and content were in place before the al-Qaeda attacks. By maintaining and strengthening comprehensive sanctions after the Gulf War, Iraq was placed under severe pressure. Iraq had been greatly weakened if not rendered helpless by the war, and its civilian population was predictably and acutely victimized by sanctions. There was no justification for such a punitive approach. The alleged concerns about Iraqi weaponry of mass destruction could have been addressed by reasonable inspection and export restrictions limiting sale of relevant technology to Iraq, but the main reliance should have been upon deterrence and containment, allowing Iraq to return to normalcy but warning its government that if they again resorted to military aggression, the response would be quick and devastating. Everything about Iraq's prior behavior suggested that it succumbed to pressure when the costs of its policies were too high. It needs to be remembered that it attacked Iran in 1980 only after being encouraged to do so by the US government, and falsely told that it would gain a quick victory. Similarly with Kuwait, the American diplomatic signals sent to Baghdad in 1990 were ambiguous at best, and there is good reason to believe that if given the chance Saddam Hussein would have pulled back to the old Iraqi borders to avert what he understood to be an impending overwhelming attack.

Tactical Ingenuity
The extraordinary execution of the terrorist operation—commandeering four commercial airliners at about the same time, carrying out the plan to fly into specific buildings sufficiently near the time of hijacking so that the chances of interception would be minimized, and managing to deliver the blow to the buildings on target with virtually full gas tanks—is staggering. Only one of the four planes

was denied success through the exploits of passengers who forfeited their lives by struggling against the hijackers, inducing a crash in western Pennsylvania, and averting an attack on a presumed Washington target, either the White House or the Capitol. Never in the history of terrorism had an operation of such stunning proportions been pulled off, although there were earlier comparable projects of spectacular scope that were foiled on a couple of occasions during the prior decade. What also made the al-Qaeda operation seem such a notable and disturbing terrorist success was that its immense results were achieved with extremely modest financial resources (one half a million dollars or less) and virtually no usual instruments of violence. Only the hitherto innocent, now notorious, box-cutters, were in the hijackers' arsenal of weaponry. Suddenly, relations of power between enemies could no longer be measured by financial capacity or shaped by the balance of capabilities. Beyond this, those who would mount such gruesome terrorist operations required no special technological sophistication other than the rather easily acquired knowledge to pilot and navigate large commercial airliners while in the air.

Writing before September 11, the conservative terrorist authority Walter Laqueur had correctly anticipated a new ethos of terrorism that prefigured megaterrorist operations. He placed major emphasis on the fact that

> [t]he ready availability of weapons of mass destruction had come to pass, and much of what has been thought about terrorism, including some basic assumptions, must be reconsidered…. The character of terrorism is changing, any restraints that existed are disappearing, and above all, the threat to human life has become infinitely greater than it was in the past.[10]

In common with the main think-tank specialists on terrorism, the danger was tactically misconceived as arising from the supposed ability and interest of terrorist groups and their state sponsors in developing and using weaponry of mass destruction, especially biological weaponry. This fear had been given mass currency when Bill Clinton, while president, read *The Cobra Connection*, a scary novel by Robert Preston, and grew personally concerned about the threat posed to American security by bio-warfare. But despite the much publicized attention to such a threat, the security bureaucracy remained complacent and gridlocked by organizational inertia and by fiefdoms that limited communication among the numerous branches of government engaged in the work of protecting American society against terrorist attack. Again, to reinforce a prior point, even if the US government had been more responsive to warnings, there is no assurance that it could stop a determined adversary from delivering bio-terrorist weaponry.

Of course, September 11 both validated the concern and undercut the exaggerated emphasis on biological war as the new and principal source of danger. It validated the idea that terrorism would shift from a primary emphasis on shock and symbolic vulnerability to a new stress on the scale of harm and substantive vulnerability of the target state, thereby blurring the boundary between war and terrorism. September 11, as widely observed, more closely resembled the Japanese attack on Pearl Harbor than any previous terrorist event, and thereby sharpened the dominant perception that the attacks needed to be treated as acts of war rather than as disruptive, essentially symbolic, terrorist incidents. Its degree of success also immediately led to a public awareness that no matter how militarily strong a modern state—and the United States was the strongest military power in human history—such strength by itself offered little protection against a ruthless adversary that was not susceptible to deterrence and possessed the means to inflict major harm. Thus the United States could not hope to overcome its condition of vulnerability to political extremism with a traditional war mentality and accompanying tactics capable of inflicting crippling substantive damage on its enemy. Striking back at what? To what end? The weaponry of the modern state was almost exclusively meant to be used against a territorial actor, and specifically, the modern state and the states system. Potential megaterrorists can choose from a wide array of comparable targets in complex modern societies. It seemed entirely possible that future megaterrorism would produce even greater damage than the September 11 attacks simply by aiming at nuclear power plants, water supply systems, electricity grids, major tunnels and bridges, seaports, crowded sports arenas, and IT networks. To even attempt to protect all such targets against attacks would inevitably push the government into an oppressive and hostile relationship with its own citizenry. And what is perhaps even more frustrating and challenging, there are few meaningful targets for the United States, with its arsenal of weapons, to strike against. As a result, relations of power between states locked in mortal combat can no longer be measured in weaponry and strike capabilities, with victory granted to the side with the largest arsenal. This traditional understanding of power was already challenged to some extent by the advent of nuclear weaponry, which significantly neutralized power differentials once a weaker state acquired a credible nuclear deterrent. The avidity with which the United States has sought to deny weaponry of mass destruction to weak states on its enemy list is in recognition of this equalizing threat to its power. As yet, however, when it comes to megaterrorism, the United States has not found a comparable strategy to that of the non-proliferation regime against the "axis of evil" countries, and thus the vulnerability revealed on September 11 persists, even if the extent of actual danger is completely unknown at this point.

The jihadist inspirational leadership of Osama bin Laden, combined with such tactical ingenuity, created a strong impression almost unanimously shared among Americans that the threat posed could not be defended against if those seeking to carry it out were left free to operate, undoubtedly motivated to strike again with equal or greater ferocity. Only the destruction of al-Qaeda's capabilities, together with enhanced preventive vigilance, gave any plausible hope of reducing the prospect of future attacks. In essence, the visionary character of the al-Qaeda threat meant that it could neither be muted by negotiations and compromise, nor deterred by containment and retaliatory threats, nor could it be minimized as insubstantial (as had been the nature of past responses to global terrorism, including that of al-Qaeda authorship). To insist that force was a necessary component of response should not be confused with launching a global war on terrorism that accepts no limits, which is what Washington has so far chosen. At this stage, the war against global terror has also been used as a justification and smokescreen for global empire-building, which seems integral to the White House game plan with or without September 11.

Unconditional Motivation

The devastation of September 11 was crucially dependent on the dedication of the participants and their capacity to remain focused on a suicidal mission over a period of several years of training and planning, including sustaining this commitment while living "normal"

THE DIMENSIONS OF MEGATERRORISM

lives in the midst of the target country's population. Without such an unconditional willingness of the perpetrators to die in the course of carrying out their mission, there would be no way to turn airliners into weapons of mass destruction.

Nineteen hijackers on four separate planes departing from three airports exhibited both competence and commitment, as well as adequate skills of organization and personal discipline. There has been some conjectures that only the lead terrorist in each of the four teams knew the precise character of the mission, but all of the participants must have realized that such a mission included a high risk of death, or an almost certain future of imprisonment for life. The sustaining basis for such an undertaking was their apparent religious zeal, their acceptance of Osama bin Laden's message as to the duty of Muslims to engage in *jihad* against the United States, including American civilian society. If bin Laden himself had only dubious religious authority, it is true that there were prominent Islamic leaders, with proper credentials, that supported bin Laden's view of the United States and the Islamic duty of *jihad* in response. As mentioned earlier, whether to regard al-Qaeda and bin Laden as a cult phenomenon, an extremist version of Islam, or a distinctive hybrid is a matter of judgment and interpretation for which no definitive answer can be given.

Suicide bombers have been a staple feature of other struggles that have involved recourse to terrorism. The reliance by Hamas, and more recently, other Palestinian resistance organizations, on such a mode of resistance has been a prominent feature of Palestinian terrorism in the last few years, and the Tamil Tigers have for decades employed terrorist tactics of resistance that depended on suicide missions. But these tactics were within a confined field of battle over specific issues that could be resolved by negotiation or by perpetuating a lethal, yet contained, cycle of violence. For the target society, the reality of terrorist assaults on its civic order and civilian populations bears many resemblances to the impact of September 11 on American society, and hence the claims of such countries as Israel, India, and Russia to have the same freedom of action in responding is to be expected, even understandable, although in the end unacceptable.

Distinctions need to be drawn. In the American case, the provocative policies being pursued by the United States are generally within the traditional framework of geopolitics, and enjoy the overall backing of the UN, with the exception of the call over many years for an end to Israeli occupation of the Palestinian territories. This UN role of backing the geopolitics of the moment is particularly lamentable in relation to the continued imposition of sanctions on Iraq. In any case, the al-Qaeda suicidal missions were not part of a specific interactive cycle of violence by enemies engaged in a conflict over territory or governance structures, but were enacting a visionary program outside the bounds of normal political conflict by relying on genocidal and terrorist means. This program included the satisfaction of some grievances widely shared in the Arab world, but its basic animus related to the ways in which Arab governments, especially Saudi Arabia, chose to seek stability and security by linking arms with the infidel. Here, the self-interested US role in the region was not by itself in violation of international law or morality. Beyond this, it seemed reasonable, desirable, and feasible to diminish the threat of future attacks by a combination of responses aimed at the destruction of the al-Qaeda network and the enhancement of American intelligence and police action that is aimed at detection, early warning, and, to the extent possible, prevention. To support such a US response does not imply denying those targeted with rights under international law, nor does it vindicate the disregard of the sovereignty of foreign countries, and even less does it endorse the widespread reliance by media and government officials on the language of a hunt or crusade to describe the process of bringing the perpetrators of September 11 "to justice."

A Resonant Message

Whether phrased as "Why do they hate us?" or by reference to the intense and widely diffused anti-Americanism in the Arab world, it is widely accepted that Osama bin Laden speaks for a large body of Islamic opinion when he denounces the American role. To admit to such a resonance is, of course, not the same thing as saying that many support a terrorist strategy of resistance or are willing to participate in a movement of such fanatical beliefs as that led by Osama bin Laden. But it would be misleading to suggest that there is not an Islamic dimension of encounter that could move either toward accommodation or degenerate in the direction of a "clash of civilizations." The religious/civilizational dimension cannot be ignored, and is an integral part of what makes the September 11 attacks historically unprecedented.

So far, the American official level of response has tried to make this resonance disappear from political consciousness by diversionary rhetoric, as well as by entirely decontextualizing the attacks. President Bush in his address of September 20, 2001 to a Joint Session of Congress addressed the issue in this way:

> Americans are asking, Why do they hate us? They hate what we see right here in this chamber—a democratically elected government. Their leaders are self-appointed. They hate our freedoms—our freedom of religion, our freedom of speech, our freedom to vote and assemble and disagree with each other.

Such an attempted deflection of Islamic resentment is profoundly misleading, entirely exempting the United States from self-scrutiny, and acknowledgement of past policy errors. As the respected Arab journalist, Raghida Dergam, pointed out at a New York conference on misperceptions between Muslims and Americans: "... the argument is not about what America is, but about what America does. Americans in their confusion must know that most Arabs and Muslims do not hate them. They do, however, have legitimate issues with American policies...."[11]

The relevance of the anti-American resentment is at once pragmatic, programmatic, and normative (touching on values and rights). It is pragmatic as the possibility of achieving cooperation in relation to anti-terrorist law enforcement in the Islamic world would be much more likely if the United States took steps to reduce low-profile, but pervasive, anti-Americanism (such as balance on the Palestine/Israel conflict, or better, working to achieve Palestinian self-determination in a manner that also served to safeguard pre-1967 Israel). It is programmatic in the sense that "winning" the war against global terror depends on removing the deep roots of terrorism, which include the valid grounds of opposition to American policies. Such a formulation suggests that there may also be invalid grounds relating to some features of the economic, cultural, and political relationships between governments, the world economy, and the peoples. For instance, to the extent that the West is blamed for the publication of literary works such as Salman Rushdie's *Satanic Verses* and films containing material disrespectful of Islam, such a result cannot be avoided if free expression is to be generally protected, which is certainly a legitimate option for a sovereign state of secular persuasion. In fact, this understanding of freedom of expression even seems consistent, at least formally, with most readings of the Universal Declaration of Human Rights, the text of which has been accepted widely in the Islamic world. At the same time, with such a high degree of cultural unevenness in the world, Islamic countries that imposed restrictions upon the dissemination of such writings on the basis either of public order or community values, could also be accepted as acting in accordance with the framework of human rights.

But the fact remains that addressing the Arab world's anti-Americanism raises a powerful normative challenge for the United States to align its policies to a greater extent than in the past with international law and morality, and with trends toward the promotion of global justice. Such a realignment has intrinsic merits based on the search for equity and peaceful resolution of conflicts in international society, but it can only become politically feasible if the domestic climate in the United States endorses moves in such a direction.

Security Crisis
As already evident, the nature of the attacks, together with the presumed will and capabilities of al-Qaeda to mount future operations against the United States and its presence elsewhere in the world, did pose a genuine security threat of an unprecedented character. No government with the capability to strike back could be expected to ignore such a challenge, nor would its citizenry accept any form of response that did not manifest a maximum effort to remove or minimize the threat. The most pressing issue facing the US government on September 12 was how to fashion an effective response, given its knowledge and resources at the time.

Such a security imperative does not do away with limits derived from international law, from morality, and from considerations of prudence. An evaluation of whether the security challenge elicited an appropriate response depends to the degree it was able to combine effectiveness while taking account of relevant limits. The essentially postmodern (it is "postmodern" because the parties to large-scale conflict were not sovereign states existing within established territorial limits) puzzle confronting American policymakers was to devise a strategy of effectiveness in relation to an adversary that could not be associated definitively with an enemy state. The initial solution was to fuse the identities of the Taliban and al-Qaeda sufficiently to make it plausible to treat Afghanistan as responsible for the September 11 attacks merely as a result of their role of "harboring" Osama bin Laden and al-Qaeda. Such an attribution was achieved by unilateral fiat in Washington, without bothering to obtain a clear endorsement from the United Nations or to put forth convincing evidence of the alleged connection in the public domain. In general, the UN Security Council did seem to endorse the right of the US to make an effective response, but in very general terms that left full operational discretion in Washington, thereby abandoning any responsibility for assuring that an American response respected appropriate limits on the use of force. From some perspectives, the US was fortunate that the source of the attack could be credibly traced back, in the first instance, to the al-Qaeda presence in Afghanistan, and not elsewhere. The very marginal legitimacy of the Taliban regime (recognized in 2001 by only three foreign countries, two of which ruptured their diplomatic relations after September 11, and denied credentials to represent Afghanistan at the UN) as a government along with its horrific human rights record made it seem acceptable to ignore Afghanistan's sovereign rights. The global problematics of an American response would likely have been far more contested if Osama bin Laden had been living elsewhere, say in Indonesia or the Philippines, and had been able to carry out global missions from such locations without any cooperative support from the governing authorities of the country, or if there had been no discernible territorial nerve center for the planning and execution of megaterrorist operations. After all, most terrorist groups survive for years, even decades, in hostile state environments, despite enormous efforts by strong states to destroy them. Spain has struggled with the ETA remnants of Basque separatism for years, despite making substantial concessions, and the Philippines, Indonesia, India, and Colombia have never been able to pacify a large portion of their own territories despite reliance for decades on harsh methods and massive military campaigns.

The challenge of megaterrorism stretched thin our conceptual framework for understanding how to maintain security in a world of sovereign states. In its essence, September 11 exhibited the catastrophic fusion of non-territorial transnational networks, political extremism, and tactical ingenuity. It also displayed the torment of an 800-pound gorilla that possesses overwhelming strength, but is unable to deploy it effectively against this new type of enemy. The initial impulse was to respond to al-Qaeda as if it were a state, as if it were a replay of Japan attacking Pearl Harbor, launching a war against Afghanistan. But almost immediately there was a realization that this would not, even if substantially successful, solve the problem. To move on from Afghanistan to Iraq is to leap from plausibility to aggressive warmaking for which there is no foundation in law, morality, and prudence, and no political backing at the UN or in international society. At this time the challenge of megaterrorism is beginning to be appreciated, but a coherent response has not yet been fashioned, and is unlikely to be by the US government, as its leading policymakers have deliberately intertwined the al-Qaeda threat with a pre-existing empire-building project of their own and with a framework of prior wars fought between territorial sovereigns.

3. APPRAISING THE
AFGHANISTAN WAR

This chapter focuses on the war in Afghanistan, its degree of effectiveness, legality, and legitimacy. To some extent, any assessment remains premature as the stability of the post-Taliban arrangements remains problematic, beset by warlordism and by pockets of armed resistance from remnants of Taliban and al-Qaeda forces. Whether this resistance will persist and become a kind of continuing struggle is uncertain. Also in doubt are the regional implications of the Afghanistan War, especially with regard to Pakistan. It is possible that Pakistan will become the scene of civil strife and provide al-Qaeda with a new base of operations that will not be as easy to disrupt, as was the case with Afghanistan. It is also possible that the outcome in Afghanistan could affect the India/Pakistan struggle over Kashmir, either intensifying tensions to such an extent as to lead to another war, conceivably fought with nuclear weapons, or, with an opposite effect, leading the two governments to moderate their enmity to the point of striking a diplomatic bargain that finally resolves the fate of Kashmir.

The American response to September 11 was designed from the outset to be maximal, that is, mobilizing of the capabilities needed to destroy those responsible for the attacks, both as punishment and as the best way to avoid future attack from similar sources. But unlike past major assaults on a leading state, the fundamental assets of the enemy could not be situated within the territorial boundaries of a sovereign state, but were spread around the world in secret cells operating underground with considerable sophistication. This fundamental reality greatly complicated the logic of response and public discussion, given the need to act effectively and in a manner that reassured the American people that their shattered sense of security was being restored as quickly as possible. President Bush did his part early on by giving speeches that signaled the seriousness with which the US government was taking the challenge of September 11, and the all-out commitment that would be made to find the perpetrators and destroy their capabilities.

It was in this sense that waging war against Afghanistan, seeking to supersede the Taliban regime, preventing Afghan territory from being used again as a safe haven from which to mount megaterrorism, and going after the leadership and headquarters of al-Qaeda, was the first test of whether the US response could be pronounced a success. To be able to attribute part of the megaterrorist challenge to a particular state, and hold its governing authorities responsible for the attacks, was extremely helpful from the American perspective. For one thing, it allowed the immediate response to be substantially fashioned as if it were a traditional war among sovereign states, seeming to overcome the perplexing problem of what to do about an enemy transnational terrorist network with large-scale destructive capabilities. It also provided the American people with a tangible battlefield on which their right of self-defense could be exercised in a vivid and reassuring manner. And as it evolved, the war in Afghanistan demonstrated the utility and superiority of American military capabilities, achieving a substantial victory in a short time at comparatively low human costs to itself, both military and civilian. But the victory was ambiguous, as well.

True, the Taliban regime was crushed, and a new American-oriented leadership emerged that was consistent with US aspirations.[1] Whether this new Afghan government can provide stability in the years ahead is highly uncertain, and will depend in large part on whether the US government invests sufficiently in post-war economic and political reconstruction, an engagement that it has not made in the recent past either in Afghanistan or elsewhere. Also, the war did not achieve its most vividly articulated goal of capturing or killing Osama bin Laden and his close associates, although it did destroy his elaborate base area in the Tora Bora cave complex. Even more problematically, the dependence on Pakistan to carry on the war in Afghanistan placed destabilizing pressures of uncertain magnitude on the secular government of General Pervez Musharraf, and it remains unclear what will be the longer-term impact on Pakistan, as well as on the India/Pakistan regional tensions that threaten the first war between nuclear weapons states.

The American recourse to war against Afghanistan had other problems, as well. The reliance on high-tech weaponry to destroy at will a low-tech society reminded even the non-Muslim peoples of Asia of colonial wars, their own struggles for independence, and of American ambitions. There is no doubt that the American intervention in Afghanistan on the side of the Northern Alliance was a denial of the right of self-determination for the Afghan people, even though the outcome was welcomed by much of the population and seems responsible for an improving climate of human rights (though one still beset by serious difficulties). Supporters of the American role in Afghanistan have begun to write openly of its "imperial" character, and urge only a willingness to recognize that imperial success depends on an accompanying willingness to devote sufficient resources so as to provide benefits to the subordinated peoples.[2]

There are conceptual issues, as well, with disturbing consequences. The ease of victory in Afghanistan tempts policymakers to continue on the same path, and may have led the American public to suppose that, after all, this war could be won in the same manner as earlier wars, that it was basically a war consisting of a sequence of territorial battlefields, with Iraq next on the list. Indirectly, a facile misperception supports those who are urging that Iraq be slated for invasion, regime change, and occupation. But the effort to treat the Great Terror War as if it resembles other wars with state enemies breaks down as soon as the logic is extended beyond Afghanistan. While viewing Afghanistan as responsible for September 11 was plausible, if controversial, viewing Iraq as responsible is implausible, and cannot qualify as an acceptable stretching of the international legal and moral constraints on the use of war or claims of self-defense.

Still more fundamental in a way is the failure, discussed earlier, to delimit megaterrorism as a distinct phenomenon requiring and justifying a particular response. The Bush administration went in the opposite direction, partly to recruit coalition partners who were faced with a variety of anti-state movements, and assimilated "terrorism" to megaterrorism. The effect of this merger was to further exempt state violence of whatever impact on civilian society from being classified as terrorism. Such a broadening of the September 11 challenge is what gives this Great Terror War both its reactionary slant and raises the possibility that America has done the unthinkable: launched a war without either boundaries or an end, a war that it can neither win nor lose, unwittingly embracing war as a permanent condition.

Against this background of cross-cutting considerations, this chapter discusses the war against Afghanistan, its initiation, its prosecution, and its provisional results. This provisionality is key, as there may occur all sorts of developments in Afghanistan and its neighborhood that will alter these assessments of what was achieved and what was lost as a result of this war.

The Challenge of September 11

Without dwelling any further on the al-Qaeda attacks, it was evident from the outset that the magnitude of the harm, together with the exposure of present and future American vulnerability, meant some form of recourse to war by the United States was inevitable. There were no credible alternatives to war, neither proceeding by way of the UN, nor through reliance on the past responses of retaliatory missile strikes and law enforcement efforts, nor by way of diplomacy reinforced by sanctions. On the basis of past experience and present prospects, each of these alternative options generally seemed unable to apprehend and punish the perpetrators or diminish the threat, and so the case for war prevailed as national policy without meaningful dissent or public debate. But war against whom? And for what objectives? With what limiting conditions?

As argued, it was the apparent good fortune of the Bush administration that Osama bin Laden had been operating from Afghanistan under Taliban rule in recent years, running a terrorist training program that apparently solicited tens of thousands of recruits from around the Muslim world in the aftermath of resistance to the Soviet presence throughout the 1980s. From an American perspective, Afghanistan was the ideal state to wage war against. It had practically no diplomatic friends in the world since the Taliban had come to power. On September 11, the Taliban government was recognized by only three countries in the world and had been refused the right to represent Afghanistan in the United Nations. Indeed, Afghanistan itself had been treated as an outlaw state for several years, a status confirmed by a special rapporteur appointed by the UN Human Rights Commission, who reported annually on the severe human rights abuses and Crimes Against Humanity that were routinely taking place in the country, including massacres of ethnic minorities and horrifying impositions of an extreme version of the Sharia (Islamic law) on Afghan women. As well, Afghanistan was the object of universal censure, including from Islamic governments, for its insistence on removing any taint of non-Islamic religious devotion by the deliberate destruction of the huge world-renowned statues of the Buddha at Budiman several months before September 11. If any state deserved the status of pariah or outlaw state, it was Afghanistan, even aside from the hospitality and free rein accorded al-Qaeda.

Against such a background it was generally credible that Afghanistan would be treated as an enemy state held responsible for the attacks of September 11. And the leadership of Pakistan, earlier the main sponsor of the Taliban when it was struggling to gain control of Afghanistan, was quickly persuaded to switch allegiance and support the United States diplomatically and logistically in its moves toward war against Afghanistan. President Bush in his September 20 address to a joint session of Congress articulated some non-negotiable demands directed at the Taliban regime that seemed to focus exclusively on al-Qaeda, seeking custody of Osama bin Laden and the al-Qaeda leadership, as well as terminating their presence within the country. When the Taliban requested evidence of bin Laden's responsibility for the September 11 attacks, their request was summarily dismissed as unacceptable, and the war was launched on October 7, 2002.

The war consisted of two main undertakings: using American tactical air power and ground-targeting guidance to turn quickly the tide of the long unresolved internal war decisively in favor of the Northern Alliance, and destroying al-Qaeda targets from the air, later with coordinated ground operations led and directed by American operatives known as special forces. The result was the total collapse of the Taliban regime and the seeming elimination of a coherent al-Qaeda presence in Afghanistan, although with the probable escape and dispersion of many members of the terrorist network, including possibly some of its top leadership, and including the dispersion within Afghanistan of militants who retain the capacity and willingness to engage in armed activities.

An appraisal of the war from a normative perspective of law and morality poses a challenge because the real enemy was not Afghanistan, but a globalized network that had centered its operations within Afghan borders. Nor was the enemy a political movement associated with a specific struggle for control or secession affecting a single state. The preliminary locus of an American response, relying on a rationale of self-defense against megaterrorism was plausibly situated in Afghanistan, and the Taliban regime's responsibility was based not on any evidence of a role in the September 11 attacks, or even any allegation or proof of any specific advance knowledge, but on complicity arising from "harboring" Osama bin Laden and his al-Qaeda operations. President Bush in his September 20 speech tied the demands directed at the Taliban regime to a wider doctrine: "From this day forward, any nation that continues to harbor or support terrorism will be regarded as a hostile regime." Such a conception stretched traditional notions of self-defense by unilaterally attributing to a foreign government ultimate legal accountability for operations emanating from its territory, regardless of whether it favors such terrorist activities or had the capacity to suppress them. As earlier suggested, the case against the Taliban was relatively strong, although far from overwhelming, and could have been made stronger had it been linked to an available rationale for humanitarian intervention, and to its seamless ideological affinity with al-Qaeda. Bush did allude to the oppressive conditions in Afghanistan, but did not explicitly connect those circumstances with the rationale for recourse to war. Interestingly, in the aftermath of the war, with the interim leader Hamid Karzai in attendance, President Bush placed strong emphasis in his State of the Union address in 2002 on the emancipatory impact of the American-led victory on the peoples of Afghanistan, particularly its women.

The Just-War Framework

In early retrospect, it is possible to appraise recourse to, conduct of, and effects of the war by relying on a flexible interpretation of the just-war doctrine, combined with a rule of reason that takes account of the new context established by a defensive war waged against a global terrorist network of demonstrated will and capacity to inflict catastrophic harm on civilian society. While the normal restraining influence of international law and the United Nations are not directly very relevant, the importance of identifying and adhering to limits is of great significance here, both to acknowledge and remind ourselves of the barbarity and non-normalcy of war as a means to resolve conflict and of the importance of not setting a precedent that unleashes the dogs of war in the future. It is relevant to note that although the UN did not directly mandate the war as falling within the scope of an American right of self-defense and that the US did not request such a mandate, there was also a relative absence of criticism of the American decision to wage war against Afghanistan in the UN or elsewhere, aside from public sentiments in Arab countries where anti-American feelings are intense and widespread. In the aftermath of trauma, the United States government was tactically innovative in devising a quick response that seemed to address the megaterrorist threat as directly and responsibly as possible, but subsequently it has been disappointingly insensitive about the need to establish limits for itself (and indirectly for others) when using force in such circumstances.

The less consequential criticisms are associated with the initial recourse to war against Afghanistan. Here, the refusal to negotiate with the Taliban over the demands issued by Washington and its rebuff of the request for evidence of bin Laden's involvement, fed an impression that seems accurate that the United States was not genuinely interested in a peaceful resolution of the crisis, and certainly fed suspicions that America's war aims went beyond neutralizing, if not destroying altogether, the al-Qaeda threat. In fact, good reasons existed not to rely on a diplomatic approach, given the unlikelihood that al-Qaeda could be seriously weakened through the efforts of the Taliban to cooperate with the US counter-terrorist campaign, but that case was never really explained in public. As a result, the impression that the United States was rushing to war fashioned an undesirable precedent. This perception was undoubtedly sharpened by the pattern of unilateralism that had been the distinguishing characteristic of foreign policy during the Bush presidency even before September 11, with its evident disdain for treatymaking, multilateralism, and international institutions. The patriotic fervor in America on nightly TV also contributed to the global image of a militarist America, a rogue superpower on the march without any regard for the constraints of international law or the views of other governments. Again, in the specific setting of urgency, with credible dangers of further attacks, the necessity for war in the context of Afghanistan seemed at the time compelling, and, in retrospect, has been conditionally validated both by the political changes in Afghanistan and by the still tentative indications that al-Qaeda's appetite for megaterrorism has been weakened. So far, the American response has reduced al-Qaeda's resistance to the level of low-profile terrorism of a traditional sort, upsetting and unacceptable, but manageable by police and paramilitary methods.

The debate on the conduct of the war raised some further difficulties, but again of a secondary character. From the outset American leaders made it rhetorically clear that they would do their best to avoid civilian casualties by using precision munitions and avoiding targets that were surrounded by civilians. Given the character of the al-Qaeda targets and the American aversion to taking casualties, the US relied upon tactics that produced skepticism about how seriously to take the American pledge to minimize civilian casualties. Especially controversial was the American reliance on discredited weaponry used in the Vietnam War—B-52 carpet bombing, cluster bombs, and huge daisy-cutter bombs containing 2,000 tons of explosives. The US also depended on targeting guidance from intelligence sources on the ground, which turned out to be deliberately misleading on several occasions, as local military leaders sought to use American military power in unresolved ethnic struggles between antagonistic warlords. Criticism also arose because the Pentagon admitted that it was keeping no record of civilian casualties, and there were scattered, but unverified, reports that the American media was being encouraged by government officials to downplay the issue. At the same time, Defense Secretary Donald Rumsfeld was widely quoted as saying, "I can't imagine there's been a conflict where there has been less collateral damage, less unintended consequences."[3] Perhaps such a claim reveals an impoverished imagination!

The issue of civilian casualties is sharply contested even among critics of the war. Carl Conetta, respected co-director of the Project on Defense Alternatives in Cambridge asserted, "[d]espite the adulation of Operation Enduring Freedom as a finely tuned or bull's-eye war, the campaign failed to set a new standard for accuracy." His institute prepared the most careful study publicly available of civilian casualties, estimating that up through December 10, 2001, in the course of dropping 12,000 bombs in 4,700 sorties, between 1,000 and 1,300 civilians were killed. Such a ratio compares unfavorably to the Kosovo War in which 23,000 bombs were dropped during 13,000 sorties, killing an estimated 500 civilians.[4] Of course, the targets and the goals were different, and the level of organized resistance was much higher than in Afghanistan, as was the civilian population density in relation to the combat zones.

There were a series of "mistakes" or "accidents" due to faulty targeting information. Michael Walzer, speaking at a Forum on Just War held at Princeton University, advanced the useful idea that the behavior of a state with respect to the conduct of war in conformity to the just-war framework could be partly assessed by its willingness to accept risks for its combat forces so as to avoid causing civilian casualties.[5] The United States record is mixed. It could and should have done more, but given the political urgency associated with effective action and compared to the indiscriminate attacks resulting in massive civilian death, displacement, and suffering in such major past wars as the Korean War and the Vietnam War, as well as World War II, there were notably successful efforts made to limit the level of civilian casualties in the Afghanistan War. Whether US behavior in the Afghanistan war should be regarded as satisfying the strictures of the just-war doctrine remains inconclusive, and it may remain so forever, certainly until more data and analysis is available.

The harsher lines of criticism on these matters emanating from anti-war and hard left sources seem well-meant, yet ill-considered. Some civilian casualties in the midst of a major war are virtually unavoidable, and such a cost, tragic as it is for those individuals involved, does not by itself cast doubt on a war undertaken, as this one was, for a just cause. Also, allegations that civilian deaths in Afghanistan equaled or exceeded the number killed at the World Trade Center and Pentagon on September 11 seem unconvincing and are based on biased and unreliable evidence. Such allegations are beside the point from a just-war perspective. The issue is whether the violence used in self-defense was proportional to the harm inflicted and to a reasonable apprehension of future harm. It is hard to contend that the level of violence relied upon by the United States was disproportionately large in relation to the ends of restored security and punitive justice being reasonably sought.

A further test of war within the just-war matrix relates to its effects, and to the restoration of peace. It was St. Augustine who in the fourth century devised the matrix of just war in the first place, and conditioned approval of particular wars as just by reference to a general view of war as an evil, but a necessary evil in certain circumstances, if conceived of as a means of reestablishing peace. It is too soon to be confident about such effects even with respect to Afghanistan, and we are certainly not able to derive even rhetorical comfort from President Bush's frequent claims that his waging of war is premised on "a vision of peace." These claims are hard to sustain in the face of the much more concerted "war talk" that is reliably attributed to the White House and Pentagon, and confirmed by the manner in which the post-Afghanistan policies are being explained.

What does seem clear is that the appalling economic incompetence and record of human rights abuse in Afghanistan during the period of Taliban rule is likely to be superseded by an improved quality of Afghan governance resulting in material and political benefits for a large majority of the citizenry.[6] Of course, part of the improvement is a result of a renewed international engagement by richer countries in the destiny of Afghanistan, contrasting with the scandalous international abandonment of Afghanistan in the afterglow of the cold war. At present, the donor states have pledged $4.5 billion in assistance as a first step in the reconstruction of the country, and there is a widespread realization that the war will not be viewed as a true success if Afghanistan becomes soon again mired in a humanitarian disaster of famine, poverty, and chaos. Despite energetic efforts and good intentions, the outcome may still be a severe disappointment if warlordism controls the Afghan future, and civil strife among competing factions obstructs and demoralizes efforts at economic and political reconstruction.[7] So far, the signals are mixed and likely to change frequently in the months and years ahead.

A Concluding Observation

The rigidities of international law associated with its efforts to regulate wars between sovereign states limit its relevance in the setting of the postmodern warfare that pits a transnational concealed network against a hegemonic state possessing a global presence. The statist temptation is to do what it knows best—namely, act as if the war is of a modern variety, that is state against state. The United States, in doctrine and practice, has wavered between a recognition of the postmodern character of the challenge it faces and nevertheless insisting that its response take the form of modern war by focusing on enemy states, while neglecting the fundamental nature of the networking challenge.

The just-war framework, although it lends itself to varying lines of interpretation, is more helpful than international law in this situation, because its basic articulation long preceded the emergence of the modern state system, and was designed to set limits on recourse and the waging of war by whatever political communities were empowered to do so. It can navigate the treacherous waters of both modern and postmodern warfare. At the very least, a just-war discourse is not invalidated because the nature of this war does not fit within the modern paradigm or template. Beyond this, although commentators will disagree on the application of just-war principles, the mere discussion of such guidelines acknowledges that even in the absence of an adapted international law framework, there are limits that apply to the way in which a state conducts its military operations in a postmodern war. The United States government has yet to make this acknowledgement, and so the issue takes on added importance in the struggle to avoid a descent into military nihilism of the sort that gave rise in the first place to the efforts to convert just-war thinking from its pre-modern moral and religious status to law. Such a conversion was needed in the early modern era to avoid the claims of emerging sovereign secular states that they were not externally accountable without their formal acceptance of international obligations. It was the great undertaking of international law in the twentieth century to induce this formal acceptance as a way of confining the role of law under modern condition, and the UN Charter expresses the resolve to reach such a goal. There are few who would claim success for international law even within the confines of modernity.

At present, the issues of delimitation are daunting. The best that can be done is to invoke the just-war framework as part of an argument that limits apply, despite the postmodern character of the war between al-Qaeda and the United States. A more ambitious response would be to devise a postmodern legal framework to govern armed conflict that seems adapted to present realities. Of course, such a framework would not be acceptable to the transnational network whose shows of potency depend on its capacity to impose its will with modes of violence that deny the relevance of limits. In this regard, megaterrorism needs to be understood as the emergence of nihilistic and anarchistic warfare on a grand scale of combat. Such a realization makes it necessary for statist adversaries and guardians of shared humane values to accept self-limiting guidelines without any expectation of reciprocity. To expect reciprocity would be to misconceive the challenge, while to meet nihilism with nihilism would be to strike a dreadful bargain with the devil.

4. THE US GOVERNMENT'S
WORLD-ORDER ARGUMENT

Despite the American reluctance to acknowledge limitations and externally imposed guidelines, its leadership was far from indifferent on the matter of mobilizing support for the war being embarked upon. Such support was seen as logistically *necessary* to gain basing and over-flight rights, and various forms of inter-governmental cooperation. Support was also seen as *desirable* so as to lend legitimacy to the American claims both at home and abroad.

Almost immediately after September 11 America found itself "at war," but without resorting either to constitutional procedures involving a formal declaration of war or international/UN requirements of seeking by all means possible a peaceful resolution. Afghanistan had been quickly selected as the primary target of the initial phase of the major military campaign. It is relevant to take note of the considerable diplomatic effort by the US government to present the war against Afghanistan as both reasonable and legitimate, both by soliciting its general endorsement at the UN and by inviting others to join in the overarching Great Terror War.

In Bush's September 20 speech the following imperative was set forth:

> Every nation, in every region, now has a decision to make. Either you are with us, or you are with the terrorists. From this day forward, any nation that continues to harbor or support terrorism will be regarded by the United States as a hostile regime.

From the very beginning, American objectives were expressed in a most ambitious fashion, contending that "[o]ur war on terror begins with al-Qaeda, but it does not end there. It will not end until every terrorist group of global reach has been found, stopped, and defeated." The American people were warned to expect a long struggle that would not be "won" in the shape of a definite ending as happened in the Gulf War, but would require a many faceted effort consisting of covert operations, financial interdiction, police cooperation, and diplomatic initiatives that extended the long interventionary arm of the United States into the domestic life of many foreign countries. These various non-military efforts were assigned important roles in the struggle, which Bush described as "not just America's fight": "This is the world's fight. This is civilization's fight. This is the fight of all who believe in progress and pluralism, tolerance and freedom."

As already noted, it has never been made clear by American leaders how such a war would end. There is a strange mixture of insight and confusion present here. What is meant by "civilization"? It is correct that world order based on the idea of state sovereignty was everywhere profoundly threatened by the vulnerability exposed in the United States on September 11, and this realization partly accounts for the degree of sympathy and support given to the United States even by governments normally suspicious of American foreign policy. But upholding the role of states in providing territorial security and meeting the challenge of networked violence is not properly equated with "civilization." The implication is that violence directed at civilians in the manner of September 11 is ethically unacceptable according to the premises of the civilization—but is it? Here, the critique of Noam Chomsky and others is persuasive on the crucial point that the state system has been consistently, for several centuries, the most persistent source of mass violence against civilians both within and without its borders, and the United States has no basis for exempting itself from such an indictment, and indeed has headed the list during recent years.[1] And it should not be forgotten that to conflate "civilization" with "states" is to imply that the many oppressive and corrupt governments around the world are entitled to consider themselves as "civilized" members of international society.

This American rationale underpinned the first phase of its response, which sought to rally countries in support of the American undertaking and to win the backing of the United Nations. In addressing the General Assembly on November 10, 2001, President Bush noted with satisfaction that emergency sessions of the General Assembly and Security Council had met on September 12, the day after the attacks, and "[b]efore the sun had set, these attacks on the world stood condemned by the world." In this UN speech Bush tried his best to rally widespread international support for the full American response:

We're asking for a comprehensive commitment to this fight. We must unite in opposing all terrorists, not just some of them. In this world there are good causes and bad causes, and we may disagree on where the line is drawn. Yet, there is no such thing as a good terrorist. No national aspiration, no remembered wrong can ever justify the deliberate murder of the innocent. Any government that rejects this principle, trying to pick and choose its terrorist friends, will know the consequences.

It is important to observe closely two features of this moral claim: that the attack on the United States must be viewed as an attack on the organized international community as a whole, and must be defended as such; and that the proper scope of response is to disrupt and destroy whatever movement anywhere relies on what is conceived to be "terrorism" by the White House and Pentagon. These are extraordinary conceptual leaps to make from simply trying to respond effectively to those who perpetrated and were responsible for the September 11 attacks and who consider themselves at war with the United States. For one thing, this enlarged concept of the response seems to imply that it should be extended in such a way as to wipe out political movements that pose no direct or indirect threat to the United States and have no meaningful connection to the ideology, the organizational reality, and the transnational ambitions of al-Qaeda. As a result, the response exceeds all responsible readings of what international law allows a state to do when it acts in "self-defense."

There is a further serious and reactionary ideologizing of the whole idea of terrorist accountability, and who is deemed a terrorist. Although terrorism has not been defined by President Bush and other American leaders, the clear implication of their words and deeds is that "terrorism" consists exclusively of acts of violence directed at civilians and civilian targets by non-state political movements, or even violence directed at military targets if they happen to be American. Thus, the attack on an American warship, the USS Cole, has been routinely, and without discussion, described as a terrorism. This selectivity is consistent with various US government definitions of terrorism that have been relied upon for decades, which treat anti-state or anti-government violence as terrorism even if directed at military personnel and government office buildings. For instance, the FBI definition of terrorism is as follows: "The unlawful use of force or violence against persons or property to intimidate or coerce a Government, the civilian population, or any segment, thereof, in furtherance of political or social objectives.[2] And similarly, the Department of Defense proposed the following definition of terrorism in 1990: "The unlawful use of, or threatened use, of force or violence against individuals or property to coerce and intimidate governments or societies, often to achieve political, religious, or ideological objectives."

In contrast, many academic specialists, especially critics of US foreign policy over the years, reject such definitional closure, insisting that whenever political violence is directed against those who are "innocent" there exists terrorism, and whoever is the actor is properly charged with terrorism. From this perspective, states are the major terrorist organizations operating on the planet, responsible for the overwhelming majority of civilian deaths from terrorism. The United States itself has extremely dirty hands considering the direct and indirect support that it has given over many years to governments that use oppressive violence against civilian targets. It is worth noting here that dictionary definitions of terrorism avoid confining the term to anti-state violence. For instance, consider the definition provided by the *American Heritage College Dictionary*: "The unlawful or threatened use of force or violence to intimidate or coerce societies or governments, often for political or ideological reasons."

Historically, as earlier noted, the use of terrorism as a term to describe political violence was initially and mainly used to describe governmental violence intended to pacify social forces in a turbulent period, most classically, in the French Revolution. Anti-state violence was more commonly associated with "anarchism." But gradually in the last half-century statists succeeded in branding their adversaries as "terrorists," most saliently with respect to Israel's struggles in the Middle East, but also in the 1970s and 1980s in Western European countries, in relation to the radical movements of the left that were seeking to shock consumerist societies into a spasm of anti-capitalist politics.

During the cold war, American think-tank militarists had waged their own wars to control the semantic terrain, relying initially on terms like "guerrilla war" and "counterinsurgency warfare" to describe revolutionary nationalism in the Third World. Gradually, the language games changed, and terrorism was effectively appropriated by Western states, especially the United States and Israel, for use in dealing exclusively with the violence of their enemies, even if the targets were of a military or governmental character. Terrorism became equated in political discourse and the media exclusively with any form of anti-state political violence, and especially in relation to political violence used against civilian targets. What makes this issue retain its significance is that governments have succeeded in having their own violence exempted from the stigma of terrorism, and treated with respect by the media and in public discussion. It is generally discussed in the West as "retaliation" or "counterterrorism," even "self-defense," implying a reactive and defensive violence that often overlooks the inflamed political context. The locus of terrorism can blur considerably depending on the identity of the party responsible for recourse to violence against civilian society. In this regard, it is one thing to denounce the September 11 attacks as immoral and as massive Crimes Against Humanity, but it is quite another to treat the United States as innocent of a massive terrorist taint over the course of decades in its own pursuit of foreign policy goals. If terrorism is to be truly eliminated from human experience, then it must be done through a process that engages all relevant political actors, and above all those states that suppress their own citizenry and play exploitative geopolitical roles on the world stage.

There is a further reason to reject the grander conception of a response proposed by the US government. By insisting on the defeat of all expressions of anti-state terrorism, there results serious, possibly decisive, interference in many long-standing struggles between states and oppressed peoples fighting for a right of self-determination. A generalized war against terrorism implies an endorsement being made of state violence as legitimate counterterrorism, and of popular movements as inherently "terrorist" if they opt for armed force even in the face of foreign occupation or persistent oppressive state violence. As became evident in the weeks following September 11, states around the world confronting a variety of armed movements of opposition have contended that their violence should be viewed sympathetically, as it is really equivalent to the US campaign against al-Qaeda, and therefore deserves a US endorsement. Such states also insisted that they were entitled to rely on the same ferocity that the United States was claiming for itself, and with a similar absence of accountability or deference to legal and moral constraints. A precedent of great significance for the future of world politics is in the process of being created through the means by which the American response to September 11 has been articulated, imitated, and operationalized.

In these respects the ideological exposition of the American response has itself acquired a visionary and ideological quality that incidentally morphed the response against terrorism into an overall program to reinstate the sovereign state as supreme being in international political life, at least with respect to traditional security concerns. Whether such a posture will have durable effects is uncertain, as the erosion of sovereign rights and the marginalization of the state is due principally to the impacts of economic globalization, non-territorial forms of empowerment, and the rise of transnational social movements that are fundamentally restructuring the political architecture of the world. Neoliberal capitalism will continue to receive enthusiastic support from American leaders, even as they seek to rely on new modalities of unchallengeable and unaccountable military superiority to dominate the planet, creating truly a global imperial presence with a rogue demeanor. Only the future will disclose whether this globalized phase of capitalism is reconcilable with the territorial locus of the American empire-building project.

As argued in the previous chapter, the root of the problematics of devising an American response is the fundamental disconnect between September 11 and the two defining templates of modern world order: (1) the framework of political relations as constituted by sovereign states exercising territorial supremacy and their interaction; (2) war as the ultimate means of resolving conflicts among such states. Neither of these templates provides the sort of guidance that could have shaped an appropriate response to the profound challenges of September 11, and yet the leaders of the United States, as well as most of its citizenry, lack the insight and imagination to formulate an alternative template that captures the new realities of conflict or, less ambitiously, to adapt the prior templates of statism and war so as to produce a response that is effective, yet respectful of normative (legal, moral, cultural) restraints. In this important sense, the US government's insistence on generalizing its enemy as terrorism, rather than the al-Qaeda network, is dysfunctional as it dilutes international political support, and makes the goal almost certainly unattainable.

The Statist Trap

States are associated with political communities residing within a bounded territory administered by governments endowed with sovereign rights. Our understanding of international conflict remains deeply associated with encounters among these sovereign states that have shaped the history of world politics over the course of the last several centuries. The idea of defending state boundaries and providing for territorial security is integral to the role and legitimacy of a given governing process. Responsibility for violating sovereignty is addressed by governments either as a result of hostile actions taken by an adversary state that produce international conflict or as the commission of a crime calling for responses based on law enforcement. In the past, terrorism associated with radical political movements operating from without the state was addressed as a form of transnational crime that called forth a law-enforcement approach depending on the seriousness of the threat and the capabilities of the target society to act effectively beyond its borders, occasionally producing intervention by way of reprisal and retaliation against the source and sponsorship of the violence.

The United States had continued to treat transnational terrorism directed at American targets mainly in this fashion until the September 11 attacks, although with some partial exceptions where there was recourse to retaliatory force and sanctions as responses to alleged terrorist provocations attributed to these countries. Reprisal raids against Libya, Sudan, and Afghanistan were undertaken by the United States on the basis of this rationale, with the intention of discouraging future transnational terrorism directed at American targets.

Arguably the 1998 retaliatory attacks on al-Qaeda training camps in Afghanistan and on the pharmaceutical plant in the Sudan for the bombs exploded at the American embassies in Kenya and Tanzania occupied a middle ground regarded as "reprisals," one-time military strikes directed at countries whose governments were complicit in allowing their territory to be used to mount megaterrorist attacks. The military strike was not intended to destroy the terrorist capability nearly as much as it was seeking to send a message to its governmental host to take effective steps to prevent its territory from being so used, or face dire future consequences. Similarly, a decade earlier, during the Reagan presidency, the United States launched an air attack on Tripoli because of Libya's alleged links to terrorist incidents involving off-duty American servicemen in a disco located in Frankfurt, Germany. Although controversy has surrounded these attacks, there are some claims that Libya became far more cautious as a result of the American attacks, and stopped lending support to anti-American terrorist groups.

Israel had much earlier and frequently resorted to such international reprisals in reaction to violence directed against its citizens and assets, in effect, holding the foreign government responsible for the failure to prevent its territory from being used as a launching pad for terrorist activities, and sending a warning that such failures would produce even more severe future responses. This Israeli anti-terrorist policy was particularly directed at Lebanon during the period leading up to the 1982 Lebanon War, which itself could be interpreted as a tactical and doctrinal precursor to the American response to the al-Qaeda presence in Afghanistan after September 11. Another blurring of lines has been associated with the American overseas approach to "the war on drugs." Such a priority in US foreign policy, especially as it is being enacted in Colombia, does conflate "enforcement" with "war." This is expressed by calling the anti-drug policy war, and by associating the goals of the policy with direct support for the Colombian government's counterinsurgency war, including its efforts to protect a strategic oil pipeline and its recourse to paramilitary violence that is highly abusive toward sectors of civilian society viewed as sympathetic with the revolutionary movement.

World Order at Bay

Devising a coherent American response to September 11 required a focused response that acknowledged the difficulties of achieving security in the face of such a dispersed terrorist network so dedicated to extremist violence and visionary goals. The first phase of a response directed at the Taliban regime in Afghanistan and the extensive al-Qaeda presence in the country was a reasonable initial response, *especially to the extent it was confined within the specific context of megaterrorism.* What was not reasonable about the American response was the depiction of the enemy as "terrorism" in general, and to associate terrorism only with the political violence of non-state actors. Already, there have been unfortunate repercussions around the world arising from the US conception of the war against global terror, as states around the world rush to invoke US definitions, policies, and practices to support reliance on violence in their own unresolved political struggles. The deepest challenge of September 11 has hardly been mentioned in the months since these transformative events took place: namely, whether the leading state or a world of states can establish security at all in the future, given the rise of networking power and organization. This challenge is multi-faceted, preceding September 11, and was earlier posed mainly in relation to the regulation of the world economy to ensure a more equitable distribution of the benefits of trade and investment, as well as sustainable growth and the avoidance of market turmoil. There were also growing concerns prior to the megaterrorist threat about an alarming rise in transnational crimes being rendered almost invulnerable to traditional law enforcement by relying on underworld networking.

The war on global terror deepens this inquiry, suggesting the possibility that only by establishing stronger international institutions and procedures, overcoming the global democratic deficit, will it be possible to ensure security, equity, sustainability, stability, and legitimacy for a world in which technology and organizational skills have so empowered non-territorial networks and disempowered territorial states. Efforts to re-empower the United States as the unchallenged hegemonic state actor seem to be accentuating the obsolete notions of statism rather than seizing the moment to move toward a truly empowering globalism that could protect all the peoples of the earth. In effect, contrary to first impressions, September 11 does not reaffirm the framework of a statist world order via the anti-terrorist undertaking led by the United States, but rather makes stark the choice for the peoples and elites of the world: *global democracy or global empire.*

5. WRECKING WORLD ORDER

Above all, and at our best, we may sometimes help question the questions.
—Adrienne Rich, *Arts of the Possible*

Over time it may appear increasingly that the greatest cost of all associated with September 11 (including the American response) for the peoples of the world will be the damage done to the global normative order consisting of international law, prudent limits on warmaking, the authority of the UN, the promotion of human rights and democracy, as well as other widely endorsed precepts of international morality associated with the alleviation of poverty and other forms of human suffering. This damage seems most directly concentrated in what was already the most problematic area of concern, that of controls associated with the use of force to pursue political goals and efforts to regulate the conduct of warfare, which in the best of circumstances are fragile. These issues are complicated by the degree to which the September 11 attacks could not be accommodated within the traditional template of international relations based on the interaction of sovereign states, upon which existing norms and procedures governing behavior in wartime were based. It is true that international law has always been tested by new situations, and has adapted by an interplay of power, reason, and general acceptance, and that in this central respect, September 11 was just another such test, although one of exceptionally wide scope and profound implications. In this chapter a red line is drawn between two sorts of developments: first, the legitimate grounds for stretching international law to enable an effective response given the originality of the al-Qaeda attacks and the continuing threats posed; and secondly, the degree to which the restraining ideas embodied in international law, the UN system, and the just-war doctrine have been treated without proper respect by the US government, both deliberately to achieve maximal freedom of action and as a result of faulty reasoning and a failure of the official analysis that has shaped the US response to delimit the threat with appropriate specificity. I would argue that international law and the just-war doctrine were flexible enough to have absorbed an appropriate response to September 11, but the response chosen by the US government did not make such an effort, thereby weakening in crucial respects the restraining claims of world order as it is now constituted.

There is another important world-order cost arising from the pressure exerted by the megaterrorist threat that could have been minimized, if it was not altogether avoidable. This cost arises from the practical need to give security considerations the highest priority both in foreign policy and at home. Such a priority followed from both the gravity of the threat and its non-territorial character, which provided the seeming justification for entering into cooperative relations with repressive governments as part of an overarching counterterrorist diplomacy. This was complemented by pressures to enhance police powers at home to detect and disrupt potential terrorist plans as early and consistently as possible. The preoccupation with security has shifted governments and civil society actors away from the promotion of a more humane world order, a movement that had been gaining impressively during the 1990s.[1]

As earlier contended, the deficiencies of the American response to September 11 were not a result of stupidity or negligence. These deficiencies are directly a result of a deliberate expansion of US foreign policy goals so as to merge the megaterrorist challenge with preexisting geopolitical ambitions to exert global dominance. It is these ambitions that are disguised from the public, in the war talk that has issued from the US government in relation to Iraq, and on such other matters as defense spending, the militarization of space, and the control of Central Asian oil and gas reserves. In short, September 11 posed and intensified two severe challenges to world order: the threat of megaterrorism and the threat of global empire-building.

International Humanitarian Law

It should be recalled that the origins of modern international law are usually associated with two events: the publication of Hugo Grotius's treatise on war and peace in 1623 and the Peace of Westphalia ending the Thirty Years War some 25 years later. Grotius observed the cruelty of battlefield behavior on both sides in this religious war that pitted Catholics against Protestants in a ceaseless struggle that, from the perspective of historical hindsight, seems to have produced nothing but a series of pointless and sickening bloodbaths. It was the great insight of Grotius to propose to substitute a framework of positive and natural law for religious and battlefield passions that knew no limits. It was the achievement of Westphalia, and some subsequent developments, to build world order in the ensuing decades on the major premise of state sovereignty associated with recognized territorial boundaries, and the minor premise of pluralism (mutual respect among members of international society enjoying a common and equal status) in the relations among these sovereign entities. Flowing from this doctrine of sovereignty were ideas of exclusive internal authority, the duty of non-intervention, the legal equality of states, and the capacity to enter into lawmaking arrangements through international treaties and other forms of agreement. Later two other ideas strengthened this normative orientation: the secular idea that the practice of religion was a matter of private conscience, with the state having the duty of fostering and implementing an ethos of tolerance; and the nationalist creed that gave states the support of their inhabitants, establishing an internal political community worth fighting and dying for and financing in the face of external threats. Historically, it should be understood that this supposed world order based on the equality of states was restricted in initial application to Europe, and was regarded as fully compatible with relations of gross inequality and exploitation of non-European countries as formalized via colonialism.

Admittedly, this normative order established at Westphalia did not make dramatic inroads in the arena of war and peace, but on most less sensitive issues the growth of international law added greatly to the stability of routine commercial and private border-crossing activities. Westphalia also contributed to the establishment of internal "peace" within its territorial and sovereign borders, a major achievement considering the degree of violence and lawlessness that existed in pre-modern Europe. Over the centuries, despite the Westphalian framework and its associated ideas about the formation of a society of sovereign states, warfare continued to operate as an incredibly bloody mode of behavior used by states to resolve their most serious conflicts and to pursue expansionist ambitions.[2] For centuries war continued to be glorified as heroic history, but there was also an underpinning of discontent that began to chip away at the acceptability and durability of war as a social institution.

At the end of the nineteenth century, the Hague Peace Conferences (1899, 1907) were convened by the leading governments of the day to set limits on the conduct of war, and although the resulting treaty documents were rather vague in content and without enforcement measures, the idea of the law of war was given a major push forward. After the disillusionment of World War I, a strong public movement arose, especially in Europe, to outlaw war as an instrument of policy and to avoid future arms races by inducing leading governments to agree to disarmament. But despite the carnage of trench warfare, the extensive use of poison gas, and such alarming developments in military technology as submarines and bomber aircraft, there was no further development in specifying and updating the legal framework applicable to wartime. A third push occurred after World War II, when a large conference of governments negotiated the four Geneva Conventions of 1949, establishing a comprehensive treaty framework accepted by almost all states for what has come to be known as international humanitarian law. In 1977 this framework was further elaborated to cover civil war (with and without international intervention) in the form of two Geneva Protocols.

Limits on War
On parallel lines, efforts were being made to restrict the discretion of states to embark upon warfare as a policy option. In the background of the legal efforts was the just-war doctrine, which owed its existence initially more to theologians than jurists, but was gradually incorporated into international law, and to secular thinking generally. The normative guidelines of just-war thinking pertaining to recourse to war were abstract and easily adapted by self-serving interpretation of facts and law to the foreign policy goals of belligerent states: no recourse to war without a just cause, either to engage in defensive activity or to enforce a legal claim. The effort of international law in the twentieth century was to impose some constraints on the war-making discretion of states, and to attach some consequences to violative

behavior. The main undertaking was by stages to circumscribe the legal discretion of governments based on the general idea of prohibiting all recourse to force except in cases of self-defense.

The UN Charter tried to restrict the discretion of states even further by limiting the right of self-defense to situations where the claimant state had been the target of a prior armed attack, but to the delight of international lawyers who advise big governments, this limitation was rendered ambiguous by the use of the phrase "inherent right of self-defense" in the key provision of Article 51. But the UN Charter in Article 2(4) does prohibit non-defensive uses of force and requires states that claim a right of self-defense to report their use of force immediately to the Security Council. The charter also confers on the UN Security Council the responsibility for approving and monitoring claims of self-defense, as well as mobilizing a collective response to protect victims of aggression.

Again, the ambivalence of the regulatory impulse was evident from the start: what seems to be taken away from states is mainly given back, as the five permanent members of the Security Council can block any determination of a wrongful use of force merely by casting a single negative vote, the so-called veto power. Also, leading states have refused to pin themselves down by adopting an agreed definition of either "aggression" or "self-defense." This wide discretion has left the application of the UN Charter at the mercy of self-serving interpretations of a contested use of force by leading states, as well as requiring on every occasion a geopolitical consensus in order to reach a Security Council decision.

At the same time, the International Court of Justice strongly reaffirmed the UN Charter framework, as embodied in general international law, in the course of assessing Nicaraguan complaints about the role of the United States in seeking to overthrow in the 1980s the Sandinista government. But, as always, when the central issues of war and security are at stake, the results were effectively nullified: the US government explicitly repudiated the decision, indeed withdrew its acceptance of the compulsory jurisdiction of the World Court, dramatically declaring at the time that no state could be expected to make a suicide pact with international law, which was ridiculous given the marginal character of the issues at stake in the conflict bearing on the future of Nicaragua and its neighbors, and the overbearing presence and power of the US in world politics at the time.

It is also notable and relevant that the leaders of the defeated governments were held accountable for their violations of the law of war and for the commission of crimes against the peace (that is, waging aggressive or non-defensive wars) in the aftermath of World War II. The Nuremberg idea of individual criminal accountability of government officials and military leaders has also given civil society a way of participating in the normative order at the global level by insisting on government compliance, and even by justifying acts of civil resistance by citizens on the basis of upholding the higher claims of international law. For example, opponents of the Vietnam War and of "offensive" nuclear weaponry have construed their activism as fulfilling the "Nuremberg Obligation."

In the aftermath of the cold war, new attempts were made to rely on this approach, especially with the Security Council's authorization in the early 1990s of special tribunals at the Hague to assess the responsibility of individuals for international crimes arising out of the breakup of the former Yugoslavia and the 1994 massacres in Rwanda. More recently, in 2002, as a result of collaboration between interested governments and many transnational citizens' associations, a treaty has brought into being the International Criminal Court, which, while weak at its inception, could over time turn out to be a radical innovation that consistently undermines the statist claims that leaders of sovereign states are above the law, or at least above international law. Although the mere establishment of such a judicial institution is an impressive achievement, it is likely to be less than meets the eye, at least in the short run. A great deal of deference in the treaty establishing the ICC is given to national courts of the countries where the alleged criminal conduct took place and where the accused is a citizen, and the most important states in the world, including the United States and China, are unlikely to become parties for the foreseeable future. Whether adequate funding and effective operating procedures can be established in the face of American hostility to the ICC remains to be seen.

The US & the Global Order

The United States in recent decades has played confusing and contradictory roles in sustaining this normative order, both championing its establishment in many respects while at the same time discrediting its application, and often withholding its own formal commitment. Those who are hopeful about recent lawmaking initiatives point to trends suggesting a gradual institutionalization of authority at a global level, especially as a result of the human rights movement, combined with a seeming shift in the role of states away from territorial preoccupations and war-making, as well as the realization that weaponry of mass destruction has made war into an irrational and exceedingly dangerous instrument of policy. Particularly important was the American reluctance post-Vietnam to become involved in ground wars fought in Third World settings, a reluctance strongly reinforced a decade ago by the effort at peacemaking in Somalia, and elsewhere. (But it needs to be understood that this reluctance never was a factor when strategic interests of the United States were seen to be at stake, as was the case in the Gulf War, where there was an expectation that heavy American casualties might result from challenging Iraq's conquest of Kuwait.) One of the likely setbacks of September 11 is the discrediting of the so-called "Vietnam syndrome," the supposedly undesirable inhibition on the willingness of American leaders to use force overseas when there is any risk of substantial American casualties or a long involvement without an accompanying assurance of victory at its end. Such caution about recourse to war seems, from a world-order perspective, to be a healthy self-imposed restraint, and its apparent absence in the past year on the American political scene has been particularly evident in the mindless manner in which the case for waging war against Iraq has been accepted without generating meaningful debate or civic opposition. Putting this point in its strongest form: if the United States is to avoid becoming even more of a rogue superpower, it needs to restore or reinvent the Vietnam syndrome, or at least subject its policy to some equivalent discipline of restraint.

This shift in concerns away from war and strategic rivalries among antagonistic states was particularly evident in the 1990s, giving rise to a focus by policymakers on "globalization," and encouraging the expectation that major warfare, and associated arms races, were passing from the global scene, and even growing obsolete as a primary institution of human security. Again, however, closer scrutiny revealed that international behavior in this period was moving in several inconsistent directions. The US was continuing to push toward the development of a national security system that amounted to a "revolution in the technology of war" resting on the military applications of information technology, the progressive militarization of space, the gradual automation of the battlefield, and guided by scenarios of global "dominance."

These prospects were initially discounted as fantasies disseminated by conservative Washington think tanks hankering after higher appropriations for the Pentagon. But this radical vision of national security goals acquired a high degree of plausibility after the battlefield success of the new styles of warfare on display in the Gulf War in 1991 and the NATO War in 1999. These wars were fought to a successful outcome at a great distance from the United States with only the most minimal casualties on the American side. Under these circumstances the war option was quietly reevaluated and decidedly upgraded, presenting itself as a "cost-effective" approach to strategic interests, provided the tactics relied on such innovative military technology as smart bombs and missiles, unmanned aircraft, and advanced information systems. This new mood of belligerency was also given a normative "cover," being proclaimed as a means of protecting weak states against territorial aggression (as with Kuwait) and as enforcing fundamental human rights by protecting vulnerable peoples (as in Bosnia and Kosovo). Such a humanitarian face for war was reinforced by the rogue state doctrine, which rested on the more familiar idea of "enemies" and "threats." The doctrine was directed at several secondary states that were accused by the US government of seeking to acquire weapons of mass destruction, and was relied upon to justify threatening such states with severe adverse consequences should they defy Washington. This American self-appointed role as the geopolitical manager of the non-proliferation regime was a unilateral initiative, and it has had the effect of reviving the relevance of war to security and the conduct of international diplomacy, after a decade of preoccupation with the world economy and the promotion of economic globalization. Not far in the background, the American military's moves to control earth from space, both with a defense shield and for the deployment of targeting satellites and offensive weaponry, underscored the scope and depth of this US pursuit of global dominance, and its seeming disbelief in the idea that war and war-making were passing from the global scene.

Cracks in the Normative Order

As of 2001, there were further indications that the apparent strengthening of the global normative order during the 1990s would not endure: one strain was associated with the widely shared view that the locus of violent encounter was shifting from international to internal conflict, and that the existing framework of international law and the UN Charter were increasingly viewed as outmoded to the extent of losing their authoritative status as guides to the behavior of states and of the UN itself. Debates in the 1990s raged about the extent of UN authority to overcome its own limitation in Article 2(7) prohibiting UN intervention in matters essentially within the domestic jurisdiction of sovereign states, especially in the context of "humanitarian diplomacy." This issue, of course, rose to a climax in relation to the former Yugoslavia, especially with respect to Kosovo. When NATO intervened militarily in 1999, without even seeking the authorization of the UN, the issue was posed in an even stronger fashion: Could a group of states (self-proclaimed "coalitions of the willing"), joined in a military alliance, ignore the sovereign rights of existing states and the charter prohibitions on intervention by acting collectively and coercively in circumstances where the territorial sovereign was violating the rights of its own people in fundamental respects?

The puzzling phenomenon of "humanitarian war" had made its controversial appearance, and the efforts to explain these developments disclosed a wide divergence of viewpoints about trends in the existing international order. For instance, the Independent International Commission on Kosovo argued in its report that the NATO undertaking was "legitimate" (reasonable and necessary to rescue the Albanian Kosovars from human rights abuses and the prospect of "ethnic cleansing"), yet "illegal" (neither defensive in the charter sense, nor undertaken with the backing of a UNSC mandate).[3] This normative incoherence was further exhibited by the inability of the critics of the NATO initiative to be able to obtain more than three votes in the Security Council for a resolution of condemnation directed at the United States and NATO, and by the willingness of the UN to take on the job of post-conflict reconstruction in Kosovo, which has effectively ratified the *de facto* secession of Kosovo from Serbia as achieved by the unauthorized war. Illegality, even as widely acknowledged, seemed to have few consequences even within the United Nations itself! As a result, the use of force for a variety of non-defensive goals seemed to occupy a gray zone of "law/no-law."

Long before September 11, the other notable area of strain was the rise of international terrorism in a wide variety of national and transnational settings. The targets of sustained terrorism with a transnational dimension always had the problem of attribution: who should be held responsible when the agents of violence are concealed and not clearly identifiable as or traceable to states? Sponsoring states have aggravated this issue by seeking to hide their financial and logistical links to such terrorism.

Throughout much of its existence, Israel has had to confront such a persistent security challenge, and has effectively abandoned the constraining impact of such charter prerequisites as "prior armed attack" or reporting uses of force to the Security Council. Neighboring countries, especially Lebanon, have been frequently attacked as the source of terrorism, and accused terrorist "masterminds" associated with the attacks have been sought out and assassinated, often by secret police and paramilitary organizations acting covertly in foreign countries. Even a UN generally hostile to Israel's security claims has been reluctant to condemn such retaliatory violence if it did seem in its specific context to be reasonably and proportionately connected with protecting Israeli society against such violence.

It is obvious that to the extent that terrorist groups operate without the support of the territorial state, the logic of attribution is dubious, and can be arbitrary and unfair, with a resulting policy dilemma for the targeted state and for the appraisal of its response. The rationale for retaliation can also be counter-productive, as was arguably the case after the 1998 African embassy attacks leading the US to strike at targets in Sudan and Afghanistan. It is now widely believed that tensions between the Taliban regime and al-Qaeda were heading at the time toward the expulsion of bin Laden and his infrastructure from Afghanistan on the eve of these American air strikes, but when Afghan sovereignty was so violated the rifts were healed, and unfortunately the rest is history. Apparently, in June 1998, the Taliban leader Mullah Mohammed Omar had agreed to and was ready to extradite Osama bin Laden for criminal prosecution in Saudi Arabia, but repudiated the deal in September 1998 after the August US missile attacks against an al-Qaeda base located within Afghanistan, which involved, of course, a frontal denial of the country's sovereign rights.[4] For perspective, one might consider the likely reaction in Washington if Cuba held the US responsible for terrorist assaults on its stability by Cuban exile groups, and launched a retaliatory attack on a Cuban training base in, say, Florida.

In essence, the Westphalian approach to security and responsibility assumes that a state controls its territorial space, and that whatever force is directed across its borders, can be properly attributed to it. But what if the state is too weak to maintain its territorial control or cannot fully control underground groups operating from within its territory? Or so strong that it is essentially off limits for retaliatory action? It seems unfair to inflict punishment only on a weak society, particularly its civilian sectors, and yet it seems unreasonable to expect the state target of such violence to refrain from seeking to retaliate and disable the threat posed by such terrorist entities.

Of course, more troublesome are retaliatory strikes that are less directed at disabling terrorist capabilities than at gaining domestic popularity by showing one's own society that something is being done to punish their enemies. There is no satisfactory way to address this dilemma, and the UN and the international community basically keep their distance, implicitly acknowledging a gap in the international legal order between "the law" and "reasonable security precautions."

Not far in the background is a profound skepticism about heeding legal and moral restraints in war, or more generally, where the fundamental interests of the state are concerned. There exists among policymakers in the United States and elsewhere a prevalent Machiavellian ethos that believes the only "morality" that pertains to such action by states is concerned with effectiveness, and whatever is conducive to such ends should be undertaken regardless of whether it conforms to legal obligations and ethical standards.[5] To complain about the lawlessness of the enemy as a means to mobilize outrage and patriotic fervor gives "law" its main utility for Machiavellian diplomats.

In contrast, the Grotian effort of international lawyers over the centuries has centered on trying to negotiate a balance between the imperatives of security and adherence to the limits of law and ethical standards, while opposing the nihilistic view that war is an inherently lawless domain of human activity (and yet resisting the naive legalistic outlook that pretends that legal rules alone can keep the peace and uphold global security). It is this willingness to condition political realism by such adherence to legal restraints and their balancing role that gives some weight to the claim of being "civilized" in the conduct of international relations.

September 11 & the Global Order

Yet despite its weakness and fragility, a normative order rooted in international law and the UN system, does exist and still plays an important role for governments and public opinion in identifying when it is permissible to rely on force in international relations. One flexible element in the normative order arises from the absence of reliable legislative institutions and interpretive procedures on a global level to fashion responses that fall outside the standard spectrum of action and reaction associated with a world of sovereign states. In this case, the criterion of reasonableness fills in the normative gap whenever a serious challenge is posed that cannot be addressed by reliance on the statist paradigm.

So understood, the normative test of the American response to September 11 cannot be understood by mere reference to the rules of international law and the UN Charter, or even the general principles of the just-war doctrine. In contrast, the response to Iraq's conquest and annexation of Kuwait in 1990 fit comfortably with the Westphalian paradigm, lending itself to standard claims of self-defense and UN collective action in response to aggression. But evaluating the response to September 11 rests rather on a more subtle and imaginative assessment of reasonableness in a context without direct precedent, generating new claims to use force and the need for new limits. It is essential to ask whether the US-led response departed only to the extent necessary from the rules governing the use of force and related matters, and whether the US government took adequate pains to explain these departures in a precise, prudent, and principled fashion by reference to legitimate security goals, given the circumstances.

Also relevant is whether the United States is willing to engage in dialogue with other governments and within the UN as to the appropriateness and character of its response. Overall, then, it is important to ask, in what respects has the response to September 11 been reasonable? In what respects unreasonable? Such an assessment can help somewhat smooth out the rough edges of international law, rescuing international political life from the twin pitfalls of a rigid legalism on the one side and lawless nihilism on the other.

My contention is that only by posing the questions in this way can the damage done to the global normative order by both the attacks and the response be properly evaluated. To ask the legalistic or moralistic questions about whether the Westphalian and Charter rules have been violated in the course of the American response ignores the problems arising from their inapplicability to the security challenge posed by transnational megaterrorism in the first place. At the same time, to treat the originality of the challenge as exempting the response from normative accountability and critical scrutiny would set and is setting a dreadful world-order precedent, suggesting the renewed vitality of the cynic's view that in international relations might makes right.

What follows is a consideration of the normative damage done by what occurred on September 11 and in its aftermath, while taking into full account the best arguments for departing from the strict application of international law, UN authority, and just-war thinking. In effect, the proposed approach is recommending an extension and adaptation of the preexisting normative order of prevailing law and morality to cover the particularities of the September 11 challenges. These include the need to protect against future attacks by al-Qaeda itself, as well as against the menacing empowerment of extremist groups, and even sociopathic individuals, that is becoming increasingly possible due to technological advances in the production and dissemination of weaponry of mass destruction. Not to mention the political problems of "loose nukes" associated with mercenary nuclear engineers and scientists, criminal thefts and sales of nuclear weapons parts and materials, and porous command and control of nuclear arsenals in several countries.

It should be evident, but in view of the controversies that have raged, it is still important to note that the attacks of September 11 were themselves norm-shattering events that engaged by their nature the most fundamental standards of law and morality operative in international society. By mounting such a deliberate attack on civilian society, massive Crimes Against Humanity were committed, and reinforced by the announced threat of waging war against the United States and its allies by reliance upon genocidal tactics, directing violence not at military or governmental targets but at people targeted merely because of their specific ethnic, national, and religious characteristics. In this sense, the planners and perpetrators of September 11 were engaged in a global criminal enterprise of a credible warlike scope far more threatening and intrusive than the piracy on the high seas to which it has been compared. Those associated with megaterrorism have been appropriately regarded as enemies of all humanity, as well as breakers of the peace.

Earlier, less focused efforts by international law to address the challenges of piracy and international slave trading in the nineteenth century rested on similar theorizing, articulated by the Latin *hostes humani generis* (enemies of all people), and essentially expanding the criminal jurisdiction of territorial states to empower global law enforcement for crimes that were threats to humanity as a whole, occasioning even recourse to war in the so-called Barbary Wars waged against North African piracy at the start of the nineteenth century. Of course, piracy and even slavery lacked the political and moral resonance for a large sector of humanity that is possessed by Osama bin Laden's basic message of *jihad* against the United States.

Reshaping and Deforming International Law

It is first necessary to deal with the threshold question as to whether the September 11 attacks gave rise to a valid US claim of self-defense under international law, and if so, what sort of action in response would be legally justifiable. The problematics of the issue arise, first, of course, because the identity of the attacking party was not a state, but a transnational political network dispersed for purposes of concealment and effectiveness in many sovereign states. The issue is further blurred because to the extent the UN Charter addresses self-defense in Article 51 it does not explicitly require that self-defense apply only to an armed attack that occurs as a result of state action. At the same time, in determining the proper target of a forcible defensive response it is necessary to fix a plausible geographic locus of attack, and that presupposes a responsible state. Such a requirement raises the issue of indirect responsibility, that is, whether a state can be properly held sufficiently responsible for an attack if it is unable or unwilling to prevent its territory from being used as a launching pad for transnational terrorism. Throughout the period of UN practice, there has been a consistent pattern of cross-border retaliation for terrorist attacks. It could either be treated as a matter of a gray-zone issue (that is, neither law nor non-law, a gap) or, more acceptably, as an adaptation of international law to fit circumstances arising from transnational terrorism that made it reasonable to loosen the seemingly rigid prohibition on the use of force in international affairs.

As has been declared from time to time, the law is not an ass, nor a suicide pact, and cannot retain respect and anticipate compliance if it forbids states from doing what is necessary to uphold the security of their citizens from externally generated attacks. Long before September 11, well-regarded international lawyers stretched the Charter language to fit these requirements of reasonableness.[6]

But there is a problem with this analysis: the geopolitical dimension and the related problem of dirty hands. The United States throughout the cold war deemed it an acceptable course of foreign policy to train and finance personnel to engage in political violence against "enemy" states, especially in the cold-war era. The School of the Americas and the CIA routinely engaged in such activity as part of foreign strategic policy, and they encouraged exile political movements to wage armed struggles against established governments treated as legitimate within international relations generally (for instance, such tactics were repeatedly authorized to achieve the overthrow of Cuba's Castro or the ouster of the Sandinista government in Nicaragua). Reclassifying "terrorists" as "freedom fighters" does not overcome this disturbing double standard, which implies one sort of legal standard for the weak and another for the strong.

This aspect of the international legal order inevitably gives rise to cynicism. It also gives rise to an apologetic interpretation that confers on leading states, what were called "the Great Powers" until the middle of the last century, a special mandate to set and interpret the rules that sustain stability, including a general managerial role that includes much more discretion with respect to the use of force. In this respect, it is a mistake to suppose that recent efforts to impose a legal regime governing the use of force on all states has been successful. Hegemonic actors have all along been "a law unto themselves," uttering the mantra of the equality of sovereign states when diplomatic ritual so required, but carving out a role for themselves premised on a geopolitics of inequality.

Contextualizing this issue in relation to September 11 points to another dimension of the existing power-driven world order. Here the geopolitical leader was the target of the attack, and thus its preeminence was brought to bear immediately, so as to loosen any bonds of constraint, either self-generated or by deference to established international norms. In any event, the United States as political actor and as led by the Bush administration was already particularly oriented toward unilateralism in the security area of global policy. Months before September 11, the Bush White House had declared its objection to several fundamental arms control agreements that enjoyed the backing of almost every other government in the world. Taking stock of these geopolitical realities is not meant to excuse the failure by the United States to offer the international community a convincing assessment of legal claims that seemed to go beyond what had previously been deemed legally permissible, but it does go a long way to suggesting why it was not to be expected. In view of this official failure to offer a principled rationale for the conduct undertaken, independent critics have a special responsibility to consider such claims, both their reasonableness in light of the attack, but also with respect to giving ground to others to invoke this precedent as support for claims of their own. How else to struggle against the general erosion of respect for international law that results from high-profile unilateralism?

What makes this issue so serious is that the United States by its actions as global leader sets precedents that are available to others for use in quite different circumstances with far less justification. Rather than offer a justification of their own, governments in such countries as Israel and India merely argue by analogy, pointing their diplomatic fingers in the direction of Washington and contending that if the United States can mount attacks without international scrutiny and restraint against their enemies, so surely can other sovereign states faced with comparable threats to their security. The problem with such reasoning is that these threats are *not* properly regarded as comparable, but the breadth of the American claims and the extravagant insistence by the US government that it is waging war against terrorism in general makes it seem arbitrary and difficult to challenge others who purport to be countering terrorist threats that are organically linked to their security. It is not only the *substantive* response by the United States that is disturbing to the normative order, but at least as aggravating has been its insistence on procedural non-accountability, even to the extent of refusing to provide evidence and reasoned justifications for disregarding the sovereign rights of foreign countries. This issue of public justification and external *procedural* responsibility is a crucial world-order concern.

It needs to be appreciated that the current world-order framework mixes legal norms based on sovereign equality with geopolitical norms and practices based on the inequality of states, and thus the degree to which the powerful are willing to submit their claims to use force to some kind of collective review, particularly within the United Nations, is the best indicator of the degree to which the rule of law is gradually superceding the rule of force. In this regard, the behavior of a state that plays the role of a hegemon is of defining importance in a particular historical set of circumstances. Public explanation and dialogue acknowledges that even the most powerful political actor accepts its responsibility to other members of the international community to show why it has chosen to act in a particular manner that seems to break the legal bonds of constraint so carefully created by the patient efforts of international diplomacy, especially in the aftermath of terrible wars.[7] Such an effort would also help identify limits that would clarify the uniqueness of the facts that justified an exceptional departure from prior legal norms governing the use of force, making it more difficult for opportunistic leaders around the world to seize upon the American response to September 11 as grounds for suppressing enemies that might have been as much (or likely, more) victims of "terrorism" as perpetrators. The US government's handling of the aftermath to September 11 displayed a relatively clear grasp of conditions for an *effective* response, but monumental insensitivity to the equally important need to fashion a *legitimate* response.

The Afghanistan Claim

As prior chapters have argued, the United States acted reasonably and responsibly when it launched its attacks on the sovereign state of Afghanistan on October 7, 2001. Some respected left critics of the American response have argued that the September 11 attacks were "atrocities" or "Crimes Against Humanity," but not an act of war engaging the right of self-defense.[8] Such proponents insist that the US government should have displayed its respect for international law by adopting "a law enforcement model" of response. Such a model would have called for a maximal global undertaking to arrange the arrest and prosecution under international auspices of Osama bin Laden and others who could be tied to September 11, followed by UN trials, and, presumably, criminal punishment if sufficient evidence was available to support a conviction. Law enforcement aimed at al-Qaeda would also have involved extensive cooperation with police and intelligence forces around the world to locate and dismantle terrorist cells and operations wherever situated, financial interdiction of flows of money supportive of these activities, covert operations as necessary for the prevention of terrorist acts in the future, and improved security at soft targets, including all aspects of commercial aviation.

Could the threats posed by the September 11 attacks be dealt with in an effective manner by relying on law enforcement, given existing global capabilities? It should be obvious that *if* law enforcement could work, it is far preferable to war as an approach to the restoration of security for the American people. If the United States could have delivered such a message to the world, its leadership role would have been instantly vindicated, and its response legitimated to all except the most inveterately hostile. Unfortunately, my answer is that law enforcement would almost certainly *not* have worked, as was apparent by its prior failure to prevent a series of prior megaterrorist incidents involving American targets during the 1990s and its inability to detect and prevent September 11.

Of course, it could be contended that this record of failure was due primarily to the incompetence of the American counterterrorism approach before September 11, including the failure (or refusal) of responsible officials to heed warnings and follow leads. Additionally, it could be argued that the law enforcement undertaking was essentially misconceived as one of *reactive* steps to be taken after attacks rather than *preventive* action to be taken to prevent attacks. But I think the elusiveness and resolve of al-Qaeda in the months since September 11, despite the severity and global reach of the American response, demonstrates beyond any reasonable doubt that even an efficient and dedicated law enforcement approach would not have been able to deal successfully with the al-Qaeda threat.

Beyond this, if the US government had opted for law enforcement, and further major attacks on the United States and American targets around the world had ensued, which seems likely, then the American reaction would have probably then produced an even more drastic embrace of war overseas and authoritarianism at home. Such an analysis should not be confused with my earlier criticisms of Bernard Lewis' counsels to the effect that al-Qaeda and Osama bin Laden were encouraged by the feebleness of the earlier American responses, but rather that the response needs to be calibrated to the nature of the threat. In retrospect, it certainly seems this threat should have been more realistically identified and interpreted earlier. United States law enforcement agencies and world society generally should have been more efficiently mobilized for a preventive response in light of the events occurring in the 1990s, but this is quite different from the civilizational argument of Lewis and others that the best response to the underlying anti-Americanism in the Islamic world is the application of overwhelming force, and not attention to legitimate Arab grievances.

Startling as it may sound, dealing in timely manner with legitimate grievances throughout the Arab world might have been the best possible form of preventive counterterrorism. Surely fairness to the Palestinians and an end to the sanctions imposed on Iraq would have softened the resentful mood and altered the hostile climate of opinion. Beyond this, such an easing of regional tensions might also have led the United States and conservative Arab governments to relax, allowing the gradual removal of provocative American military bases in Saudi Arabia and elsewhere in the Middle East. We cannot know, of course, the effects that such initiatives might have had if taken years ago, either on Arab attitudes in general, or, more specifically, on the outlook, tactics, and strategy of al-Qaeda.

The American recourse to self-defense and related decision to wage war against Afghanistan was all but inevitable. Afghanistan was the apparent principal al-Qaeda nerve center and the place where its most prominent leadership resided. All indications are that Al Gore, had he been president at the time, would have shaped a similar military response directed toward Afghanistan and would have adopted the same tactical goals of overthrowing Taliban rule and destroying the al-Qaeda presence. These comments are all matters of conjecture, of course, but I think that it is highly likely that any state with the capacity to wage a reactive war would have done so if attacked in the manner of September 11, and particularly if there existed every reason to expect more of the same, or worse, at any point in the future.

The generalized US response directed against Afghanistan seemed reasonably connected with a claim of self-defense. It also seemed reasonable to regard the Taliban as indirectly responsible for the attacks, and therefore subject to accountability in the furtherance of defensive claims. And it further seemed reasonable to think that a comprehensive attack on Afghanistan that destroyed its operational infrastructure and killed, captured, disabled, and dispersed the al-Qaeda leadership was the most effective short-run American approach to threat reduction in the immediate aftermath of September 11. Affirming the broad contours of the American response that initiated war against Afghanistan in October should not be understood as an endorsement of what was done in its entirety, especially the combat tactics relied upon in Afghanistan and elsewhere. These criticisms appear to gain in weight as the evidence of civilian casualties and societal disruption mounts and casts a shadow backward, to raise the question anew as to whether the war against Afghanistan was carried out in a reasonable and responsible manner. I will first set forth the principal legal justification for attacking Afghanistan, and then indicate that this justification, while persuasive as an underlying claim, is itself subject to serious qualifications with respect to its implementation.

Afghanistan as Self-Defense

The question posed by most critics in the West was directed at the way the US government responded to September 11, especially the resort to war. Although the Bush administration explained the war, at first, as essentially a mission to catch Osama bin Laden, the overall effort was to destroy the al-Qaeda presence in Afghanistan and, by political restructuring, to make the country unavailable in the future for transnational terrorism. It seemed reasonable to seek these goals by means of a military campaign, though only by reliance on tactics, as mentioned, that sought to minimize the Afghan civilian loss of life, while seeking to be as successful as possible in incapacitating al-Qaeda. The September 11 attacks were on a massive scale, were carried out with a pronounced intention of achieving "victory" over the United States, managed to undermine America's sense of security, and included every prospect of being repeated in the future, possibly with even more disastrous damage. As earlier indicated, no state had ever mounted an attack on the United States that inflicted comparable harm, much less trauma, and only Pearl Harbor was remotely comparable. As with Pearl Harbor, there was never seen to be an alternative to war in self-defense for the United States, despite the grassroots strength of pre-existing isolationist sentiments at the time.

The only significant difference was the nature of the assailant and its apparent goals, and the aggravating reality that the harm was inflicted at points of maximal symbolic importance, and in the most densely populated and substantively vital urban centers of territorial power and authority. In such circumstances, stretching the international law doctrine of self-defense to include a non-state actor seemed reasonable and necessary. Such a conclusion is bolstered by the related acceptance of four other points: it was not plausible to expect the US to seek a negotiated solution; al-Qaeda demands went beyond the scope of diplomatic normalcy; the organization gave every indication that it would seek to strike again with as much deadly force as it could; and it seemed intent on obtaining and using biological, chemical, and nuclear weaponry of mass destruction in the future. The vulnerability so vividly disclosed on September 11 seemed to suggest some future attacks of this sort were likely to succeed.

On this latter point, American leaders have issued periodic frantic warnings indicating their expectations that such attacks would be attempted, that some would do great harm, that weaponry of mass destruction would be relied upon, and that other devastating assaults would be directed at Americans before long by suicide bombers. In

Vice President Dick Cheney's words, "[t]he prospect of another attack against the U.S. is very, very real... Not a matter of if, but when." In those of Defense Secretary Donald Rumsfeld, "[t]hey have chemical weapons... some shortly will have nuclear weapons." And most chilling of all, the words of FBI Director Robert Mueller, "[i]t's inevitable. There will be another attack. We will not be able to stop it. I wish I could be more optimistic."[9]

It is possible to discount partially such dire warnings as leaning over backward in compensation for the failure to anticipate September 11. Such warnings also provide officialdom with insulation from future criticisms should another attack occur. It is possible, too, to associate the timing of the warning as too conveniently coinciding with accusations made by FBI agents and others that their pre-September 11 warnings had been ignored at the higher echelons of government and that on some occasions their efforts at tracking leads were actually blocked by the Washington bureaucracy. But at this point it is appropriate to be on guard and to refrain from the view that success in Afghanistan has basically removed the threat of future attacks. There are too many indications that the Afghanistan campaign did not destroy significant portions of the al-Qaeda network, as well as evidence that its operatives have not abandoned their *jihad*, nor are prepared to renounce terrorist tactics.

The necessity of self-defense seemed strongly grounded in reality, but the question of exercising such a right via recourse to war against Afghanistan raised additional legal concerns. Would it be effective? There were two broad sets of concerns on this score. First of all, the so-called Vietnam syndrome seemed relevant, namely that interventionary operations of this kind tend to get mired in a quagmire, rely on tactics that inflict devastating damage on civilians in the target society, produce many casualties on the American side, and generally end in political frustration and domestic turmoil. In essence, the argument being made by some critics was that a military intervention of this kind does not work, as was allegedly demonstrated by the Soviet defeat in Afghanistan a little more than a decade earlier.

During the early weeks of the Afghanistan war, the inconclusiveness of the air campaign appeared to confirm these fears. Prominent skeptical voices began to be heard, especially from Europe, on such matters as excessive reliance on an air war and the use of such legally dubious battlefield weaponry as cluster bombs and B-52 carpet bombing, which caused heavy Afghan civilian casualties on the ground. Some of the criticism was directed at the war itself, some at the indiscriminateness of the tactics generating still more anti-American resentment, and some at the disposition to strike from the air and at a safe distance, which rendered the operations less successful in relation to their main goal: the capture and neutralization of as much of the al-Qaeda presence as possible.

The combination of the American air campaign and use of indigenous Afghan forces with mixed loyalties and their own priorities on the ground facilitated the cross-border escapes of a large proportion of the al-Qaeda forces, including evidently much of their top leadership. The bombing campaign directed at the Tora Bora cave complex, which served as headquarters for the al-Qaeda operations, particularly exposed the weaknesses of the American approach. American ground forces could clearly have been more effective in surrounding the area and closing off escape routes, particularly across the border to Pakistan, but there would surely have been higher American casualty totals.

Despite these early anxieties, the Afghanistan War appeared to achieve significantly relevant results in a short time. Innovations in military technology, especially in relation to targeting and unmanned aircraft, both minimized civilian damage and enhanced the effectiveness of air operations. Further, ground campaigns directed at the al-Qaeda concentrations of forces, around the Tora Bora region and elsewhere, seemed to have some of the desired effects of destroying their Afghanistan infrastructure, killing and capturing large numbers of operatives, and dispersing the Afghan remnant of the network into a condition of deep concealment. True, much of the al-Qaeda leadership still remains unaccounted for at this point, either escaping or possibly killed, but the operations of the network appear to have been seriously disrupted, at least temporarily. The absence of megaterrorist incidents in the months subsequent to September 11, despite the provocation of the American response, suggests provisionally the effectiveness of the US strategy to attack Afghanistan. At the same time, note needs to be taken of a spread to Pakistan of grisly forms of terrorism (assassination of journalists, attacks on churches during hours of worship, and even on a hospital) associated with Islamic extremism and al-Qaeda in response to the attack on Afghanistan.[10]

An important aspect of the American success, was to turn the tide of the civil war rapidly and decisively in favor of the Northern Alliance, leading to an abrupt Taliban collapse, the initiation of a political process to reconstruct Afghanistan, and a rescue of its peoples from the deep abyss of impoverishment, humanitarian disaster, religious autocracy, and political oppression into which they had fallen. These positive results, although not explicitly relied upon by the US government in advancing its justification for recourse to war, except after the fact when it was hailed as an emancipatory event for the Afghan people, especially women, enables the Afghanistan War to be considered a successful "humanitarian intervention." There are ambiguities here too. It is far from certain what will happen in Afghanistan during the months and years ahead, and whether the United States will play a constructive role in the peaceful reconstruction of the country. It is also not agreed that a use of military force without the explicit endorsement of the UN should be labeled an humanitarian intervention on the basis of its rationale and results.

Beyond this change of governing regime, the American strategy seems to have been a reasonably effective set of moves designed to ensure that the country will not serve as a future haven for transnational terrorism as it had during the Taliban years of rulership. The prospects for Afghanistan remain murky and will so continue for a long time.

The second set of objections relating to effectiveness was generally concerned with an anticipated backlash in the Islamic world. This backlash was believed to risk, above all, the destabilization of Pakistan, with the prospect of either civil war or an Islamic takeover. Such a course of events was also feared as likely to raise tensions still further in the region, risking an Indian "preventive war," and increasing the possibilities of a regional nuclear exchange. Such fears have materialized to a degree, although with an uncertain linkage to the Afghanistan War. It remains controversial as to whether the increased militancy of Kashmiri activists, including their training in and infiltration from Pakistan, can be properly regarded as a Pakistani side-effect of the al-Qaeda/United States encounter. It is further complicated by the degree to which the Bush approach to counterterrorism emboldened India to step up its oppressive rule in Kashmir, prompting an escalation in resistance activity. At minimum, it seems that the unsettling developments associated with the response to September 11 pushed India and Pakistan closer in the spring of 2002 to unleashing nuclear war than any two countries have been since the high drama of the Cuban Missile Crisis in 1962. The outcome of the regional confrontation, along with domestic turbulence in Pakistan, has posed unresolved questions about the stability, and even the viability, of the pro-American leadership in Islamabad.

Additional anxieties about thousands of fresh al-Qaeda recruits who would conceive of the assault on Afghanistan as the beginning of an inter-civilizational war by the infidel West against Islam, have not been realized, at least not directly. Even the Arab street was not greatly energized by the Afghanistan War. The Islamic world was itself somewhat surprisingly divided, with Iran pursuing a vigorous anti-Taliban line. It is correct that the great majority in the Arab world opposed the American-led war and were moved to reaffirm their anti-American sentiments by the nightly emphasis on civilian casualties shown on TV by al-Jazeera, but this opposition did not translate into eruptions of political outrage in the Arab world. (It needs also to be understood that the great majority of the Arab world, despite its anti-Americanism, also repudiated the megaterrorist attacks of September 11, although not accepting the American version of al-Qaeda responsibility or even of the Arab identity of the perpetrators.) Much more consequential with respect to Arab attitudes has been the unwavering US support for Sharon's upsurge of anti-Palestinian extremism in this period, which has exerted considerable pressure on the neighboring Arab governments to adopt much more engaged anti-Israeli postures, while diplomatically moving to find some path to a defusing solution for the Palestinians. Again, on balance, the fears of those who opposed the Afghanistan War based on a backlash theory have not yet been borne out.

Having provided this qualified endorsement of the first phase of the American response to September 11, it now seems appropriate to consider some of its problematic aspects, not so much only in relation to Afghanistan, but more generally as incubating American imperial dreams and designs, as well as intensifying violent forays by other governments around the world against societies whose peoples are struggling for elementary human rights, including the right of self-determination. These wider ramifications of the American response were hidden beneath the self-defense banner and will be discussed critically and in more detail in Chapter 7.

A final point on these issues: causal connections are hard to discern in international relations. Real motives are concealed, and the rationalizations that are given out by governments are self-serving, often with an intent to deceive. The upsurge in state violence may not be in each instance explicitly justified or explained by reference to the American response, but governments around the world know that their critics can be put in an untenable position as soon as the justification of state violence is couched in the language of counterterrorism or defense against terrorism. Also, action and reaction cycles are difficult, if not impossible, to disentangle. There is no way to conclude whether India or Pakistan should be held primarily responsible for moving to the very brink of regional warfare that would almost certainly have ended in mutual catastrophe. Similarly, the extent to which suicide bombings inside Israel were the cause or pretext for Israel's offensive operations carried out against West Banks towns, cities, and refugee camps would be impossible to determine, even if governments were far more transparent in their security policy. It does seem reasonable to conclude that the American mismanagement of the response to September 11 has contributed substantially to the intensificiation of state violence in several existing conflict situations, especially in several Asian countries.

Rhetorical Overkill

From the outset, the Bush administration specified the goals and intentions of its response to September 11 in a flamboyant political language that exhibited no sense of limits or restraint and contained some dangerous policy implications. This disposition, whether unwitting or primarily related to the wider American global agenda of dominance, can be illustrated by reference to a few notorious examples. Of course, it is to be expected that any American president would rally domestic unity and patriotic sentiments in such a moment of indisputable national crisis. And further, the American way of war, except during the cold war when a series of stalemates resulted, has been to go all out for victory, and to define the belligerency in terms of our good and their evil.[11] The abruptness, shock effect, and apparent source of the attacks accentuated this disposition to regard the United States as a savior nation, an avenging geopolitical angel engaging the forces of evil in epic battle. As Osama bin Laden, by temperament and language, presented the conflict in equally ultimate terminology, battle lines on both sides were drawn in an abstract, totalizing rhetoric.

The first official name given to the American response by the Pentagon, Operation Infinite Justice, expressed the true spirit of the American claim, which was to regard itself as the chosen vehicle of history for the worldwide destruction of the great evil of this era, namely, terrorism. President Bush, in his "with us, or with the terrorists" speech, declared "[t]his is not… just America's fight. And what is at stake is not just America's freedom. This is the world's fight. This is civilization's fight. This is the fight of all who believe in progress and pluralism, tolerance, and freedom."

If this kind of summons had been directed at al-Qaeda and the threats it posed, then it would have seemed appropriate, and would not have conveyed an impression of an unfocused response of disproportionate magnitude. But from the beginning the scope of the undertaking was grandiosely (mis)conceived. As Bush expressed it, "[o]ur war on terror begins with al-Qaeda, but it does not end there. It will not end until every terrorist group of global reach has been found, stopped, and defeated." Again, one might have breathed more easily if the words "global reach" had been understood in accordance with their common meaning. By indicating that the Middle East and South Asian groups concerned with unresolved regional and national issues, including those dedicated to Palestinian and Kashmiri self-determination, were on the list of prohibited organizations, it became clear that this war on terrorism was being waged against all non-state revolutionary forces perceived as hostile to American global interests. It should be noted that some of these groups identified with the September 11 enemy posed no threat, lacked any pretense of global reach, and were as much, or more, victims of unacceptable state violence as they were perpetrators.

On November 10, speaking at the United Nations, Bush underscored the unbounded nature of this new war against terrorism: "We're asking for a comprehensive commitment to this fight. We must unite in opposing all terrorists, not just some of them." The once seemingly limiting notion of global reach is completely abandoned in this formulation. In keeping with the prior US government's approach to counterterrorism, "terrorism" is understood in this usage to refer only to political violence used by non-state actors, movements, and groups. States are indicated only as *sponsors* or *havens* for such groups, but not as themselves engaged in terrorism. This one-sided definition of terrorism has extremely serious real world consequences, operationally giving a green light to states opposed by internal political forces that have long been oppressed by state violence. A more evenhanded view of terrorism would regard any violence directed at civilian society as terrorism, which would be reflected in the media and public attitudes. It would no longer be possible for a leader such as Ariel Sharon to defend Israeli high-tech violence against Palestinian civilian society by insisting that there is no equivalence between Israeli "self-defense" and Palestinian "terrorism." Beyond this, each instance of political violence needs to be assessed as to the character of its goals, the degree to which peaceful methods have been tried in the past, and the extent to which the scale and tactics relied upon seek to restrict direct harm to non-civilian targets.

The culmination of this mobilization of language was to merge the war against terrorism with the geopolitical agenda associated with the alleged threats posed by so-called "rogue states." The hostility toward these states, which are also principally in the Islamic world, preceded September 11, but was reasserted with more threatening implications in the months following, especially as the Afghanistan war seemed to be in its last stages, with the destruction of the Taliban regime. The rhetorical trope relied upon to link these two undertakings was, of course, "the axis of evil" passage in Bush's State of the Union Address on January 29, 2002:

> States like these [Iraq, Iran, North Korea] constitute an axis of evil arming to threaten the peace of the world. By seeking weapons of mass destruction, these regimes pose a grave and growing danger. They could provide these arms to terrorists, giving them the means to match their hatred. They could attack our allies or attempt to blackmail the United States.

The rhetoric used is part of the demonstration that the war on global terror did not end in Afghanistan, but the argument rests on a blend of unconvincing speculation and the widening of the agenda. These states so identified are not guided by visionary leaders with a penchant for martyrdom. Even Iraq has consistently behaved as a "normal" state acting on a calculative basis of gains and losses, giving way when defeated in the Gulf War and negotiating in a traditional manner, observing diplomatic protocol at the United Nations and elsewhere. To the extent that Iraq harbors revisionist ambitions and hostile intentions toward its neighbors, it seems capable of being contained by deterrence, which includes a threat of an overwhelming devastating response in the event of unacceptable provocations. The power disparities are such that any external aggressive act of war by Iraq would result in an overwhelming and immediate response, which would further reduce an Iraq already crippled by war and sanctions, to ruins and helpless destitution. There is no evidence to suggest that Saddam Hussein harbors such a suicidal disposition. Even the war Iraq launched against Ayatollah Khomeini's Iran in 1980 was done only with US encouragement, and under the impression that an easy victory would be quickly achieved. When a stalemate resulted, Iraq accepted a UN-brokered restoration of the status quo.

In general, the rogue states are far more threatened than threatening, and to the extent their governments seek weaponry of mass destruction, it is for deterrent purposes in the face of asymmetric aggressive moves made against them, mainly by the United States, which enjoys both a decisive military advantage in every sphere of war-making and a homeland beyond reach. There is no basis for thinking that such governments are seeking or would invite their own destruction by providing such capabilities to an organization such as al-Qaeda or some similar terrorist organization. The axis of evil countries are more intimidated, not less, by the US reaction to September 11, but threatening them in such an intense manner is the most extreme expression of American unilateralism to date, and troubling to most foreign countries, including European allies, with the limited and partial exception of Britain. If and when such threats are converted into military action, there is likely to be a strong anti-war upsurge on several levels: within the Arab world, in Europe and other parts of Asia, and quite likely in the United States itself.

By using inflammatory and inflated rhetoric to explain the American response to September 11 there are several general consequences: a loss of convincing, and thus justifiable, rationale for reliance on the right of self-defense (there is no such legal basis for invoking the right against rogue states); an expansion of the scope of military operations with a seeming indifference to the scourge of war; a green light for state terrorism; a disregard for the relevance of legal and ethical limits on the use of international force; and the pursuit of geopolitical ambitions by the United States under the guise of waging war against "evil" and "terrorists." This combination of effects does great damage to the always fragile normative order in world politics, especially by its refusal to validate recourse to war in the most minimalist terms consistent with the approach taken in international law and the UN Charter, which, while not pacifist, both seek to restrict state use of international force on a discretionary basis. This substantive assault on normative restraint is greatly magnified by the repeated indications that the United States will determine by itself the role of force in fulfilling its security goals, and has no need to gain approval either internally from its own citizens or externally from other governments or from the United Nations.

Such a posture contrasts in style and substance with the frantic diplomacy used to prevent the outbreak of regional war between India and Pakistan in May/June 2002, which was based on a rejection of unilateralism, and the logic of self-help with respect to security policy. Both states were asked to cool their passions, to seek accommodation, and India, unlike Israel, was not given authorization to treat terrorist provocations as the occasion for conducting a defensive war. At the same time, Pakistan was urged to back down on Kashmir, and to avoid provoking India. The underlying rationale for the American approach is clear: Pakistan, the source of transnational terrorist activities in Kashmir and India, is needed in the campaign against al-Qaeda, and this will only be possible if President Pervez Musharraf holds onto power, which would become unlikely if a war with India occurs and Pakistan loses. Beyond this, a nuclear war between these two densely populated countries would probably cause catastrophic damage, diverting attention from American priorities and exerting great pressure to achieve nuclear disarmament.

In terms of security policy in this period, it is evident that the US government is pursuing a three-track approach: rogue states are coercively denied self-help options based on weapons of mass destruction even if faced with credible threats mounted by militarily superior potential attackers; middle powers, especially if related to the United States in a positive manner, are subject to diplomatic pressures to modify security and self-help on the basis of pragmatic considerations (e.g. an interest in sustaining positive working relationships with *both* India and Pakistan); and the United States itself, which is the architect of its own self-help posture, reliant on weaponry of mass destruction, and resentful of criticism by others and resistant to diplomatic efforts to inhibit its geopolitical operations.

Secondary Effects: Escalating State Terrorism

One of the worst spillover effects of the manner in which the US government has orchestrated its response to September 11 has been the hunting license issued to states around the world to intensify violence against their opponents, and to validate such action by claiming to be fighting against terrorism, helping the American-led global war on terror. India, Russia, and China have all stepped up their violence against internal movements for self-determination that have been engaged in resistance to state power for decades. In effect, the American leadership, expressed by rhetoric and through the generality of its own military campaign, with its many fronts and its absence of specific goals, has been read (correctly) as an unconditional authorization for state violence, which often is best understood as terrorism. If terrorists are equated with evil, and their governmental opponents are regarded as inherently good, then it is obvious that violence by the latter against the former is never excessive or wrong. Such is the fundamentalist logic of the Great Terror War.

Nowhere has this impact been felt more harshly than in Palestine. Bush's bonding with Ariel Sharon (christened by the White House "a man of peace," despite a spate of military operations causing severe harm to Palestinian civilian society) has given Israel the room to maneuver it needed to launch a devastating attack on the cities, towns, and villages throughout the West Bank in March/April 2002, using tanks, helicopters, and missiles against essentially defenseless Palestinian communities. The Israeli pretense has been the destruction of "the terrorist infrastructure," but the nature of the operation seems designed to crush the Palestinian spirit, destroying ministry records and educational facilities, interfering with medical services, and inflicting unspeakable hardships and numerous daily humiliations on the long-suffering Palestinian people. The United States, made conscious of the adverse regional effects of such Israeli aggressiveness, has from time to time made tepid countermoves calling for Israeli withdrawal and the establishment of a Palestinian state, all the while reiterating its inane insistence that Arafat do more to stop Palestinian terrorism, while basically allowing Sharon to call the shots. Despite the intensity of domestic pro-Israel support, as in relation to India/Pakistan, the US approach to Israel/Palestine is subject to pragmatic countermoves that reflect wider regional interests in the stability of pro-Western Arab governments and assured access to Gulf oil at moderate to low prices. Even such a mild White House posture has been derided as cynical and hypocritical in the Islamic world, and as incoherent by mainstream critics who argue that it is not consistent to enlist countries in the global war against terrorism and then complain when they adopt the sort of totalistic tactics relied upon by the United States in Afghanistan, especially in the Tora Bora area, to destroy al-Qaeda with as few American casualties as possible.

The incoherence is a consequence of cross-cutting geopolitical pressures needing to be reconciled with ethnic politics at home. It would be a major setback for US regional objectives if its support of Israeli state terrorism destabilizes moderate pro-Western Arab governments in Egypt, Jordan, and the Gulf. But Bush invited this policy dilemma by casting the anti-terrorist net so broadly, and without specific linkage to al-Qaeda and kindred fanatical movements with both an anti-American animus and a genuine "global reach." The consequence was to stigmatize popular movements that were engaged in self-determination struggles in which both sides were relying on criminal tactics, attacking civilians and imposing the burdens of war on innocent civilians. Again, nowhere is this observation more true than in relation to occupied Palestine where the UN has been calling for Israeli withdrawal for more than 35 years, and where Israel's settlement policies and reliance on collective punishments imposed on the Palestinians as a whole are flagrant, massive, and continuous violations of international humanitarian law, as embodied in the Fourth Geneva

Convention. To paint Palestinian armed resistance under these conditions as "terrorism" is to do violence to language and to the cause of justice. At the same time, Palestinian violence that deliberately targets civilians *is* terrorism, just as Israeli punitive action against the Palestinian civilian population *is* terrorism.

In sum, the United States did have a valid claim of self-defense given the scope and impact of the September 11 attacks and the nature of their perpetrator, but such a claim cannot be properly extended to justify state violence against civilian society, to allow for the disregard of the sovereign rights of foreign countries, to threaten or use force against "rogue" states, or to make acceptable recourse to a war mode in circumstances of unresolved self-determination struggles. In this sense, neither can the United States convincingly rely on self-defense to justify uses of force in states other than Afghanistan, nor can other states be allowed to rely on the American war against Afghanistan in the context of their struggles—even if their opponents engage in terrorist acts.

Faustian Bargains

To pursue the military campaign against Afghanistan, and more generally against global terrorism, the US government immediately gave priority to its strategic interest in obtaining foreign military bases and allies, as well as governmental cooperation and diplomatic support. The repressive governments in Central Asia with lamentable human rights records were immediate beneficiaries, as was Pakistan. In exchange for varying degrees of tactical and diplomatic cooperation, not only were concerns about human rights or proliferation suspended, but hundreds of millions in foreign economic assistance was gratefully conferred. It is difficult to assess the reasonableness of these initiatives, and the extent to which such undisclosed agenda goals as future dominance of Caspian Sea oil and gas were a large part of the picture. But what seems clear is that as during the cold war, the strategic opportunism of the new geopolitics takes precedence over earlier efforts to promote human rights and democracy. Such moves reinforce realist conceptions that all that matters in world politics are relations of power. It further highlights the role of the United States as the dominant military actor in the world, and puts in the background earlier growing concerns about global governance, overcoming poverty, distributing more equitably the benefits of globalization, and environmental protection. Further in the background are the "blowback" concerns associated with the unanticipated negative consequences of opportunistic diplomacy, prime instances of which are the two main current tormentors of the United States: Osama bin Laden and Saddam Hussein. Arming and equipping unpalatable governments and movements in the present setting could also eventuate in actions directed against American interests around the world.

Weakening International Humanitarian Law

As mentioned earlier, the conduct of the war in Afghanistan relied on tactics and weapons that seemed to ignore to varying degrees the underlying prohibition against indiscriminate uses of force or force directed at non-military targets, thereby shifting risks of loss of life to the extent possible to the Afghan side. In mitigation, the reliance on accurate targeting and munitions, the difficulty of effective combat operations against a concealed adversary in a rugged mountain terrain, the urgency of the operation in view of the threat of further attacks, and the rapid success of the basic commitment to drive the Taliban regime from power need to be taken into account. It has been difficult to assess accurately the number of Afghan civilians killed in the main war operations by American military action, but what studies exist estimate the number to be at least 2,000–3,000, some eleven months after the initial attacks in October 2002. Some of these deaths resulted from faulty targeting based on misleading ground intelligence supplied by Afghan sources more interested in their own ethnic conflict than faithfully pursuing the American objectives relating to the Taliban and al-Qaeda, again reflecting the US reliance on war-fighting modes that minimize their own casualties even if it means raising risks to civilians present in combat zones.

More flagrant, more obviously deliberate, has been the American refusal to apply the Third Geneva Convention relative to the treatment of prisoners of war (POWs) in relation to captured and detained combat personnel. To begin with, the US invited worldwide criticism by its initial mode of transporting those detained—hooded and in heavy chains and manacles—and then placing them in open air cages at the

Guantanamo base in Cuba, aptly called Camp X-Ray. The US government then denied the prisoners formal POW status, claiming that those detained did not qualify as lawful combatants, since they lacked uniforms and were not part of a chain of military command. Article 5 makes it clear that where there is doubt as to POW status "such persons shall enjoy the protection of the present Convention until such time as their status has been determined by a competent tribunal."

After an international uproar, the US government partially relented, drawing a distinction between Taliban detainees, who would be treated as POWs within the Geneva framework and al-Qaeda fighters, who would continue to be denied such status. There is some legal justification for drawing such a distinction, especially as al-Qaeda forces, as part of an avowed terrorist network, did not comply with the requirement of Article 4(A)(1)(d) "conducting their operations in accordance with the laws of and customs of war." Further, given the continuing threats posed by al-Qaeda and their concealment, it was within reason to seek information by sustained interrogation, which could arguably be hampered by the strict application of the Article 17 guidelines, which required that POWs only disclose their identity and their role in the military organization; they could not be subject to any "physical or mental torture, nor any other form of coercion" so as "to secure from them information of any kind whatever." These individuals were seen as dangerous beyond their combat role in enemy forces, being regarded as members of an extremist organization devoted to inflicting harm on civilians and not acknowledging themselves the relevance of international humanitarian law or even a distinction between war and peace or between civilian and military targets. Under such circumstances, the American commitment involved a belligerent intention to keep such individuals permanently confined, and to the extent possible, charge them with "crimes" under US law and international law.

To carry out this latter intention, President Bush authorized by executive order the establishment of military commissions to prosecute non-US citizens accused of being terrorists. These tribunals operate secretly and without according due process to a defendant or any right of appeal, and were empowered to impose death penalties. Again, the American approach was widely criticized by human rights organizations at home and abroad. The case made for such an approach was essentially one based on military necessity given the distinctive character of such international terrorism. Reassurances of fairness were provided by the Pentagon, but rested on trust that broad discretionary powers of the US government would not be abused at the application stages. Again, the precedent is not a worthy one, and if the situation were reversed, the US would be most uncomfortable, to understate, about relying on vague assurances cut off from the Geneva framework. It is worth recalling in this context that the US has enacted into law authority for the president to authorize the use of force to retrieve Americans facing war crimes prosecution by the International Criminal Court, whether or not they are responsibly accused.

Here, again, the issues of appropriate treatment standards for detainees is somewhat complicated due to the novelty of the threat, and its relationship to reasonable efforts to uphold the security of territorial societies. How should such captured al-Qaeda operatives be handled in the absence of specific evidence linking them to terrorist acts and activity? Would it be reasonable to treat mere al-Qaeda membership as tantamount to participation in a criminal conspiracy to engage in terrorism? It seems reasonable to believe that so long as al-Qaeda (or some equivalent network) persists as a reality, the release of such individuals or their repatriation to the country of origin would be imprudent, and possibly dangerous. Again, the template of international law does allow a threatened state to act in accord with its rules, and the humane values they embody, and yet take reasonable precautions to uphold the security of its society in the face of unprecedented circumstances. The best approach under these circumstances is to fashion a new template for humanitarian law that takes into account the special circumstances of megaterrorism that call for new standards, while seeking to maintain the humane values of protecting the vulnerable (disarmed enemy combatants) that is the essence of the Geneva approach.

In light of the distinctive challenges associated with megaterrorism, the Camp X-ray extravaganza appears to have been almost totally unjustified and quite unnecessary, while the other aspects of the American approach are more understandable, but have never been explained in a clear and persuasive way so as to engender confidence and public understanding. It would seem appropriate to demand more in the way of information from individuals clearly associated with al-Qaeda, especially if exercising command responsibilities, as well as to hold them accountable and detainable in a manner that exceeds what is permissible with respect to combatants who had been part of the Taliban military effort that seem limited to participation in an unresolved civil war. From such a perspective, there seems no persuasive reason to deny Taliban detainees full Geneva treatment, including their repatriation to Afghanistan at the earliest possible time considering that the Taliban has been removed from power in Afghanistan, and that their role may have been involuntary, and in any event, unrelated to the September 11 events. It may be reasonable to detain such individuals until the collapse of the Taliban has been fully consummated, and until the possibility of some sort of resistance movement that joins together Taliban and al-Qaeda remnants has been effectively precluded. It also makes little sense, and lacks any justification, to treat al-Qaeda foot soldiers as if they were valuable sources of information merely because they had been recruited into the organization.

As in other matters, the challenge of September 11 can neither be adequately addressed by relying on the pre-existing framework of international law, nor should this framework be entirely discarded. What is required is the reasonable adaptation of this framework to the urgencies of this new modality of warfare, namely, a terrorist worldwide network guided by visionary goals in opposition to an established territorial state. In this regard, it does not seem appropriate to view Taliban soldiers as part of the network, or to treat them as dangerous unless specific evidence exists of participation in Crimes Against Humanity that can form the basis of criminal charges. Also important would be a principled and persuasive explanation for why the traditional template of humanitarian law is insufficient, and must be adapted to meet specific needs. My argument is that the US failures of reasoned explanation for its action are as consequential for the weakening of international humanitarian law as its substantive disregard of legal restraints on its behavior.

Any evaluation of the US refusal to deal responsibly with international humanitarian law is further complicated by the unilateralism of the US approach in general to its conduct of foreign policy, especially, but not only, during the Bush presidency. Under these circumstances, there were never grounds for having confidence that the US would expand its options under international law in a manner that is as sensitive as possible to humanitarian considerations, as set off against the urgency and special character of security requirements. Especially in the aftermath of September 11, the US response is widely perceived, especially overseas, as vindictive, punitive, and excessive, as well as being an understandable and necessary effort to protect itself against further terrorist strikes. There are also grounds for thinking that warnings from official Washington about the imminence of terrorist threats are being exaggerated so as to prolong the mood of crisis and its accompanying patriotic support for whatever the government undertakes. Such an atmosphere provides an ideal political cover for empire-building activities.

Bypassing the United Nations

From the outset of the September 11 attacks, the US government made it clear that it would fashion its response outside of the institutional framework of the United Nations and without external guidance, but would at the same time seek to bolster the legitimacy of its response and reinforce its call to others to join in the campaign against global terror by recourse to the UN. Acting with unusual dispatch, the UN Security Council on September 12 already adopted Resolution 1368 condemning the terrorist attacks "in the strongest terms," defining them as a threat to international peace and security, calling upon all states to act "urgently" to bring those associated with the attacks to justice, and acknowledged the legally important US contention that the attacks validated a claim of self-defense under the charter. This was followed up on September 28 with Resolution 1373, which obligated all states to prevent and suppress the financing and any form of support of terrorism, deny safe haven, cooperate in anti-terrorist law enforcement, and strengthen border controls to impair the mobility of terrorists. It also imposed on states the duty to make diligent efforts to deny asylum or refugee status to individuals with terrorist affiliations, and, significantly, the resolution established a committee charged with monitoring implementation of its provisions.

On October 7, 2002, the day that the war against Afghanistan began, the permanent US Representative to the UN, Ambassador Negroponte, sent a letter informing the Security Council that the US government was exercising its rights of self-defense based on "clear and compelling information" that al-Qaeda had been responsible for the September 11 attacks and that this organization had the support of the Taliban regime, but failed to disclose the evidentiary basis for such an incriminating conclusion. The letter also indicated that the US was entitled to invoke its rights of self-defense in the future in relation to other organizations and states associated with terrorism, but it failed to specify what was meant by such a claim, and whether any limiting conditions applied.

When President Bush addressed the General Assembly on November 10, he reiterated his call to war, thanking the UN bodies for their "strong and principled stand." At the same time, Bush repeated his earlier warnings to states that they would suffer the consequences of failing to join in the global campaign being led by the United States. More specifically, Bush asserted that

> even beyond Resolution 1373, more is required...We're asking for a comprehensive commitment to this fight. We unite in opposing all terrorists, not just some of them. In this world there are good causes and bad causes, and we may disagree on where the line is drawn. Yet, there is no such thing as a good terrorist. No national aspiration, no remembered wrong can ever justify the deliberate murder of the innocent. Any government that rejects this principle, trying to pick and choose its terrorist friends, will know the consequences.

This passage contains the three standard tenets of the US approach that seem particularly dangerous and regressive: the generalization of the September 11 threat to embrace all terrorists, the identification of terrorism as anti-state violence and the exemption from scrutiny of state violence, and the threat to those governments that are seen by the US government as somehow acting beyond these guidelines.

It should be noted that by adopting the third guideline as a principle of its own foreign policy, the United States would be subject to censure or even attack for the aid and support that it was routinely giving covertly and overtly to anti-Marxist armed struggles around the world during the latter stages of the cold war, including several movements in Central America and Southern Africa that systematically engaged in terrorism on a grand scale. Such support was even officially endorsed and proudly embraced during the 1980s, becoming known as the Reagan Doctrine, a US commitment of support for "freedom fighters." As I have argued throughout, there is a distinction between supporting terrorism and megaterrorism, but such a distinction is repudiated by the manner in which the US government has itself defined the September 11 threat.

The public mood, especially in the United States, was such at the time that no adverse reaction to such ideas was widely voiced to this anti-terrorism war that itself seemed to pose new dangers of its own to international peace and security. As earlier argued, the US had solid grounds for claiming self-defense, for acting against al-Qaeda on the basis of necessity and urgency, and of retaining operational control over this initial phase of response outside the UN. Its efforts to rally support and approval in the UN met with considerable success and no opposition, an impressive acknowledgement of the novelty and gravity of the situation arising in the aftermath of September 11. The generalized challenge to states also encouraged this early show of solidarity in confronting such a concealed network that itself refused subordination to any particular state.

At the same time, at first, the lack of US respect for the role of the UN in relation to peace and security was effectively ignored by the UN and its membership. All along there was almost no effort made by the US government to comply with the fundamental UN Charter idea of treating recourse to war, even in self-defense, as a last resort, after all reasonable avenues leading to a peaceful solution had been tried and failed. In the background, here, was a rush to war by Washington, a refusal even to respond to the Taliban request for evidence of Osama bin Laden's and al-Qaeda's responsibility for the attacks. At the very least, an explanation of why such an approach needed to be taken should have been provided so as to show that special circumstances dictated this departure from the charter aversion to war, and to reaffirm the American recognition of the importance of not allowing war/peace decisions to be made by governments on their own without Security Council approval. As the leading state in the world, this reversion to non-reviewable self-help by the United States is unfortunate in relation to global governance. As its diplomacy in the 2002 India/Pakistan crisis suggests, American geopolitics are shaped by a dual hegemonic role:

self-help for itself and diplomatic leverage on others to accept an international duty to do everything possible to avert war, including an acceptance of a mediating role by a powerful state or a representative of the United Nations. The UN, itself mired in weakness and dependency, has been disappointingly passive about responding to this central assault on its most basic mission.

But by far worse than this early failure of respect for UN norms and procedures, was the American claim that "self-defense" could validate post-Afghanistan reliance on force to wage war in other settings where terrorism was allegedly an issue. There is no UN or international law justification, for instance, for supposing that the al-Qaeda threat covers a pre-emptive war launched against Iraq, or other "axis of evil" countries. And there is certainly no basis in the UN authorization of the US response for allowing leaders of other states to draw analogies to September 11 to validate launching their own attacks against nationalist movements of self-determination. By unilaterally expanding the orbit of its war beyond the reasonable self-defense claims directed at Afghanistan, the US has been severely compromising and damaging the authority and role of the UN in the area of peace and security, which was at best of only modest proportions. The United States seems to be acting on a presupposition that the pursuit of its strategic goals is now by itself a sufficient justification for war, provided only that a rhetorical link with September 11 is asserted.

The Just-War Doctrine: Use and Abuse
Both as reinforcement of international law flexibly adapted to the urgencies and originality of visionary megaterrorism and as a parallel source of normative guidance, the just-war tradition of thought and doctrine makes an important contribution, as has been described in the prior chapter. Just-war thinking is rooted in the dominant religious and ethical traditions of the West, yet finds sufficient complementary ideas in other major civilizations to avoid being dismissed as Western thinking. To a large extent, international law superseded just-war thinking as diplomacy became increasingly shaped by the interaction of sovereign states, and as secularization placed a greater premium on the formal expression of governmental consent, especially in international treaties, as the basis of international obligations.

But just-war thinking never departed altogether from the stage of global policy. During the 1980s, when there was much societal ferment and discussion relating to the permissibility of nuclear weaponry, the Catholic Bishops applied just-war thinking to their own assessment of these issues and attracted a great deal of attention. In contrast, the effort to address similar issues by the World Court in an Advisory Opinion issued in 1996 attracted much less serious response, as nuclear weapons were widely regarded as not being capable of regulation within the statist framework of international law, which absolutized security claims associated with the survival of states, not people. My point is that just-war approaches reemerge prominently whenever the statist framework is strained by the novelty of the challenge. September 11 exerted precisely such a strain.

There is a further reason to prefer, or at least pay close attention to a just-war rationale as, in effect, "an exception" or supplement to international law. Most interpretations of international law resist the sort of flexible adaptations based on an assessment of reasonableness in the context offered above. Such an approach is particularly opposed in European legal circles, which generally consider international law in a stricter posititivist manner, and criticize harshly the more adaptive view of international law rules and principles as opening the way for politicization, converting international law into a geopolitical instrument at the sole disposal of the strong, whether church, state, or market. In the present setting, it is dangerous in substance and as a precedent to validate the American claims against Afghanistan by reference to international law. Taking seriously the idea that for a state to be guilty of aggression it must mount an armed attack against another state, be so regarded by the UN Security Council, or, at the very least, collaborate so closely with the attacker as to be co-responsible. None of these conditions was genuinely satisfied in the context of the American response to September 11, although the UNSC could itself be regarded as derelict by failing either to mandate the Afghanistan response or condemn it, thereby tacitly acknowledging either a gap in the law or an irresolvable encounter between international law and geopolitics.

The just-war tradition makes no claim to pin down the discretion of political actors exercising authority on behalf of a political community to any great degree. It relies on generalized principles to help identify the dividing line between permissible (just war) and impermissible (unjust war) violence. Recourse to war is based on the legitimacy of defensive force, the absence of an adequate alternative to war in the pursuit of justice, the primacy of the security of the state, the treatment of war as a last resort, and the authority of the actor to represent the community opting for war. In the setting of September 11, as with international law, the American decision to respond by recourse to war against Afghanistan seems generally vindicated by just-war thinking, although there seemed to be some question about the purity of such a conclusion in the Afghanistan context.

My argument is that just-war thinking, properly interpreted, can provide ample grounds for recourse to a just war, but only if its authorization of war is balanced by a specification of limits that upholds the war against Afghanistan, but nowhere else. No other country possesses a sufficiently close link to al-Qaeda operations to make it accountable enough for either past attacks or a threat to facilitate future attacks. Without such linkage is would be unjust to target a country for military attack. Such a limiting consideration does not, of course, preclude anti-terrorist undertakings in additional countries that occur with the consent of the territorial sovereign or, in exceptional circumstances, narrowly focused covert operations even without such consent.

It is disappointing that the April 9, 2002 response of 128 progressive intellectuals to the centrist letter, "Why We're Fighting," was itself fundamentally deficient by denying altogether any valid basis even for the war against Afghanistan, as well as offering no credible antidote to the persisting al-Qaeda threats. To rely on "criminal law enforcement" and the UN is to insist that the American government not take necessary and reasonable preventive action in circumstances where its citizenry is at serious risk. Such an imperative to act responsibly in relation to genuine security threats takes precedence in thought and action over distrust of American motives and criticism of its past behavior in the Islamic world and elsewhere. But to the extent that the anti-war letter of response calls for public debate in America and invites European criticism of American war policies, it provides a useful alternative to the sort of "hyper nationalism" so powerfully mobilized by George W. Bush with the help of mainstream America media.

The turn from recourse to war to its conduct helps clarify the sort of limits that do pertain to any international war, even if it is being waged on the basis of a persuasive just cause. Four principles emerging from the just-war tradition set limits on the conduct of war, and have also been influential in structuring the international law of war:

• Discrimination: Any use of force should discriminate between military and civilian targets, and unconditionally avoid targeting the latter regardless of military necessity; civilian innocence should be respected without exception in the course of waging war;

• Proportionality: Any use of force should have some reasonable relationship between the responsibility, resistance, and capabilities of the target state and the level, intensity, and goals of response by the state acting in self-defense;

• Necessity: Any use of force should be essential to the attainment of legitimate military objectives; excessive force should be avoided.

• Humanity: Any use of force should uphold international humanitarian law, and avoid any human suffering not reasonably related to necessary and reasonable military objectives.

The principle of proportionality is of the greatest importance in the present setting of post-Afghanistan discussion. Besides lacking a just cause or falling within the right of self-defense, an American attack on Iraq is impossible to justify as a proportionate response to September 11 or because Iraq might in the future help al-Qaeda launch future attacks. In this regard, the reasonable attribution of responsibility for the attacks to the Taliban regime in Kabul is not at all persuasive in the context of Saddam Hussein's Iraq (a fact that in no way is meant to exonerate this regime of past wrongdoing.) To shift the rationale in relation to Iraq to one of preventive and preemptive war directed at hostile countries allegedly seeking to acquire weaponry of mass destruction seems totally at variance with just-war thinking, as well as a denial of the self-help foundation of security in a world still dominated by sovereign states.

President Bush's words delivered at the Commonwealth Club in San Jose in April 2002 set forth the American public rationale for war: "We will not allow the world's most dangerous regimes to threaten American friends and allies with the world's most dangerous weapons."

Such a rationale is completely at variance with UN Charter restrictions on the use of force, as well as having no reasonable relationship to the threats or attacks on September 11. What would be proportionate would be a series of non-military moves connected with international police cooperation, intelligence-gathering, covert operations, and law enforcement that was clearly focused on destroying the surviving capabilities of the al-Qaeda network situated outside of Afghanistan. This is being done by the United States, although here too the justification is being clouded to the extent that American capabilities are being used in a series of foreign countries to help a range of states suppress nationalist armed opposition movements. Even if such movements use terrorist methods, their conduct is essentially unrelated to the September 11 attacks or to future dangers.

It is possible to imagine a scenario in which preemptive war is necessary and just, but it would require overwhelming evidence to set aside international law restraints. It could be the case that political extremism is merged with menacing capabilities at the level of the state in such a way as to make recourse to war a practical necessity, but despite the rhetoric that has been relied upon to justify a war against Iraq, neither the past behavior of Baghdad nor its likely future behavior provides any persuasive grounds for abandoning reliance on deterrence, containment, and diplomatic normalization.

Conclusion

This chapter has sought to walk the tightrope between permissible and impermissible uses of force, taking account of the distinctive challenge of September 11, but not losing sight of the long struggle to minimize the role of war in the lives of the peoples of the world. As such, it acknowledges reliance ultimately on the self-help character of world order, and the responsibility of states to take reasonable measures to ensure the security of their citizens in the face of genuine threats directed at their well-being. International law and the just-war tradition, in many respects complementary to one another, seek to balance the reasonable concerns of sovereign states in the face of aggressive enemies against the effort to impose clear and meaningful limits on recourse to war and the conduct of war. The United Nations was established in 1945 largely to help with this process, and to entrust such decisions to the extent possible, to the collective wisdom of an executive body that contained representatives of the most powerful countries along with a series of countries chosen from international society as a whole. The first group of five leading countries as of 1945 would be permanent members of the Security Council, while the latter group comprising all the rest, raised to ten, would rotate on the basis of General Assembly elections for two-year terms. The modesty of the UN incursions on the self-help structure of international relations is underscored by giving the permanent members a veto over any decision on the Security Council, which effectively acknowledges the primacy of geopolitics.

Since September 11 this primacy has been evident from the moment the US government started to explain its response. What this chapter has argued is that the effort to put limits on the rights to wage war are important in clarifying self-help options in specific contexts of challenge. It also concludes that the US government has not crafted its response to September 11 in a manner mindful of such limits. What has been especially disturbing is the evident intention to extend the rationale for war beyond its proper scope by attacking Iraq. As of now the full range of consequences of such an impending attack cannot be foreseen, but the damage to world order is likely to be great, as is the likelihood of much death and destruction for the people of Iraq, who have endured more than a decade of harsh sanctions imposed in a setting of devastation and disruption brought about by the Gulf War.

It is time to wonder why such a rush to war has generated so little resistance on the American home front. An immediate casualty of the atmosphere is the US Constitution's fundamental idea of separation of powers in the context of committing the country to war; Congress has not asserted the letter or spirit of its prerogatives. After all, even aside from the merits as argued in this chapter, one would have expected the isolationist elements in American political culture to raise some uncomfortable questions about "Why Iraq?" and to hear much louder protests from those many Americans who still retain bad memories from the Vietnam era ranging from distrust of the government to an unwillingness to die and kill in a distant Third World country already beset by massive human suffering. The next chapter contends that some part of the answer has to do with the blinding surge of patriotism that has flourished in America since September 11, making Americans far readier than earlier to deal decisively with potential adversaries and easily convinced that waiting to be attacked is not the way to go about achieving security in the age of megaterrorism.

6. CHALLENGING THE
NEW PATRIOTISM

A country is the things it wants to see.
—Robert Pinsky, *An Explanation of America*

A mainstream refrain to the tragedy of September 11 is that it has had its good sides, including the reawakening American patriotism, reminding us of the great good fortune of living in the best country that ever existed. Such patriotism is understood as a celebration of the nation as it is and was and will be, coupled with an adamant refusal to admit historical blemishes or to tolerate self-criticism. With such an outlook, criticism of past and present policy, acknowledgement of legitimate grievances on the part of some anti-American outlooks, is impatiently brushed aside, generally without even a reasoned response, as simply "unpatriotic."

It is not a love of country that I am questioning, but the sort of blind love that in a time of warfare gives rise to fundamentalist nationalism and imperial overreach, a crusading mentality that is unconditionally self-serving and completely oblivious to the harm inflicted on others, or for that matter to the prudent limits on one's power and resources. It is such a mentality that promises to bring us war without end as a response to the September 11 attacks, in the process making peoples and governments around the world—and not only Muslims—fear, resent, and resist what American seems to stand for on the global stage.

It needs to be understood that territorial citizenship and nationalist modes of patriotism had been on the wane in the more developed and affluent countries, including the United States, but especially Europe. Globalization and regionalism weakened territorial and nationalist bonds for many persons who belong to the most influential strata of citizens. As well, a range of experiences from surfing the Internet to frequent air travel have de-territorialized political identity still further. Beyond this, the religious upsurge, combined with heightened ethnic consciousness and an array of micro-nationalisms spread across the planet, was giving rise to what was often called "identity politics," which above all meant a much more fluid and less territorial and statist locus of loyalty that had been prevalent in the Age of Nationalism.

At the same time, former colonies throughout Asia and Africa were experiencing a rising nationalism as among the first fruits of their political independence and sovereign status, and often found the overlay of globalization in its various dimensions a new danger in the post-colonial world, making the overall global tapestry complex and confusing. And also contradictory, as globalization offered some countries unprecedented opportunities for rapid economic growth and sustainable development.

For America and Americans, especially, the response to September 11 represented, among other things, a dramatic reversal in the decline of traditional nation-centered patriotism, and for that reason the manifestation of patriotic sentiments may have been more fervent than otherwise. The trauma of the attacks, and their penetration of domestic space, presented an intense emotional occasion for the reaffirmation of their values for those conservative forces still attached to the territorial trappings of modernity, and they were joined by many who as late as September 10 had conceived of themselves as "globalists" of various stripes with only the vaguest of patriotic sentiments.

The Challenge of September 11

From the morning of the attacks on the World Trade Center and the Pentagon, the American people and their leaders seemed unified in their resolve to respond as effectively as possible, whatever the costs—a national climate of opinion that combined fear, anger, pride, a thirst for revenge, and some unacknowledged global ambitions. As President George W. Bush expressed this resolve in his September 20 speech: "Tonight we are a country awakened to danger and called to defend freedom. Our grief has turned to anger, and anger to resolution. Whether we bring our enemies to justice, or bring justice to our enemies, justice will be done." This call was immediately expressed in the language and urgency of war, a position that seemed correct, even unavoidable, given the magnitude of the harm inflicted and the obvious intent of the perpetrators to wage a merciless war with no holds barred, directed at all Americans, Jews, "Crusaders." There was an immediate governmental policy and a societal consensus that the

American military response should be immediately focused on the extremist Taliban regime and the al-Qaeda headquarters in Afghanistan.

It was against this background that there occurred in the United States an unprecedented display of flag-waving patriotism, an affirmation of America linked in the political and moral imagination with the evil "other," the demonization of Osama bin Laden and all those who perpetrated or supported in any way such a massive crime against humanity. But the American mood was also an affirmation of the bravery and sacrifice of the several hundred firefighters and police officers who died at Ground Zero, while making heroic rescue attempts under perilous conditions that saved many innocent lives otherwise trapped in the collapsing towers. This exemplary behavior by ordinary Americans was taken by the president and media as a demonstration of the true American spirit, which justified the surge of national pride, as well as reinforced the resolve to do whatever necessary to avenge the deaths from the September 11 attacks and avoid a future attack as a matter of urgency that took precedence over all other concerns of national policy.

This patriotic fervor needs also to be understood as a response to the realization that bin Laden's attack on America appeared to be greeted positively in many parts of the Islamic world, especially in Arab countries. In that same speech, President Bush blandly explained this anti-American hatred: "They hate our freedoms." Such a self-serving explanation further encouraged the American understanding of the challenge of September 11 as essentially a geopolitical soap opera pitting good against evil. The mainstream media in the US reinforced this moralistic imagery by cheerleading the moves toward war, while excluding any expression of dissenting or skeptical voices, and did not attempt to probe the motives of the attackers and their sympathizers. This unconditional celebration of American life, values, and institutions, without a scintilla of willingness to listen to the anti-American grievances so prevalent in the Arab world, along with the absence of any receptivity to self-criticism, has produced an intense and highly nationalistic patriotism with dangerous implications for ourselves and others.

Again, these implications can be most vividly apprehended by the manner in which President Bush has rallied the country in two major speeches setting forth the American response to September 11. I would highlight here three disturbing expressions of this mode of perception. In the initial address on war aims to the Joint Session, Bush laid down a challenge to the rest of the world in highly charged hegemonic language: "you are with us or you are with the terrorists." Such an approach is understandable from the narrow perspective of countering megaterrorism: to be effective it is helpful to fashion a response that is global in scope. At the same time, unless qualified, such language coming from the most powerful state on the planet seems oblivious to the existence of moral and legal limits on the use of force and exhibits no respect for either the sovereignty and security interests of others or for heeding their views on how best to achieve global security.

This unilateralist tenor, while slightly disguised by the efforts to construct an inclusive counterterrorist coalition of states, was given a more disturbing twist in Bush's State of the Union address (January 29, 2002) when he directed belligerent warnings at North Korea, Iran, and Iraq, calling them an "axis of evil," a rhetoric recalling both the World War II fascist coalition of axis powers and Ronald Reagan's designation of the Soviet Union as "the evil empire." Such threats were being directed at governments that were not generally seen as posing threats against the United States, and were in no meaningful or manifest way connected with the al-Qaeda network. For the United States president to threaten other countries in this manner would seem to be itself a direct violation of Article 2(4) of the UN Charter that obligates states to refrain from "the *threat* or use of force against the territorial integrity or political independence of any state." Some lawyers might contend that the Bush polemic was not specific enough to be a threat, but in the context of an ongoing war, such talk seems threatening in the extreme, and especially in an atmosphere where there is a constant buzz about Pentagon discussions of military options and the preparation of war plans to attack Iraq and overthrow Saddam Hussein.

The patriotic moment is so dominant that it allows such an aggressive and dangerous foreign policy to be put forward by Washington with hardly a whimper of protest or doubt expressed either by the opposition party or prime time television. The respected British military commander, Sir Michael Rose, has tendered the opinion that if the United States goes ahead and wages war against Iraq it could turn out to be as monumental a blunder by the United States as was Hitler's attack on the Soviet Union in 1940! This may sound like hyperbole, but the decision is surely weighty for the country and for others, and yet American war plans seem to have been evolving for months without the slightest willingness on the part of the White House to engage the public and the political opposition in genuine discussion of whether such an American recourse to war is necessary or legitimate. This circumstance also reflects the failure of the Democratic Party to function as a responsible opposition. When finally in the summer of 2002 the Senate Foreign Relations Committee under Democratic Party leadership held hearings, the witnesses uniformly accepted the goal of regime change in Iraq, discussing only issues of feasibility, strategy, cost, and risk. Such a misleading discourse gives the impression of debate, but functions as a ritual of public justification. Such staged presentations should not be confused with the reality of an open exploration of policy alternatives.

It needs to be appreciated that even the contemplation of such recourse to force is an undertaking in blatant defiance of the most basic restraint on war-making as embodied in international law. It would seem that the war diplomacy that has been waged against Iraq is already tantamount to the commission of a Crime Against the Peace in the Nuremberg sense. It should be recalled that the defeated German and Japanese leaders were punished individually not only for waging aggressive war, but for *planning* and *conspiring* to engage in aggressive war.

And finally, the patriotic moment has been variously invoked to stifle criticisms of state security measures that interfere with normal civil liberties of Americans, and especially of resident immigrants from the Islamic world. The notably reactionary Attorney General John Ashcroft, reacted in a venomous vein to the most mild criticism of his proposed measures giving the government extensive police powers— "My message is this: your tactics only aid terrorists" and "give ammunition to America's enemies." A similar vindictiveness designed to intimidate and silence critics has been consistently expressed by US officials in their unrelenting moves to prosecute and punish to the full extent of the law, John Walker Lindh, the 20-year-old American convert to radical Islam, for his participation on the side of the Taliban in their struggle against the Northern Alliance, which after September

11 became the military ally of the United States. In the end, for reasons still not entirely clear, Lindh pleaded guilty, accepting a plea bargain that resulted in a twenty-year prison sentence.

The essential message being sent to the citizenry by US officialdom, and dutifully transmitted by the media, especially primetime TV, is that there are no legitimate reasons for any expression of doubts or opposition by true Americans to the militarist course being charted by the White House. And as a result, responsible discussion can be confined to the feasibility of means and tactics, while avoiding any serious assessment of their legal and moral acceptability, and without listening to foreign doubts about the American reliance on a war strategy to meet the megaterrorist challenge.

Patriotism, Citizenship, and Nationalism

The basic energy of patriotism is of course emotive, understood as love of country, an affirmation of a bonded political community of fellow citizens proudly sharing memories and identities, as well as a willingness to make sacrifices for the sake of their collective well-being, and especially on behalf of the security and survival of the country. In the modern era, in which political community has been based on a secular consensus, the sovereign state has become the main focus for these sentiments, especially for large and well-governed states that are not afflicted by the presence of restive minorities or secessionist movements. States have also tried, with mixed results, to resolve and mute issues of multicultural and national identity by conferring nationality as a matter of law, issuing passports based on a legal concept of "nationality," and above all claiming to be nation-states.

In fact, the psychological foundations of group and national identity may not correspond with state boundaries, creating a variety of tensions, including in their most intense forms separatist struggles for national self-determination and claims for the protection of minority rights, including the cultural rights related to separate national identities. Much of the bloodshed in the world during the last decade or so has resulted from such conflicts. The "nationalist" character of these tensions has been blurred and confused by using the word "nation" in two quite distinct senses: as descriptive of the citizens of a territorial state that share a common nationality based on law; and as identifying those individuals with a psycho-political sense of shared nationality resting on common memory, cultural artifacts, possibly language, and a proclaimed destiny. When the second type of nation does not coincide with the first type, there is bound to be tension, which, if acute and compounded by structures of domination and economic exploitation that favor the dominant ethnic or religious grouping, creates in the subordinated people the mentality of a "captive nation" or, from the viewpoint of the established order, "a menacing separatism."

Citizenship in a secular state implies full and non-discriminatory membership and rights of participation in a political community, the most important by far being sovereign states. The idea of citizenship is increasingly being applied to political communities other than states, lending political significance to the notion of a European citizen, and even a world citizen. One impact of globalization and the rise of regional political communities has been to establish multiple identities and a non-exclusive sense of citizenship. War as an undertaking of the state is a throwback to simpler times of exclusivity and territorial preoccupations, when there reigned a tribal sense of passionate solidarity incapable of objectivity, a monolithic world-view that lent to its participants a willingness to fight and, as necessary, die. War creates a special regime of intensified patriotism and nationalism and maximizes the duties of the citizen, especially the obligation of young males to serve in the armed forces. This most serious claim of wartime over the life and destiny of such young citizens makes it crucial for the community as a whole to believe ardently that the cause is necessary, and thus worth the dying and killing. Opposition is betrayal.

A further implication of such wartime patriotism is to consider acts of overt support of the enemy as constituting the capital crime of treason. The ideological climate of wartime has also been used by political leaders to encourage a powerful, often jingoistic, symbiosis between nationalism as ideology and patriotism as creed. It is notable to observe that when this symbiosis is absent from the American political scene, the US government cannot gain domestic support for a war policy. This was evident in relation to the American-led humanitarian peacekeeping missions of the 1990s, most notably in 1993 in Somalia under UN auspices, when even eighteen American combat deaths generated a populist backlash that almost instantly rendered the undertaking politically unacceptable. The patriotic idea is only mobilizing when it can draw convincingly on nationalist security goals, giving rise to the emotional and uncritical partisanship of a war mentality. There is little doubt that traditional patriotism remains mired in an anachronistic statist vision of world order that has not yet adapted to the fundamental changes wrought by globalization and networked empowerment, although arguably this adaptation was underway in Europe and North America until it was abruptly challenged by the events of September 11 and, even more so, by their aftermath.

It is at least conceptually possible to imagine a response pattern to megaterrorism that would have nurtured global patriotism by immediately endowing the United Nations with the mission and capabilities to manage the response to September 11. Such a response would have been logically plausible and politically inspirational. It might also have been functionally rather more effective than what unfolded, and continues to do so, but its enactment was beyond the boundaries of the political imagination of ruling governmental elites in America and elsewhere. In crises affecting security, those elites automatically rely on the affective bonds of nationalism, as strengthened by the deliberate invocation of traditional patriotism. In such circumstances, the sovereign character of a state comes to the fore, making deference to constraints of law, morality, and world opinion seem far less appropriate than in normal times. This insistence on non-accountability becomes even stronger if the state in question is the self-proclaimed and acknowledged global leader, and happens to be governed by a leadership that appears to be particularly chauvinistic.

The United States is a prototypical successful sovereign state, rich and powerful, enjoying the undivided support of the overwhelming majority of its citizens, despite an exceptional degree of ethnic, religious, and cultural diversity within its boundaries. Its foundation myths and historical experience generate pride and love of country that is genuine for most of its citizenry on most issues, despite some terrible dark corners associated with memories and residues of slavery, lynching, and the dispossession of native Americans. The American Civil War and the defeat in Vietnam, as well as the Great Depression of the 1930s, have more recently tested national unity, but the outcome in each instance has borne witness to the resilience of the country as a coherent entity. Its republican form of government associates patriotism with the affirmation of the freedom and rights of individual citizens, including their right to dissent from national policy. Despite this democratic creed, the suppression of opponents in wartime has been the practice whenever the United States has been at war or in a serious struggle with a foreign adversary.

Part of the self-glorifying American epic narrative is the supposed reluctance of the United States as a country to engage in warfare but, once engaged, to view the conflict as one between its forces of good and the enemy's forces of evil. This polarizing and moralizing of conflict has produced a historic unwillingness to settle for compromises, which appear to the morally driven warrior as nothing less than pacts with the devil. World Wars I and II were both so conceived, as were the cold war and the Gulf War, and so is the current war on global terror. Victory is thus seen in totalistic terms, unconditional surrender demanded, and normal constraints governing conduct in war are largely ignored so as to reach sooner and at less cost to the virtuous side (ours, of course) a victorious outcome. Negotiation, diplomacy, and deference to international law and the United Nations are consistently subordinated to military effectiveness and the almost religious degree of assurance that whatever is done is in furtherance of America's just cause, and of benefit to the world as a whole. No dose of historical objectivity has been able to weaken this self-redeeming and seemingly endlessly self-renewing sense of American moral exceptionalism and innocence. Such talented "communicators" such as Ronald Reagan, and now George W. Bush, have always known very well how to tap into this seemingly infinite reservoir of American self-esteem and call forth patriotic and nationalist responses of unquestioning approval for policies however dubious from the perspective of law and morality, or even prudence.

Such a background does not tell the whole story. The United States has emerged over the last several decades as the unquestioned leader of the world, a position based on military power, technological innovation, economic prosperity, diplomatic authority, and cultural vitality. The significance of this role has been highlighted since the end of the cold war and the disappearance of the Soviet Union as a credible challenger. At the same time, the complex developments understood beneath the rubric of "globalization" has de-territorialized all states, including the United States. Such de-territorializing has given great historical weight to networked forms of organization, changing the nature of conflict, and creating this new phenomenon bureaucratically described in the United States as "asymmetrical warfare," better conceived as warfare by the weak designed to probe the vulnerabilities of the strong. The spokespersons of the Department of Defense have popularized this term as a way of seeking to call attention to new vulnerabilities in American security that are not addressed by reliance on traditional military capabilities, thus giving rise to an American need for different types of combat training, weaponry, and tactics to meet these new threats. But asymmetric warfare is a two-way street. The weak are also rendered acutely vulnerable by the destructive capabilities of the strong to strike accurately from a distance, to "see" in the dark, to target from high altitudes, and to wage many types of one-sided warfare without risking high casualty levels. It would be more accurate to reserve the term "asymmetric warfare" to describe the extreme vulnerability of weak countries to the military capabilities at the disposal of powerful states, especially the United States, but it has been generally used in the opposite sense to argue for bolstering the capabilities and changing the budgetary priorities of the strong so as to restore and solidify the significance of power inequalities as measured by military capabilities.

September 11, of course, epitomizes the clash of these two interpretations of asymmetric warfare. The response exhibits the dynamics of superpower asymmetry, with the technologically more powerful established state wreaking havoc and devastation anywhere on the planet at virtually no human cost to itself. The type of tribal patriotism that has emerged in the United States since September 11 has displayed almost no capacity to interpret the world scene in light of these new realities, but has shaped a nationalist mood that is rooted in the mainly obsolescent attitudes and perceptions of a territorially constituted world order. Such perceptions have been further encouraged by the US response that has moved from war to war as if the al-Qaeda challenge could be addressed within the traditional war framework of a struggle among territorial actors enjoying the status of sovereign states.

There is also a normative dimension that needs to be considered in clarifying concerns about the impact of this still prevalent type of American patriotism. To begin with, there has been a long struggle during the past century to limit recourse to and conduct of war as much as possible. The carnage of the world wars encouraged an idea of world order that sought to minimize the role of war in regulating the relations among states. Limiting war to conditions of self-defense and in situations authorized by the UN Security Council expressed these aims in a form that was geopolitically ineffectual. As earlier discussed, the UN role was hampered, and rendered ambiguous, at its inception by the veto given the permanent members and by its not being entrusted with independent financial and enforcement capabilities to challenge the ethos of sovereignty. It was also hampered by the gridlock resulting from the cold war, making it almost impossible to create a consensus in the face of any international conflict. If major wars were to be avoided under these conditions, it was not because of constraining legal rules and the existence of the UN system, but because of the prudence of political leaders at the level of the state, especially associated with the adoption of deterrent approaches to security induced by the presence of nuclear weaponry.

The existence of this weaponry on both sides of the cold-war cleavage, as well as the modest geopolitical stakes at issue, meant that the United States had to accept compromises and stalemates, if not worse, as in the Korean and Vietnam Wars. The unconditional commitment to victory in war turned out to be politically unacceptable during the cold war, with the catastrophic risk that pushing too hard could result in nuclear war. At the same time, these outcomes of armed conflict in Third World countries were disappointing and unsettling, being inconsistent with the standard American approach to its wars—namely, fight only just wars, but then go all out to win. In these instances, the anti-Communist wars were never fully "sold" as just and necessary, so as the human costs to America of these wars mounted, their overall worth was increasingly called into question. The inconclusive endings, which was humiliating in the setting of the Vietnam War, made many American citizens disillusioned and convinced that young Americans had died in vain, and should do so no longer. It also made large portions of the citizenry extremely distrustful of the government, its competence and integrity.

With the collapse of the Soviet Union, earlier American attitudes toward war have re-emerged by stages and then have been radically extended with dogmatic clarity in the struggle against global terrorism. During the 1990s the revived moralism of American foreign policy was explained to the public either as a defensive and strategic response to aggression, as in the Gulf War, or in the ethical language of humanitarian diplomacy, as in Somalia, Bosnia, and especially Kosovo. The attacks of September 11 on the symbolic and substantive core of American primacy in the world, together with the genocidal ethos of the perpetrators, has generated a reversion to the traditional American response to war as committed to total victory, even without having a clue as how such a conflict should be concluded and victory declared. Such a commitment takes on added credibility because the visionary outlook of Osama bin Laden and al-Qaeda cannot be deterred (as was the Soviet Union, and even Iraq in the 1990s) and apparently they have at their disposal a large cadre of suicidal warriors prepared to attack the United States and its citizens in the future. Beyond this, more than in past wars, there are no battlefields or delimited enemy territories, and so it is more difficult to achieve a consensus as to what the war is about. The global terrorist network can be anywhere, but is definitively nowhere. Its operational units can lodge themselves as sleeper cells in the midst of the United States itself.

Under these conditions it is to be expected that Americans will pull together at home (except against "suspicious" aliens in their midst) and pursue all-out victory in the war. Patriotic zeal lends enthusiasm to the undertaking, recognizing and validating the sacrifices made by those who fight and pushing the citizenry to mobilize the resources needed to win the war, including a novel vigilantism that enlists citizens in the search for potential terrorists by reporting on neighbors and others who for one reason or another evoke suspicion, maybe their name or appearance or reading habits or their "unpatriotic" political views. Big Brother has been enlisted in the war against megaterrorism.

Why, then, should there be so much concern about these roles of patriotism in the setting of a response to September 11? In essence, these concerns arise because waving the American flag so vigorously has made it more difficult to set proper limits on the response, and these limits are necessary for both pragmatic and normative reasons. It has seemed that the American leadership has itself been genuinely engulfed in this tidal wave of patriotic feelings, which is both allowing and encouraging it to undertake a far wider war than is necessary given the scope of the threat, although possibly this wider war is instrumental to unacknowledged goals associated with the geopolitics of energy and with empire-building. There has been a consistent unwillingness by American leaders to define national goals and defensive responses with precision. This has led to the adoption of foreign and domestic policies of a dubious and dangerous character that adopt extravagant goals unrelated to the genuine challenges posed by the September 11 attacks, goals that seem to make effective responses much less likely. Perhaps it is naive to expect wartime goals to be focused only on the genuine security threat when the role of power in the world has to do with resources and patterns of influence.

Patriotism Reformulated

In times of crisis, when a society is threatened by an external enemy, there has existed for centuries a strong tendency to express patriotic feelings through tribal displays of unconditional support. The extremity and traumatic character of September 11 accentuated this tendency, quickly reviving what had seemed to be a diminishing nationalist ethos. The anthrax scare weeks later consolidated these largely spontaneous sentiments of nationalist solidarity, which were still further strengthened by periodic messages from the US government to the citizens to stay alert because additional attacks were in the offing. The patriotic mood was both a result of the extreme circumstances and a cleverly contrived campaign to mobilize popular enthusiasm for the war policies that was brilliantly coordinated by the White House and the mainstream media, expressing itself in part by a sudden rise in American citizens' support for and trust in the leadership of the country and of government generally. These attitudes have somewhat weakened over time as information has revealed the extent to which the government failed to heed advance warnings or to exercise due vigilance in light of information at its disposal, as well as by the marked downward drift of the stock market and the value of the dollar in leading currency markets.

If the United States was truly a beleaguered country fighting for its survival against far stronger adversaries, such a fusion of nationalism and patriotism would not only be natural, but it would probably be of great functional value. One thinks of the Vietnamese or Palestinian struggles for self-determination against overwhelming odds as important historical examples. But the post-September 11 realities facing the United States, and indirectly the rest of the world, were decidedly different, both more complex and demanding, essentially a struggle on uncharted territory pitting against one another rivals with radically different styles of combat and tactical advantages. In a fundamental sense, this new war is the first postmodern war testing the capacities of both networking and geopolitical power as deployed in an essentially borderless world.

Because the US government mobilizes for war in an ultra-nationalist manner, it is disabled from reflecting upon its own conduct, and it is unwilling to take steps that might address those Arab grievances that are just and in accord with international law and morality. Worse than this, the White House is seduced by its own hyperbolic and hypocritical rhetoric about terrorism, so it throws its weight behind oppressive policies of great severity. Instead of confining its defensive claims to the specific threats posed by the al-Qaeda network, the Bush administration has generalized its struggle so as to take on "terror" in general, although selectively defined to reflect geopolitical alignments. At this point, a justifiable defensive posture by the US morphs into an interventionary enterprise directed at the unfinished struggles of several national movements struggling against great odds to achieve self-determination. To add Hamas, Hezbollah, Islamic *Jihad*, and Jaish-I-Mohammed to the "terrorist underworld," as Bush did in the State of the Union Address, is to associate terrorism exclusively with non-state actors, when in fact violence against civilians is deliberate on both sides, and with far greater ferocity by the states in question, whether Israel or India. The proper role for the United States in these conflicts is to work as consistently as possible toward realizing just solutions that bring peace and accommodation, and not to confuse its response to September 11 with the adoption of a morally and politically incoherent approach that amounts to an endorsement of state terrorism.

The point about patriotism here is that the United States as a global leader is not just defending itself, but is inevitably through its actions setting rules of the international game for others and thus has a particularly serious responsibility to ensure that these rules do not perpetuate and aggravate ongoing wars, thereby adding to injustice and suffering. When, as has been the case, such a leader has dulled its power of judgment by indulging patriotic enthusiasms, it inevitably sends a message to other governments around the world that they are free to whip up comparable patriotism on their own soil, and engage in extreme violence. We may be witnessing a new paradoxical manifestation of globalization: patriotism as a geopolitical tactic. It is paradoxical, because the main thrust of globalization is non-territorial, while the domain of patriotism is first and foremost territorial. The originality of this Great Terror War is this confrontation and interplay between territorial and non-territorial force fields. The winds of patriotic fervor are blowing across national boundaries causing a dangerous heightening of tensions around the world. From another angle of interpretation, this resurgent patriotism/nationalism provoked in the United States by September 11 is a perfect match for the rhetoric and extremism of bin Laden and his cohorts, especially in its tendency to essentialize good and evil and its unconditional and simplistic commitment to engage in a violent and morally pretentious struggle until the evil other is exterminated.

The further point is that when patriotism disguises a huge empire-building project that becomes the subtext for a war against global terror, the war itself is likely to go badly! This is because energies and resources are not sufficiently focused on the specific threat, but dispersed, and directed at establishing a global control mechanism, what amounts to a dominating geopolitical network. In effect, the United States transforms itself into a global network that has an American state-centric nerve center and a territorial base of operations. This combination of capabilities and ambitions is best understood as a postmodern type of empire, foregoing formal arrangements of control while exercising global dominion, which is challenged, if at all, by a rival underground network of comparable ambition. This American project is being perceived by other states as threatening to their sovereignty and independence, generating counter-moves, and a reluctance to cooperate fully in the common struggle of states against megaterrorism. At the same time, other states are inclined to back away from directly challenging this American role: partly because the US is defending statism in general against the system-transforming revisionism of the al-Qaeda network and partly because US power and wealth remain the linchpin of stability and prosperity for the world as a whole.

Traditional forms of patriotism can be effortlessly morphed from a legitimate defensive response into a self-destructive undertaking of national expansionism, hegemonic pretension, and imperial overreach. President Bush's designation of North Korea, Iran, and Iraq as "an axis of evil" implies that such countries might in the near future become targets for preemptive military attack and coercive diplomacy if they are perceived as making moves unwelcome in Washington. This is one of the more egregious examples of this sort of thinking, which is an unsavory mixture of self-serving moralism and over-reaching geopolitical ambition. These governments have never even been seriously accused of involvement in September 11, and they pose no threat to the United States, but rather are threatened *by* the United States and its arsenal of nuclear weaponry. By and large, to the extent such countries seek weaponry of mass destruction, it would seem to be for deterrent purposes. As one prominent war hawk, Charles Duelfer, acknowledges with respect to Iraq, "Hussein surely also realizes that there would be no talk of invasion now if he could threaten American forces or Israel with nuclear incineration." If such weaponry were ever to be acquired and then used aggressively by Iraq, or even threatened, the backlash would be swift and decisive, leading to the annihilation of the government in question. Such a logic is so obvious that its operative relevance can hardly have been ignored by the leadership of these countries. But the Iraqi motivation to develop nuclear weapons, as Duelfer contends, to the extent that it exists, is to deter its adversaries from the sort of attack being contemplated by Washington throughout 2002. To deprive Baghdad of achieving this capability it is necessary to attack it soon before the costs to the United States become unacceptable.[1]

I am not suggesting that this entire litany of concerns can be attributed to the surge of nationalism and patriotism, but these sentiments have paved the way, at least in the United States and to some extent in Europe, for war and a statist revival. The strength of this patriotic mood has been such as to incapacitate the Democratic Party as a source of principled opposition, raising for debate vital matters of public policy, none more important than whether to go to war. Patriotism has induced a spirit of bipartisanship in the United States that has reached such extremes that the Democratic Party leadership has been mainly eager to present itself as beating the drums of war as loudly, or even more so, than its Republican counterparts. Citizens generally have been half scared and half convinced that the call for unity is properly understood as requiring a suspension of criticism and conscience, as well as an agreed acceptance of limitations on their traditional freedoms. Even the lamentable treatment of Taliban/al-Qaeda prisoners at Guantanamo and the refusal to accept the application of the Geneva Convention raises only the mildest domestic expressions of criticism, and then only at the margins of permissible discussion. In this instance, the failure to uphold international standards is an instance of self-defeating arrogance, as it is Americans who would benefit most from maintaining Geneva standards, given the American military, economic, and diplomatic presence around the world. If the United States can decide when captured individuals are "unlawful combatants," why can't others do the same—or worse? Such patriotism acts as a powerful vaccine that immunizes the body politic against self-criticism, and it often weights policy toward short-run goals at the expense of a longer-run, more enlightened, pursuit of its best interests.

In a globalizing world there exists another way of being patriotic that reconciles love of country with responsibility to humanity: a cosmopolitan patriotism. Such attitudes have started to form in the midst of the de-territorializing of economic, social, and cultural life and seem to have affected segments of public opinion in Europe. Cosmopolitan patriotism accepts the right of a people and a country to defend their fundamental existence in accordance with international law, whether struggling for self-determination or dealing with a foreign state that is an aggressor. At the same time, such a patriotic outlook sees the self from without, as well as from within, and welcomes criticism while seeking to live by the rule of law and a geopolitics of mutuality (treating others as we would have others treat us; not doing to others what we would not want done to ourselves) rather than dominating by the rule of force. The citizenry of the United States is being tested in this period to shape a response to September 11 that restores its security, but also contributes to peace and justice in the world, and especially helps the Arab and Islamic world to overcome its current plight. Such a response would mean doing more to ensure that the poor benefit from future economic growth and emerging patterns of globalization, using diplomatic muscle to end tragic encounters of the sort that have cast such dark shadows over Palestinian and Israeli lives for decades, working for more capable and trusted international institutions, especially the United Nations, and supporting the deepening of respect for human rights, democracy, and the international rule of law.

In important respects, this plea for cosmopolitan patriotism is a return to the original American vision so powerfully devised and presented to itself and the world in the Declaration of Independence. It is to use the authority of government and the power of the state to promote and protect its citizenry, as guided by the great goals of "life, liberty, and the pursuit of happiness." It is to act in the world with "a decent respect for the opinions of others." Cosmopolitan patriotism engages country and world with eyes wide open, and cherishes and honors those noble sentiments that animated the founders of the American republic who were so impressive because they exhibited humility as well as pride. If American exceptionalism is to amount to anything positive in coming years it must be guided by what Lincoln so memorably called "our better angels."

A United States guided by the spirit of cosmopolitan patriotism could turn the tragedy of September 11 into an inspirational moment in the history of the early twenty-first century. At the moment such a prospect is as remote as landing a man on the moon must have seemed in the 1930s. As the old world order of states and wars is being transformed by networks and digital potency, we must indeed reconceive politics as the art of the impossible. After all, by 1969 Neil Armstrong did land on the moon.

7. THE ECLIPSE OF
HUMAN RIGHTS

U ndoubtedly, part of the hidden cost of patriotic excesses is the tendency to become insensitive to infringements on liberties at home, and human rights generally. To the extent this pattern can be attributed to the impact of September 11, it represents an indirect victory for the al-Qaeda attacks, compromising the most legitimate elements of the American reality, including its own proudest traditions as first enunciated in the Declaration of Independence, heroically enacted in the Revolutionary War, and enshrined in the Constitution on the basis of the Federalist Papers and an exemplary constitutional convention. At the same time, it is important to avoid self-congratulatory assessments of America's human rights record, which has throughout its period as a coherent country been beset by glaring contradictions between proclaimed values and actual practices at home and abroad.

Michael Ignatieff observed that "[s]ince the end of the cold war, human rights has become the dominant vocabulary in foreign affairs. The question after September 11 is whether the era of human rights has come and gone."[1] To the extent this statement had any purchase on reality whatsoever, it was a question that could be put only to American policymakers. It is questionable whether Ignatieff's eye-catching assertion captured more of political reality than the earlier highly dubious American pretensions of serving as the governmental torch-bearer for the global human rights movement. What is perceptive about the observation is that human rights, if understood broadly as encompassing the entire humanitarian agenda of world politics (and not just the norms contained in international human rights instruments), had been achieving an increasing policy salience with each passing year during the 1990s, exhibiting a welcome shift of concern associated with the end of the cold war.

At the same time, caution and analytic clarity about even this positive assessment are needed to make sense of the role of human rights in the pre-September 11 world. Human rights, although ardently affirmed in this period throughout the world, never became the "dominant vocabulary" for the foreign policies of most countries, including even those of liberal democratic persuasion. Governments in the North were cautious about stressing human rights to the extent of interfering with their sometimes inconsistent economic and security goals, which continued to enjoy a higher policy priority in most capitals of the world, including our own, despite Washington's occasional opportunistic and strident insistences to the contrary. The fact is, in the active pursuit of economic and strategic goals, most governments generally overlook gross abuses of human rights, or at best exert a quiet influence behind the scenes. For the United States the opportunistic profile of its approach can be seen by its willingness to blink at China's far worse human rights record, while holding Cuba's to a higher standard for reasons of domestic politics and because the economic interests at stake were rather trivial.

The criticisms by countries in the South directed at American-led attempts to promote the coercive implementation of human rights were deeper and more widely supported. Many of the governments in the South, especially in Asia and the Middle East, not surprisingly distrusted this American foreign policy emphasis on human rights, contending that it was both overbearing and hypocritical. The American approach in the 1990s appeared overbearing because it seemed so patently interventionary—or at the very least, hegemonic in its reliance upon strategic manipulation from an overall geopolitical posture of dominance and in support of a controversial linkage of human rights with neoliberal market economics. The advocacy of human rights was seen from such selective vantage-points as allowing the United States to pick and choose its targets, as well as to disregard the sovereignty of weaker countries whenever it suited its purposes to do so. At the same time the US government annoyed many governments with these moralizing pretensions, given its own record. The US had not itself even ratified many of the leading human rights treaties, and yet it claimed the moral high ground for itself, from which it delivered lectures to governments around the world, imposed harsh sanctions self-righteously on economically vulnerable adversaries, and even threatened military interventions in support of human rights goals. At the same time, the mildest criticisms of US human rights practices from overseas sources about, for example, the frequency of capital punishment and the unreliability of its application, were sure to drive the US Congress into a nationalistic frenzy. While rather arbitrarily imposing sanctions on countries around the world in response to their alleged human rights deficiencies (on Castro's Cuba, for example), the United States continues to view its own behavior with respect to human rights to be exclusively a matter for *domestic* concern.

The US position also struck many foreign governments as hypocritical, due to the US's unabashedly adopting double standards to craft its approach to human rights. The US has been calling attention repeatedly to the human rights deficiencies of a few states treated as enemies, especially such "rogue states" as North Korea and Iraq, while treading ever so lightly on such friends and allies as Israel and Turkey. To be selective in this way is to admit tacitly that the promotion of human rights is expedient, driven by strategic interests and domestic politics, rather than a principled respect for the values of justice and human dignity. Such glaring inconsistencies in practice decidedly undercut the moral authority and political influence of American objections to human rights abuses even when those objections were well taken in relation to particular circumstances. The US diplomacy of double standards has become quire shameless in the last year or so, rising to new heights of normative arrogance by claiming an exemption from the jurisdiction of the newly established International Criminal Court for American members of UN peacekeeping forces, and even conditioning its continued support for the Bosnia peacekeeping presence in 2002 on the acceptance of this American demand, leading after much maneuvering to a bargain that accepted American demands on a year-to-year renewable basis. It is quite extraordinary to insist upon such special treatment, especially as it is most unlikely that any American peacekeeper would be indicted and prosecuted, given the limitations on the authority of the ICC and the likelihood that the US would evade the issue by mounting a prosecution of its own, which would then take precedence.

Beyond this tainting of American human rights credentials *before* September 11, it is important to realize that much of the positive political energy that has placed human rights on the global policy agenda has never really come from the governmental representatives of sovereign states. The emergence of human rights as a serious issue in world politics is mainly a result of deeply rooted civil society initiatives and pressures that were sustained for decades with little encouragement from powerful governments. Most states, including the US, were latecomers to this historic effort to transform human rights from a collection of pieties that were initially officially endorsed to satisfy public relations needs in the aftermath of World War II. The justifiably celebrated Universal Declaration of Human Rights was adopted in 1948 *only* because the non-obligatory document made it clear that enforcement of the standards agreed upon was entirely a matter of voluntary action. There existed at the time an uncontested conviction that the implementation of human rights should be regarded as an internal issue, and not allowed to intrude on the domain of serious diplomacy, which was viewed as serving national interests, the interaction of sovereign states, and not universal values or internal state/society relations. The UN accepted this limitation on implementation by writing into its charter a pledge "not to intervene in matters essentially within the domestic jurisdiction of any state," which was lawyerly language for conveying the sense that human rights and civil strife were to be resolved exclusively by the play of domestic forces. Such ideas have been challenged in recent decades as human rights became more widely supported as *political* projects, and as civil strife generated humanitarian catastrophes made visible to the world by real time TV coverage.

Despite these extremely low initial expectations for the Universal Declaration of Human Rights that existed when it was adopted in 1948, this widely endorsed instrument set minimum international standards for acceptable behavior, which, somewhat unexpectedly, were gradually viewed with increasing seriousness by many political actors around the world. The NGO community, as well as opposition groups in countries governed in an oppressive manner, seized the formality associated with the widespread acceptance of these inter-governmental norms to push for compliance in various settings. That is, even though governments had given their approval because they considered the Declaration to be nothing more than a feel-good document, human rights organizations and political movements regarded the development as an invitation to mount pressures on governments for compliance by the means at their disposal.

The United States, again surprisingly, did eventually make a major contribution to this transition of the human rights movement from piety to policy. It was in the presidency of Jimmy Carter, especially during its first two years (1976–78), that an innovative and suddenly high profile US commitment to promote human rights in its foreign policy was unveiled with fanfare. Such a step was viewed cynically in many quarters at the time, seen as little other than a White House trick to distract the citizenry from the American defeat and loss of face in Vietnam. To affirm human rights as integral to American foreign policy was to take a step to restore the confidence of Americans in the essential benevolence of their country. It also facilitated the renewal of American claims of moral exceptionalism on the world stage. Soon, however, the Carter advocacy became controversial precisely because, whatever its motivations and goals, the effects on other societies were real and giving rise to unwanted strategic outcomes.

The Carter administration's support for human rights was attacked by conservatives as contributing to the 1979 fall of Shah's regime in Iran. This momentous development deprived the US of an important strategic ally and substituted a hostile and revolutionary Islamic government led and inspired by Ayatollah Khomeini, which first brought political Islam onto the stage of contemporary geopolitics, and must be viewed as a forerunner of al-Qaeda. This major setback for US foreign policy, whether attributed or not to the Iranian Revolution, quickly led to a reevaluation of the relevance of human rights to the goals of American foreign policy. It was evident that the Carter presidency never had the intention of allowing its human rights advocacy to promote regime changes that had adverse strategic effects on US interests, as was dramatically the case in Iran. As was true earlier, support for human rights was never expected to have any serious *behavioral* consequences, but just as civil society activists had earlier breathed life into the Universal Declaration of Human Rights, so opposition groups around the world endowed the Carter human rights initiative with political effects, treating it as a green light to intensify their efforts to challenge oppressive regimes. Given this analysis, it is hardly surprising that the White House significantly muted the human rights advocacy that was so strident in the early Carter years. The result was that human rights were once more put on a back burner as far as US foreign policy was concerned, and the subordination of human rights to strategic priorities was strongly confirmed. But again the ebb and flow of such adjustments is often more than meets the casual eye.

Congress, acting out of a mixture of motives, tied most foreign economic assistance to the human rights records of recipient countries, and required the State Department to prepare annual country reports analyzing degrees of compliance with human rights norms and year-to-year progress. This process by itself has become a resource for human rights NGOs, and it exerts a degree of pressure on foreign governments to avoid the embarrassment and consequences of criticism. Also, governmental bureaucracies generally do not backtrack on policy as readily as politicians, and the human rights machinery put in place by the Carter administration within the US government continued its efforts to strengthen support for human rights, especially calling attention to the deficiencies in Communist countries, despite Carter himself backing off. The encouragement given to human rights nationally and internationally by the early Carter presidency had developed a momentum of its own that continued despite the White House shift of mood. Some foreign policy contexts, including Eastern Europe, Communist China, and, to some extent, apartheid South Africa, suggested that American strategic goals were often quite consistent with the objectives of the international human rights movement. And so right up until and beyond September 11 the official embrace of human rights by the US government continued, although in light of the Carter experience, which was later discounted as unsophisticated, adjustments were made to make sure that US action did not undermine friendly foreign governments. Subsequently, the US promotion of human rights became self-consciously more differentiated to ensure that strategic interests were not being unwittingly undermined, and also more dedicated to the inclusion of private property and market forces in the operational definition of human rights.

During the 1990s, the US government in the Clinton years again made human rights and the expansion of democracy a centerpiece in its approach to the world, a validating feature of its status as the sole surviving superpower and unchallenged global leader in the main spheres of public policy, but the understanding of what is meant by human rights was subtly changed and expanded in scope. The ending of the cold war helps explain this development. The emphasis shifted from the earlier human rights focus on abuses of civil and political rights, especially for the populations living in Communist countries, to both a more generalized concern about the spread of electoral democracy and a less focused preoccupation with regimes that threaten their citizenry or an ethnic minority, with repeated Crimes Against Humanity and even genocide. The most prominent human rights issue of the decade became humanitarian intervention on behalf of peoples facing disaster as a result of internal developments. This undertaking was staunchly defended by the Clinton administration in the setting of the Balkan Wars as intervention to uphold the most fundamental rights of a people, even if it required acting on the particular occasion of protecting the Kosovars without a formal UN mandate and involved encroaching upon the territorial sovereignty of former Yugoslavia. Part of the wider understanding of this post-cold war decade was the degree to which the main global security challenges of the future would arise from unresolved internal conflict, including the repression of minorities and severe deprivations of human rights. In a sense, the issue of human rights, as associated with ethnic cleansing, genocide, and failed states, was partly perceived as the new strategic interest of leading governments in an emerging era of globalization, which placed a premium on political stability as a precondition for an expanding global economy. Such an assessment gave the US hegemon the task of directly and indirectly pacifying those situations that threatened the profit margins, investment prospects, and economic confidence of major players in the world economy. In this sense, human rights did assume unprecedented importance because they were being reinterpreted from the new economistic prism of realist perspectives as being of strategic importance. During this period even the Pentagon established within its midst a new bureaucratic entity devoted to humanitarian peacekeeping operations, but the mission was less idealistic—to make the world as safe as possible for the steady expansion of trade and investment.

Worldwide, the human rights movement had been for some decades making impressive progress before September 11: the anti-apartheid campaign was basically mobilized around human rights objections to South African racism; the development of a European framework of accountability for human rights allowed citizens to challenge their own governments; the liberation of East Europe was achieved, in large part, by the mobilization of the citizenry in support of human rights demands; and various calls for humanitarian intervention in the Balkans and sub-Saharan Africa were based on an international duty to rescue people from abusive governments. Even the pressures to hold truth and reconciliation commissions in the aftermath of oppressive rule, and the push for an international criminal court, were associated with a widening international consensus that the boundaries of sovereign states should not be respected if the territorial government fails to uphold minimum human rights standards.[2] During the decade of the 1990s, the movement toward an international human rights consensus was initiating a normative revolution in international relations that was beginning to supersede realist calculations of power and status in the political imagination of observers and policymakers. But this journey toward humane global governance shaped by a consensus of values and an acceptance of law-governed procedures for change and dispute settlement, even optimistically viewed, was always bound to be a long one, and it had barely commenced when it was derailed by the events of September 11. The derailing reflected a renewed preoccupation with security concerns, as well as total reliance on an American blend of war mentality and imperial ambitions to frame a global policy agenda that focused on megaterrorism.

Promising Developments Before September 11

A series of peaceful transitions from authoritarian rule took place in the 1990s, especially early in the decade. These political changes resulted in substantial progress from the perspective of human rights, democracy, and constitutionalism. Particularly notable in this regard was the consolidation of democratic governance throughout much of Latin America, especially Central America; the collapse of Communist rule in Eastern Europe and the Soviet Union; and the extraordinary bloodless repudiation of apartheid by the previously ruling elite in South Africa. These were historically significant achievements that fostered the impression that an important trend was underway, linking *legitimate* government to a minimal regard for human rights and democracy.

Also significant, if more problematically so, was the rise of "humanitarian diplomacy" relating to two sets of circumstance: "failed states" where domestic chaos was burdening the civilian population with starvation, lawlessness, and disease; and states, most notably in the Balkans and parts of sub-Saharan Africa, where severe patterns of human rights abuse were taking place, often with the intent of "ethnic cleansing" and even genocide. The United States started the decade as the champion of these international efforts to respond to such humanitarian catastrophes, but got badly burned in Somalia in 1993 after an attack cost American lives and domestic opposition to the political ramifications of the American presence grew. Then just months later the US government turned its back on an unfolding massive genocide in Rwanda.[3]

In Bosnia, the United Nations was given a peacekeeping role, but without a proper mandate or sufficient capabilities, resulting in the persistence of mainly Serb ethnic cleansing under its nose, culminating in the terrible massacre of 7,000 Muslim males trapped in the UN "safe haven" of Srebrenica in 1995. These issues persisted, producing a debate about the foreign policy of the United States and the ability of the UN to cope with humanitarian catastrophes. Washington, for mixed reasons, bypassed the UN when mounting a humanitarian intervention to save the Kosovar Albanians from the prospect of "a second Bosnia," acting in 1999 effectively, yet controversially, under the auspices of NATO. Before September 11 there were frequent heated discussions about whether patterns of humanitarian diplomacy were evolving in a generally useful way, with many governments especially in the South concerned that the geopolitical embrace of human rights was being used to circumscribe sovereign rights and leading to uses of force that could not be reconciled with the UN Charter or international law. Critics contended that such actions could be best understood as a kind of humanitarian imperialism or, in Noam Chomsky's phrase, a highly discreditable "military humanism." At the same time many progressive voices, while acknowledging impure motives on the part of the intervenors, nevertheless supported these interventions that seemed to offer a measure of relief for beleaguered peoples and societies at severe risk with respect to basic human rights. This argument reached shrill heights in relation to preferred policy options in relation to the Balkans, first for Bosnia and later Kosovo, and, although never resolved, its salience greatly diminished after September 11, and seems now to lack political relevance altogether. It is hard to contemplate any major international initiative calling for humanitarian intervention so long as the war on global terror is being waged.

A generally more positive experience arose during the decade with respect to international accountability, starting in the early 1990s with the establishment by the UN Security Council of international criminal tribunals for the former Yugoslavia and Rwanda, indicating that the most serious human rights abuses were to be treated as international crimes for which responsible individuals would be held directly responsible. Here, as with humanitarian intervention, the motives were suspect and seemingly contradictory, reflecting both a repudiation of reprehensible behavior, but also exhibiting a guilty conscience on the part of the Western liberal states about their failures to do more in the face of prolonged ethnic cleansing in Bosnia, massive genocide in Rwanda, and terrible civil violence and chaos in several other sub-Saharan African countries. This process of combining support for criminal accountability of abusive leaders with geopolitical opportunism reached its climax when Slobodan Milosevic was indicted during the midst of the NATO War on Kosovo, marking the first time that a current head of state had been so charged. There were few respected international voices who doubted Milosevic's criminality as a political leader, but many who viewed the timing of the indictment by a tribunal funded mainly by the governments then at war with Serbia as eroding the legitimacy and objectivity of the judicial process.

This dramatic break with sovereign immunity occasioned by the indictment and prosecution of Milosevic seemed less abrupt than it might have otherwise because of the prolonged legal fight associated with the 1998 detention of General Augusto Pinochet, the Chilean dictator between 1973 and 1990. He was held in Great Britain, while Spain's extradition request was reviewed. The former dictator was to be prosecuted for a series of crimes, including "political genocide," committed while he was head of state. This historic incident energized

THE ECLIPSE OF HUMAN RIGHTS

people around the world in relation to crimes of state and their perpetrators, raising hopes that human rights were coming of age and that the global rule of law was beginning to get the upper hand in its struggle with sovereign prerogatives. In a series of widely discussed British judicial proceedings, the Pinochet controversy was thoroughly explored, culminating in a House of Lords decision that found that Pinochet could be extradited, but only for torture at the end of his rule, since Britain had accepted in its domestic law an international treaty making torture an international crime. In the end Pinochet was sent back to Chile for medical reasons, where he was then pursued on a multitude of criminal charges until finally declared by the Chilean Supreme Court in June 2002 to be unfit to stand trial.

The Pinochet litigation stimulated further efforts, especially the pursuit of other notorious figures alleged to be legally responsible for Crimes Against Humanity committed while holding official positions in government. Belgium was the surprise site for such innovative judicial undertakings due to a Belgian law that gave its national courts broad authority ("universal jurisdiction" of the sort previously used against piracy on the high seas) to prosecute individuals alleged to have committed such crimes anywhere in the world. Prosecutions were launched against an array of political figures, including most prominently Saddam Hussein, Henry Kissinger, and Ariel Sharon.

In separate decisions in 2002 by the World Court and by Belgian courts there has been a partial retreat, confirming an earlier view that criminal prosecutions of public officials accused of crimes of state could not be pursued while they were holding office, and in the absence of their being in the physical custody of the prosecuting authority. In effect, further efforts to use existing national judicial institutions to impose standards of accountability on leaders accused of crimes has been procedurally stymied, especially since September 11. At the same time, the earlier initiatives are continuing to have some effect. The mere threat of prosecution has had some notable results and has encouraged widespread discussion of broad questions of individual accountability for abuses of power. One consequence of this raised consciousness has been an elaborate scholarly effort to provide guidelines for national courts asked to decide such cases on the basis of claims of "universal jurisdiction."[4]

Also impressive has been the impetus given to the movement joining many governments in a collaborative relationship with a large coalition of civil society organizations around the world, first, to promote a treaty conference designed to establish an international criminal court, and then, to obtain the sixty treaty ratifications needed to bring this new institution into being on July 1, 2002. Such efforts achieved great success in the treaty conference at Rome and managed to acquire more than the needed number of ratifications in about three years, which is surprisingly fast given the way governments deal with prospective treaty obligations, particularly here where a sovereignty-eroding subject-matter was involved. The process was, however, beset by American arm-twisting to discourage participation. Of course, the United States, China, and Pakistan are among the important rejectionist states, and the United States has signaled its extreme distress by withdrawing Clinton's earlier signature of the Rome treaty text at the end of 2000. Clinton's gesture was itself a gratuitous and ambiguous act as there was no immediate prospect that two-thirds of the US Senate was ready to give its advice and consent to have the US so bound, and the accompanying White House message indicated lingering official US concerns about the ICC. This American refusal to go along with what most of the rest world regarded as a constructive initiative, fully consistent with seeking accountability under international law, was one more big American slap in the face of the world community, seemingly intended to dramatize the extent to which the Bush presidency was opposed to the International Criminal Court and unwilling to lend the institution any support whatsoever. This obstructionist effort has generated criticism from America's closest allies who perceive Washington's stand as partly petulant and partly undermining of the whole enterprise of law in human affairs.

Somewhat more successful and less controversial (as not linked to geopolitics) were the various initiatives in the 1990s that sought redress of historic grievances, instances of past injustice that had not been rectified. Holocaust survivors and heirs were successful in recovering gold that had been held in Swiss banks, as well as monetary deposits. Compensation was also negotiated on behalf of victims of forced labor during the period of Nazi rule. Similar efforts were undertaken in the Asian context to impose responsibility on Japan for various abuses before and during World War II with less concrete success, but with consciousness-raising effects all the same. Indigenous peoples also raised awareness of the degree to which they had been dispossessed by force from their lands and reduced to poverty, and confronted by the reality of ethnic extinction in many instances. The plight of indigenous peoples gained a certain measure of international support for the protection of their remaining survival rights. Descendants of African-American slaves also mounted a campaign to receive monetary reparations for the severe and multiple wrongs inflicted. Even if the material goals were not achieved, a greater awareness was highlighted by the pronouncement at the 2001 Durban Conference on Racism that the institution of slavery was a Crime Against Humanity.

There is no doubt that the September 11 fault-line has derailed, at least temporarily, these lines of development and has, in effect, dramatically slowed, if not altogether halted, the normative revolution that was just getting underway, and of such promise for the most victimized and vulnerable peoples in the world. Instead, the struggle for human rights in this country and elsewhere has reverted to a battle against regressive policies of governments that challenge minimum standards of respect for human dignity. At most, attention is given to whether the US is conducting its military and non-military campaign against global terror overseas and in relation to tightened security at home in a manner that exhibits reasonable sensitivity to human rights standards and procedures. What has been lost, not irretrievably one hopes, has been the energy associated with an incipient normative revolution, which was seeking to establish humane forms of global governance for all the peoples of the world, thereby challenging the predatory features of economic globalization and political oppression. This normative revolution held in its unfolding great promise for the peoples of the world an emphasis on the accountability of leaders, on participatory democracy at all levels of societal interaction, on the global rule of law, and on the extension of human rights to issues associated with economic, social, and cultural rights. A vision of a hopeful future was beginning to form, and it was this vision that lay shattered among the ruins at Ground Zero on that fateful day in September.[5]

In sum, while it was certainly an exaggeration to dramatize the global role of human rights to the extent suggested by Ignatieff, there definitely was a human rights momentum building that might in time have transformed the tone and substance of world politics in beneficial ways. Beyond this, it seems proper to recognize that human rights had become much more important by the end of the last century for policymakers and citizens than anyone could have predicted in its middle. Human rights as generally understood have evolved first to place constraints on the state as political actor, later to impose some affirmative duties on the state to ensure the well-being of persons living under its authority, and still later, to encompass the elements of humane global governance. These preoccupations presuppose the dominance of the state as an organizing force in the world, which was true in a historical interval that started some centuries ago and now seems to be ending, but not conclusively or without an ebb and flow of perceptions and a welter of contradictory geopolitical interpretations.

If modernity in world politics is associated with the dominant role of the sovereign state, with its accompanying preoccupation with territory and boundaries, then postmodernity can be understood as a loss of such primacy for states and bounded territory. At first, this kind of postmodernity seemed to be reducing the state to what one commentator called the "virtual state," displaced by economic globalization, the Internet, and the general rise of market forces.[6] Then came a second challenging form of postmodernity: globalization-from-below, with its emphasis on values and law, its engagement with human rights and global democracy, and its vision of an emergent global civil society. And finally, or so it seems, September 11 involved two more clashing postmodernities: the transnational networked power base of al-Qaeda combined with the visionary goal of a reconstituted Islamic *umma* that would supersede the destructive barriers on Muslim community erected on the model of the Western secular state; and the global empire-building response of the United States, with its disregard for sovereign rights and territorial boundaries in its complementary resolves both to wage war wherever al-Qaeda has a foothold and to informally dominate the earth as a whole via space-based weaponry and an overwhelming control over innovations in military technology that render futile efforts of armed resistance by rival states.[7]

If this analysis is correct, then, at the very least, the modern human rights era is coming to an end, and if human rights are to be sustained

THE ECLIPSE OF HUMAN RIGHTS

and strengthened in the future, a *constructive* postmodern framework must be created that possesses several interrelated features:

—it revives the normative revolution of the 1990s in the altered, post-September-11 global setting;

—it protects individual persons and groups against a variety of transnational abuses associated with a climate of global war that pervades societal relations by invoking a new range of territorial and non-territorial security justifications for constraints on freedom;

—it recognizes the emergence of new threats to human rights as arising both from the activities of terrorist networks and an emergent global empire that cannot be understood by conceiving of world order as constituted by the interaction of sovereign states.

Such a potential postmodern framework for human rights is offered as an alternative to George W. Bush's project of an American empire, to Osama bin Laden's vision of an Islamic global community, or to the borderless world still being touted by neo-liberal militants mindlessly promoting economic globalization as shaped by the market logic of capital efficiency.

On a more prosaic level, it is important to take note of the various negative impacts of September 11 on the specifically *modern* (that is, state-oriented) human rights project. Part of the overall argument of this book is that megaterrorism augmented and somewhat transformed the role of the hegemonic state (but not states in general, or statism), but at the same time accelerated the process of the annihilation of a statist world. It did this by exposing the acute vulnerability of *all* states to attack by non-state enemies with modest capabilities, thereby underscoring the inability of states, even the most powerful, to provide acceptable levels of security for the territorial community. And beyond this, the inability of states to find sufficient suitable targets of retaliation, thereby weakening the role of military superiority in relation to security and drastically altering the calculation of power differentials in world politics, or, more significantly, calling into question whether "war" as traditionally conceived can deal with such an enemy. With the rise of networks devoted to megaterrorism, the viability of the future of the liberal democratic state is being tested in several of its crucial dimensions, especially with respect to its capacity and willingness to sustain an atmosphere of constitutional liberty, as well as its ability to provide tolerable levels of security for its inhabitants.

There is a puzzle here that is profoundly disturbing, whatever the political outlook. If the modern era is ending, and if human rights as we know them are an expression of normative growth or ethical evolution as an antidote to the sovereignty of states, then can human rights be adapted to the realities, whatever they turn out to be, of postmodern world politics? Or must human rights, as security, be substantially reinvented rather than merely adapted to function in such an altered political setting? Ken Booth has influentially indicted the state system as providing over the course of several centuries a safe house for "human wrongs" by way of its deference to and refusal to challenge the territorial supremacy of the state.[8] In a sense, the human rights movement has been trying, with only limited success, to reduce, if not overcome, the incapacity of the state system to protect the human dignity of threatened persons and peoples. Its failures to do so even without taking account of the intrusion of the postmodern element are dramatic and widespread: an unwillingness to challenge large states that torment separatist minorities (China on Tibet, Russia on Chechnya, India on Kashmir); and its refusal to engage deeply where strategic interests of major states are not at stake (Sub-Saharan Africa, Balkans). Despite these persisting failures, progress was being made during the final decades of the prior century, mainly because transnational civic pressures were collaborating with sympathetic governments to respond to abuses in many settings, and vulnerable groups, sometimes assisted by TV, were making their grievances better understood. In Europe, particularly, the political culture was beginning to challenge in pervasive ways the idea that territorial supremacy is an intrinsic aspect of statehood, giving human rights a sovereignty-transcending quality facilitated by the gradual emergence of a multi-state European sense of political community underwritten by growing confidence in a regional rule of law.[9] Of course, such a radical shift in political community arouses intense opposition within Europe itself, especially at the grassroots. This becomes especially evident if the economic burdens of Europeanization are seen as heavy and unfairly distributed, as has been the case recently in Europe, particularly the radical step of moving toward a common currency. At present, Europe is experiencing a political backlash in several countries that has given the reins of government in most important European states to so-called Euro-sceptics.

Despite these issues and concerns about the limited success of the modernist human rights movement to reach its goals, the passing of modernity is highly relevant. It often makes actors other than states the efficient cause of some human rights abuses, and blurs the lines of responsibility for addressing human wrongs. Before September 11, this postmodern perspective mainly focused its attention on abuses attributable to market forces operating globally according to a neo-liberal regulatory logic, what in an American setting might now be appropriately called "Enron Capitalism." Since September 11 this postmodern perspective, especially in the United States, has shifted gears, focusing on security and the challenge of megaterrorism. The main criticism in earlier chapters of the official US response to this challenge has been its dysfunctionality, especially the unwillingness to specify the threat convincingly and to address the deeper causes of Arab/Islamic extremism, including responses to legitimate grievances. In the spirit of this chapter, the criticism needs to be reformulated: Washington has a misplaced and excessive reliance on the partially outmoded security apparatus of state sovereignty in a setting where its applicability, although undeniable to a certain extent, is ill-suited to address the core challenge posed by an extremist concealed networked adversary. The Bush administration since September 11 has combined two extremely dangerous tendencies in this regard. First, the government has argued that the novelty of the threat justifies the suspension of the application of international constraints (both substantive and procedural) on the use of force and also subordinates and narrows the rights of citizens and non-citizens. Second, US officials extend this novelty argument in such a way as to validate an erosion of the modern international law framework of constraint on recourse to and conduct of war, even in contexts where the applicability of rules of restraint remains persuasive, as in state-to-state relations (for example, to overcome legal and moral objections to preemptive war against Iraq).

What do these broader framing considerations relating to the modernist/postmodernist interface have to do with human rights? It is my contention that lifting the modernist limits on respect for human rights exactly parallels lifting the limits on recourse to war and international force. The US government's argument and practice implies that human rights considerations can be ignored to serve the higher interests of security given the threats posed by megaterrorism. This erosion and suspension of human rights is being justified by the exigencies of being "at war." My response, prefigured in earlier chapters, is that there can be some carefully delimited justifications for weakening deference to human rights at home and abroad, but only in cases of genuine necessity with a strong burden of persuasion on the government to establish such grounds in specific contexts. This burden has not been accepted in form, much less discharged in substance, and as a result there is an impression created that human rights have been vindictively and gratuitously abridged by the US government in relation to those suspected of al-Qaeda sympathies or involvement, whether the target of suspicion is American (John Walker Lindh, José Padilla) or the prisoners captured in Afghanistan and elsewhere being held in Camp X-Ray. As well, in the interests of an anti-terrorist alliance, as earlier argued, opportunistic deals have been struck that appear to overlook human rights consequences to an extent that seems unwarranted by the practicalities associated with achieving international cooperation in the struggle to defeat megaterrorism. The fundamental flaw in the American approach has been its insistence that the September 11 events have unleashed a war on "terrorism" in all of its anti-state forms, including those associated with traditional territorially based conflicts, which should continue to be treated within the modernist framework of control and resistance. Such an insistence on merging the modernist with the postmodernist challenge has the damaging side-effect of aligning the United States with all states confronting any armed opposition, even in instances, as is the case with the Palestinians, where recourse to force involves an exercise of a right of resistance to an illegal and oppressive Israeli occupation that has been maintained for more than 35 years. (Needless to say, affirming the Palestinian right of resistance is consistent with the condemnation of Palestinian tactics that involve the deliberate targeting of civilians, as in suicide bombing, which is unconditionally prohibited by both international law and morality.) Similarly, in Kashmir, where India has used oppressive tactics and has refused over a period of decades to implement agreed international procedures designed to achieve conflict resolution, the dynamics of regulation and territorial security need to be set off against both legitimate rights of resistance and impermissible recourse to terrorism.

There is also a conceptual point that needs to be clarified. "Human rights" is used here in its broader sense that became gradually accepted during the 1990s. It includes not only the human rights treaties that have been incorporated into international law, but also international humanitarian law that extends protection to combatants and civilians caught in war situations. It also encompasses the efforts of the 1990s to hold leaders accountable for abuses of power and authority while holding official positions in government, as in the Pinochet litigation or the Milosevic prosecution. In this broader usage, human rights also concerns a range of efforts to redress historic grievances endured by specific constituencies of victims. And finally, the concern of human rights extends to participation in UN peacekeeping and post-conflict activities that are related to the protection of populations that have suffered past abuses, as in the case of Bosnia and Kosovo. In this regard, the US refusal in July 2002 to authorize an extension of the UN peacekeeping mandate in Bosnia without an assurance of immunity for America personnel from criminal prosecution before the newly established International Criminal Court is highly relevant to an appraisal of the US human right record.[10] It underscores the self-serving application of double standards: the US insists on an exemption from legal accountability appropriately applied to others, while at the same time selectively applying legal obligations to others based on geopolitical calculations.

Concrete Human Rights Impacts of September 11
Even if human rights are conceived narrowly and legalistically in relation to the Universal Declaration and the two main international treaties, the International Covenant on Civil and Political Rights (1966) and the International Covenant on Economic, Social, and Cultural Rights (1966), there are several specific concerns that have emerged in the period since September 11. One of these concerns, which parallels a more discretionary approach to the use of force, is reliance on the threat of megaterrorism as a pretext and rationale for taking steps in local and national policing that conservatives have long

favored. Even before September 11 anti-immigrant feelings were growing in the United States, again allowing the ultra-nationalist mood to provide a patriotic cover for restricting the rights of immigrants, engaging in a much expanded approach to deportation for visa violations unrelated to any allegations or evidence of links to terrorist activities. As in other aspects of the analysis offered here, there is a legitimate concern with security that arises due to the character of the al-Qaeda threat, its use of Islamic extremists to penetrate American society as a stage in the mounting of megaterrorist attacks and the inability to guard all major points of vulnerability. American governmental institutions must be empowered to take *reasonable* and *necessary* preventive steps that may involve weakening prior restraints on privacy and the use of illegally obtained evidence, but only on the basis of *specifically demonstrated need* and in a manner that seems likely to reduce the threats posed. Of course, the reasonableness of restraints on freedom is directly related to the gravity of the threats, which is elusive, especially for the public. In many respects, an evaluation of reasonableness has to be based on high degrees of uncertainty as to the gravity of the risks, and the acceptance of restraints is highly dependent on trusting the good faith of the government and the commitment of its top officials to the ideals and practices of freedom. From this perspective, it is most unfortunate that the Attorney General and the newly appointed chief of homeland security do not inspire such confidence.

When it comes to American foreign policy, September 11 seems to have made the high-profile pursuit of international human rights almost a matter for nostalgia to be associated with a simpler, gentler world that no longer exists. Diplomatic support, overseas basing rights, and inter-governmental intelligence and police cooperation are given such a pronounced primacy at this point as to cancel out misgivings about the poor human rights records of foreign governments. There are reports, indeed, that such poor records are being exploited, turning individuals detained in America who are suspected of having useful information over to governments, such as Egypt, that have few, if any, scruples about relying on torture as part of their normal interrogation process.

But the impact on American domestic policy has been even more dramatic, and generally foreboding. The fears of penetration and of concealed terrorists lurking within American society has encouraged the government to take extreme action against those it deems suspects, including detention without charges, deportations of non-citizens without due process, the arrest of citizens on suspicion, and a variety of harsh initiatives impossible to reconcile with the values associated with constitutional liberty. The notorious and comprehensive USA Patriots Act of 2001, which, incredibly, was adopted by Congress without the benefit of hearings or detailed vetting, has also dangerously beefed up the government's police power to compromise the rights of American citizens, by engaging in surveillance and intruding on privacy in a variety of ways, and generally by empowering the forces of homeland security to obstruct and act almost limitlessly without the discipline of accountability even to American judicial institutions. This entire innovative regulatory framework is made more menacing by the legislative adoption of an exceedingly vague and elastic definition of "domestic terrorism," a Pandora's Box for governmental abuse.

To what extent the new authorizations are reasonable responses to the sorts of threats that exist in the post-September 11 world is difficult to evaluate without greater access to intelligence information, including objective assessments of the periodic dire warnings made by high officials as to the severity of the danger now and in the future. And even then, evaluations would vary greatly depending on the weighting of such information and on the mix of values being brought to bear by the evaluator.

What does seem to be the case is that, especially with regard to non-Americans, there is a degree of insensitivity to rights that is extremely disturbing: holding individuals for long periods incognito, not allowing representation of counsel, deporting without charges or evidence, suddenly heightening Draconian enforcement of INS regulations despite cruel and arbitrary hardships on immigrant families, and creating a climate of intimidation that does not seem functionally required by the security challenges posed, and thus appears excessive and discriminatory.

The Lindh and Padilla cases, although the latter is unresolved, reveal disturbing confirmation of a worst case scenario with respect to human rights. In the Lindh case, an extremely young and idealistic American convert to Islam who apparently aligned himself with the Taliban cause in Afghanistan, and who had some contact with al-Qaeda, was being prosecuted to the full extent of the criminal law before being unexpectedly persuaded to enter a guilty plea. The US government seemed to be relying almost exclusively on evidence obtained after Lindh's capture, in humiliating circumstances while in captivity to the Northern Alliance in Afghanistan and on the brink of death.[11] The plea bargain outcome obscures the degree to which judicial institutions would have protected Lindh's human and constitutional rights if the trial had gone forward.

The case of José Padilla presents different issues. Padilla appears to be loosely accused of a connection with an al-Qaeda plot to set off dirty bombs (that is, bombs containing radioactive materials) in American cities, with the intent of causing widespread panic and harm. Of course, the prevention of such dire and frightening mega-criminality is a most urgent concern of government, but whether there are ample grounds for pressing this case depends on the quality of the evidence, which has not been disclosed. To authorize prolonged detention and coercive interrogation without such evidence is to establish the wrong kind of precedent. In the current atmosphere of fear and apprehension, the danger of national hysteria is substantial, and that could easily take the form of false accusations, intimidation of Islamic residents, a law enforcement process giving rise to a general mood of ethnic and religious hatred. The handling of such cases as Padilla's will reveal the extent to which the US government is disposed to strike an acceptable balance between protecting the precious, yet periodically precarious, tradition of American liberties against the adaptive needs of meeting the megaterrorism threat.[12]

The case of the so-called twentieth hijacker, Zacarias Moussaoui, is also worth watching, again for somewhat different reasons. Moussaoui is being charged with complicity in the September 11 attacks, and he faces a possible death sentence, but to date there is no indication that the US government possesses any convincing incriminating evidence aside from some indications of al-Qaeda contact and sympathies, as well as reports that the suspect enrolled in an incriminating form of flight training (operating a plane in the air without seeking instruction on takeoff and landing). Moussaoui makes no secret of his allegience to Osama bin Laden and his acceptance of its genocidal politics, but his world view is not what he is being prosecuted for, and hostility to this world view should not be allowed to become a substitute for a demonstration of substantive complicity in the crime charged, nor should it overcome the presumption of innocence, all the more so given the seriousness of the charges being brought and the inflamed trial atmosphere.

At the same time the case poses some perplexing issues. If Moussaoui is found innocent, should he be set free given his endorsement and embrace of such extremism? It is in such instances that the argument for preventive detention poses a potentially tragic dilemma for a free society under serious and credible threat. The least bad solution might be to enact some sort of mechanism for such detention under exceptional circumstances, where there is enough evidence of dangerous proclivities to lead a reasonable person to deem detention as an appropriate safeguard, but for how long? Under what conditions? These are questions that will need to be addressed if the megaterrorist threat persists, or worse, becomes magnified in the months and years ahead.

If we consider the wider global picture bearing on human rights, there are a few counter-trends to the dismal picture presented above that might yet turn out favorably in relation to the international protection of human rights. As was earlier suggested, Afghanistan, despite a host of persisting problems and uncertainties, seems much better off from a human rights perspective as a result of September 11.[13] Although the situation there remains deeply confused by the revival of warlordism and the related absence of a governing process whose writ runs much beyond Kabul, Afghanistan has managed to achieve some positive results relating to religious tolerance, cultural freedom, women's rights, political democracy, and freedom of speech, as compared to the repressive Taliban rule that governed Afghan society on September 11. Perhaps even more consequential for most Afghans than the recovery from oppressive rule, has been rescuing the people from a regime unable to address the minimal material needs for food, health, jobs, education, and housing that are associated with economic and social rights. As matters now stand, the new Afghan leadership is receiving significant developmental and emergency assistance from international society, which should be converted into a better life for most of the population, and which would certainly not have been as forthcoming if Taliban rule had continued.

More broadly, American concerns about allowing poorly governed and destitute countries to become havens for transnational political extremism may encourage a greater commitment of resources and energies to state-building and development assistance. In many ways, the post-conflict approach to Afghanistan will reveal the degree to which there are strong indications that the American approach to counterterrorism is connected with the struggle against world poverty, and especially with an acceptance of international responsibility to sustain the viability of economically disadvantaged states. This perspective is associated with the realization that meeting the challenge of megaterrorism requires addressing the deep roots of political extremism and societal despair, and it also presupposes a political awareness not trapped in the modernist paradigm of militarism and coercion as the foundation of global security.

A Concluding Comment

The sacrifice of human rights associated with the developments since September 11 can be assessed from at least three perspectives:

—the heavy dose of cold water that has temporarily extinguished the forward progress being made with respect to extending and deepening the reach of human rights as epitomized by the normative revolution underway in the 1990s;

—the willingness of the citizenry to forego the vigilance required to protect constitutional liberties at home, being reduced to passivity by a combination of fears about future megaterrorist attacks with an uncritical patriotic fervor that presently endorses as beneficial virtually anything that the government seeks to do in the name of security and counterterrorism;

—the new geopolitics of empire-building that fosters alliances and submission, a global game of power and control, that consigns matters of values and ethics other than opposition to the "evil" of terrorism, to inoperative status.

These concerns about the directions taken by American policy do not address in concrete terms the genuine need to stretch the paradigms of legitimate response so as to find effective ways to address megaterrorist threats that can probably not be eliminated by relying on the rights and duties embodied in traditional international law, as well as in the UN Charter. These threats seem to include the potential catastrophic prospect of suitcase nuclear bombs being exploded in large cities, and a variety of dangers associated with large-scale attacks on vulnerable American targets that could cause massive casualties and produce general panic. To what degree is preemptive law enforcement justified by these dangers of catastrophic harm? Debate and reflection are needed, as well as procedures by which some sort of civilian review is associated with exceptional claims to abridge rights. In effect, a new balance needs to be struck between the goal of protecting American society and the importance of upholding the rights of individuals and groups alleged to be posing threats.

Past experience suggests the importance of remembering the constraint side of the security equation. In times of crisis, repressive tendencies become more robust, taking advantage of the climate of fear and accompanying patriotic fervor. It is well for Americans to recall the shame that is now associated with two such phenomena that occurred under the cover of World War II, and later, of the cold war: the forcible relocation of Japanese-Americans in concentration camps and the destructive McCarthy-era practice of a ruinous blacklisting of loyal and prominent Americans accused of Communist sympathies. Because September 11 was a dagger struck at the exposed flesh of the American body politic, and because that dagger apparently remains poised to strike again and with frequency, the emotional case for taking whatever preventive action is urged by the government is far greater than what it was during World War II and during the cold war. And for these reasons the need for some monitoring of this process is crucial.

There is also reason to distrust governmental authority in relation to the protection of the rights of citizens. An authority or discretionary power granted for one purpose is often used by those in government for quite unrelated reasons. Whether it is the classification of information to withhold awkward failures of policy from the citizenry or it is security claims that are used by politicians to undermine their opponents, the importance of governmental transparency is difficult to overstate. The governmental rationale for non-disclosure based on the protection of sources or relying on secrecy to avoid helping enemies turns out to be often invoked as pretexts for illicit ends, sometimes merely to hide embarrassing past failures of governmental policy.

During the Vietnam War, the government vigorously challenged the release of the Pentagon Papers, but their content revealed nothing of benefit to the foreign adversaries of the United States. These policy documents *did* contain massive amounts of information embarrassing to policymakers and useful for critics of the Vietnam War, both to demonstrate the degree to which the leaders were misleading the public and the extent to which tactics were being used that could not be reconciled with the law of war. The whole Watergate exposure of the Nixon White House illustrated the degree to which the power of the presidency was being deployed to hamper critics of the US approach to ending the Vietnam War. To the extent that information is genuinely sensitive, it makes the case for independent monitoring procedures, not for conferring unconditional authority on governmental bureaucracies, however strong are traditions of constitutional government and however often the public is reassured by leaders of their respect for these traditions. It is only a vigilant citizenry that can hope to counteract the instinctive law enforcement biases of government and preserve human rights in times of stress, and limit departures from the normal expectations of freedoms to an absolute minimum.

8. FACING THE FUTURE

Now let us begin.
Now let us rededicate ourselves in the long and bitter,
but beautiful, struggle for a new world.

—Martin Luther King, Jr., April 4, 1967
Riverside Church, New York City

In a fundamental sense, the challenge of megaterrorism, urgent as it is for the well-being of Americans and others around the world, is diversionary. More accurately, it reinforces a wide array of transformative forces at work in this historical period that are overwhelming the problem-solving capacities of territorially based sovereign states. Ironically, the response to September 11 has so far produced an ideological and structural reaction that seems to move resolutely in an opposite direction—not only has the most powerful state ever claimed an unprecedented extra-territorial breadth as needed to uphold its security, but it has successfully mobilized hyperbolic nationalist passions to produce a patriotic frenzy that has marginalized the relevance of international law and the United Nations, and effectively silenced or ignored its critics. These dynamics are regressive so far as the requirements of world order are concerned, as well as dysfunctional in relation to the specific threats posed by al-Qaeda.[1]

Whether our concerns are those associated with protecting the global environment against climate change for present and future generations; regulating a runaway world economy; acknowledging the relevance of the religious and civilizational resurgence with respect to political identity; controlling transnational criminality, illegal immigration, and human trafficking; or protecting the vulnerable from Internet abuse, the capacities of the sovereign state, even operating at its most legitimate and responsible levels, are being overwhelmed. It is thus a historical irony of epic proportions that the United States should seize this moment to mount its empire-building effort on a global scale. In a sense, such a project amounts to a gigantic geopolitical denial of the gathering evidence that the state and a world order based on territorial states can no longer cope successfully with international political and economic life in an acceptable manner, and that a drastically different form of global governance needs to be established to create a tolerable future for coming generations. It is perhaps to be expected that the guardians of the established order, when challenged deeply, fall back upon the familiar; they may acknowledge the severity of the challenge, but not by responding creatively, which would involve taking into account the distinctiveness of the situation. Instead, an easier, familiar, yet disastrous path is chosen, intensifying what has seemed to work in the past. So conceived, such intensification translates into a lethal embrace of a doctrine of unconditional and perpetual war.[2]

This imperial project is almost certain to inhibit the sort of adjustments in the organization of world order that are both needed and increasingly desired by the peoples of the world. For one thing, as suggested earlier, if the statist ethos continues to infuse hegemonic geopolitics, it will almost certainly, and soon, produce a backlash in the form of states and popular movements uniting to resist the American empire-building project, injecting tensions and rivalry of a particularly dangerous character, given the weaponry at the disposal of all major and an increasing number of minor states, and soon to be within easy reach of non-state actors as well. It is likely that China would spearhead such a reactive formation aimed at containment of the US, possibly joined by some combination of Europe, Russia, or Japan. Such a renewal of global rivalry among leading states could waste huge amounts of resources, risk the recurrence of major strategic warfare, and divert attention from the issues—such as global warming, the growing scarcity of fresh water, and the rise of transnational networking—that are rendering a verdict of dysfunctionality on world order and on the ways international life is currently organized.

This backward turn appears to reverse a series of encouraging trends, as described in the prior chapter, that had been visible during the twentieth century's last decade: efforts to redress past injustices suffered by groups (indigenous peoples, Holocaust victims, colonized peoples, descendants of slaves); moves toward the accountability of political leaders (Pinochet, Milosevic); inquiries into the indictability of world leaders such as Henry Kissinger, Ariel Sharon, and Saddam Hussein; the establishment of an International Criminal Court; demands for participation and democratic procedures (civil society militancy at UN conferences on women, development, human rights, environment; anti-globalization movement; proposals for the creation of global peoples parliament); and regional innovations (the European Union, especially the European Parliament and the European Court of Human Rights). Such developments were mainly undertaken as a result of citizen activism in transnational settings, concrete expressions of the emergence of global civil society.[3] But these developments also expressed an interest of a large number of moderate governments in expanding the rule of law at a global level, partly in an effort to counter the detrimental impacts of the American superpower approach to world order. In the background before September 11 was the growing realization by business and financial elites of the importance of finding ways to increase the public acceptability of economic globalization, expressed in a variety of ways, such as by entering into a global compact under UN auspices and adopting voluntary codes of conduct pledging corporate respect for environmental and labor standards, as well as for human rights.[4]

It is, of course, arguable as to whether these trends—globalization-from-below—were anything more than ripples of resistance incapable of arresting the powerful drift toward a market-based globalization of an essentially anti-democratic, anti-environmental, and unfair character, which would need to have its stability underwritten by a gendarmerie administered from Washington. Providing security for markets rather than for territorial societies would convert the state into a global service provider, leading quite likely to a gradual weakening of nationalism. From this neo-realist perspective, September 11 merely tilted the balance further, seemingly giving the US a more active role in shaping the process, and anchoring globalization in the territorial soil of American militarism and a revived nationalism. In effect, such an American global empire could be best understood as itself a type of global network of extra-territorial control that operated informally and without claiming any authority to impose its version of global governance. What was claimed was a rulemaking and enforcement capability controlled from Washington with respect to political communities throughout the world, and a denial of sovereignty everywhere except with respect to the imperial actor and its friends.

In any event, those who were active before September 11 in supporting moves toward global democracy and humane global governance are themselves now deeply challenged to resume the struggle under these altered circumstances. It would be all too easy to become co-opted or pacified by this new atmosphere of statist intimidation and wartime security prerogatives. The first step in the dynamics of renewal is to relate critically to the present set of rapidly evolving circumstances, but at the same time not to become so preoccupied with criticism of the American response as to deny the overarching imperative of addressing the megaterrorism threat in a credible manner. As is evident in earlier chapters, I do not share the view of various anti-war activists here and abroad that the war-inducing impact of September 11 should have been unconditionally opposed from the outset. My position is bound to be contested, and to confuse, as my support for a limited military response is coupled with a sharp critique of American militarism as well as an indictment of the stubborn US refusal to address the legitimate grievances of the Arab world. In my view, this complexity of outlook is reflective of the originality of the situation, which calls for as much clarification as can be attained, but no easy embrace of an anti-government or anti-war stance. It is this task of clarification that occupies the remainder of this final chapter. It is not necessary to revisit the earlier more specific discussion of September 11 and its aftermath. The focus here will be upon the more generic world-order issues raised by megaterrorism and by global empire-building.

What is New

The template of international conflict has been shifting for the last several decades from the Westphalian template of conflict among sovereign territorial states to an emergent structure of influence associated with the organizational strength of information-based non-territorial networks, although the pattern is confused by the contradictory moves during the same historical interval toward the universalization of statism as a consequence of the decolonization process.[5] This conceptual inquiry into the changing structure of world order has long been at the edges of international life with respect to such diverse matters as the regulation of transnational business and banking, environmental protection, and the interdiction of drugs and arms flows. Also under consideration, especially recently, has been the realization that transnational political violence directed at an established state from sources outside its territory can exert a devastating and intolerable impact on the security and peace of mind of a society, and that reactive responses can provide, at best, temporary relief from the threats posed. The impulse to strike at the source has been tolerated by the UN and by the assessments of most international law specialists, who have endorsed departures from the literal requirements of the UN Charter in order to give governments the authority to deal reasonably and proportionately with grave breaches of their territorial security. The defense of the US war on Afghanistan rests on such a line of argument, but the magnitude of the attack, harm, and threat generate a sense of major war, if not world war, calling into question the traditional diplomacy of conflict by highlighting the potency of non-territorial networks in undermining the capacity of even the most powerful states to provide for the security of their territorial communities.

Such a new sense of essential chaos recalls the world of medieval Europe, which provided much of the political impetus for the emergence of order-producing sovereign states organized along territorial lines. Might the chaos wrought by megaterrorism generate a sense that world order based on the political fragmentation associated with territorial sovereignty is no longer capable of providing order at tolerable costs, pointing to the need for political unification as the foundation for viable global governance? What seemed utopian before September 11, became a practical necessity on the next day! Or at least there was opened the possibility of the need for such an adjustment, and the American response implied that the entire world was a potential battlefield. Actually, even before September 11, there were comparable globalizing voices to be heard in civil society, worried that without an effective global strategy of regulation global warming, pollution, and freshwater shortages would lead to societal collapse and civilizational disaster.

But let us refine the narrow argument further by supposing there had been no Afghanistan/al-Qaeda linkage. Suppose there was no identifiable territorial actor so closely associated with the violence of

September 11 that could plausibly be held accountable and no state where a coerced change of government could be reasonably believed to reduce significantly the threat of future attacks. Then what? There would be no acceptable target, no way to reduce future risks by recourse to war, and no way to reassure a threatened public that the state under attack could deal with the threats posed. And indeed the very attempt would turn the state into a virtual prison. It could be asked whether a megaterrorist operation can be effectively organized without a territorial base, and fortunately this cannot be known at this time. But what if there should occur future major attacks by al-Qaeda, with no territorial state acting as a safe haven, then what? There are disturbing reports now circulating that al-Qaeda has regrouped in Pakistan and elsewhere since being driven out of Afghanistan, and that it retains much of its ability to produce transnational havoc around the world.[6]

To some extent, a comparable problem has haunted security planners since the dawn of the nuclear age. If a nuclear weapons state launches a major attack on another nuclear weapons state, what should that state do? The presumption of deterrence has been a credible threat of maximal retaliation, but to what rational or ethical end? The response would not help overcome the catastrophic experience of the attacked country, but would merely inflict a comparable or greater ordeal on masses of innocent people, and perhaps even provoke a second wave of devastating attacks. If deterrence fails, then carrying out its threat seems both futile and criminal. The structure has long been understood by strategists to be incoherent, and depends on what has aptly been described as "the rationality of irrationality," hopefully inhibiting every leader of a nuclear weapons state until the end of time.[7]

Even worse than the dilemmas associated with nuclear weaponry, in some respects, is declaring war on a concealed network. How can its existence as a dangerously dispersed adversary be anything other than a prescription for perpetual war? Normally a major war cannot be ended without either the utter defeat of the other or a negotiating partner arranging a terminal ritual such as a peace treaty, or at least an instrument of surrender. The only way of approaching this problem *within the Westphalian template* is to set the anti-terrorist goals as the extermination of "the enemy," which immediately puts the undertaking outside the framework of law and just-war thinking. This problem of discovering parameters has been imprudently further accentuated in the September 11 context by generalizing the enemy to encompass all forms of terrorism. The refusal to treat Taliban and al-Qaeda detainees as prisoners of war while still maintaining the posture of being at war underscores the willful confusion that results from the US wanting it both ways.

In prior circumstances of major war, its statist character framed our understanding of an ending, of defeat and victory, and of a peaceful settlement. By and large, such wars have had non-exterminist goals even if the demand of the winning side was on some occasions for "unconditional surrender" so that it could dictate the terms of peace. The stakes of the conflict could be very high as was the case in World War II. This war was a primary instance of "just war" because the defeat of the Axis challenge was a just cause that could not be achieved without recourse to war, a conclusion that stands up to analysis despite the reliance of the just side on unjust means.[8] The normal objective of a peace settlement is to restore balance and stability by reintegrating the defeated states, although sometimes after a punitive interlude, as with the Versailles Peace Treaty, or on the basis of occupation and domestic political restructuring, as with Germany and Japan after World War II. The idea that the defeated side, in this case al-Qaeda, must be eliminated after the end of a major war is essentially a throwback to the pre-modern idea of conquest and destruction, but with the added difficulty here that there exists no reliable way to gauge their elimination.

These novel features of this disintegrating world order call for humility and a capacity for acknowledging the non-contradiction of opposites. Such an acknowledgement does not come easily in the West, which since the Enlightenment has accepted a kind of either/or rationality that cannot accommodate contradiction. We find ourselves in a situation that both calls for reliance on war to achieve tolerable levels of security and insists that such an unusual war poses an impossible set of questions about scope, tactics, and termination of conflict for which we have no genuine answers. A large part of geopolitical humility in this global setting of transition, being situated between a dying order and an unborn one, is to place emphasis upon the minimization of disruptive violence, and on a receptivity to post-

Westphalian alternatives.[9] Because of the familiarity of the Westphalian template, and its plausible extension to Afghanistan, there has occurred the implausible extension of this template to encompass the axis of evil states, giving an unwarranted territorial locus to the continuation of an American-led military response. The implausibility of this extension casts doubts on the coherence, and even the good faith, of the earlier phases of the US response to megaterrorism. This pervasive failure to sustain coherence and growing evidence of geopolitical hubris by the US government have made the response to September 11 deeply disturbing and dangerous to a widening circle of observers in America and around the world. Humility in this setting of geopolitical novelty would mean adopting the narrowest war aims possible, identifying limits, seeking closure, and exploring alternatives to war-based security policies, as well as exploring seriously long-term arrangements for global governance that are animated by seeking to promote and sustain the well-being of all peoples on the planet.

Focus

Because the terrain of megaterrorism is both slippery and largely unknown it becomes especially important to focus clearly and narrowly on goals. Without such a focus there is no way to distinguish between reasonable and unreasonable response strategies. The dangers of an unnecessarily broad and prolonged conflict are considerable, especially to the extent that the alleged threat is extended to "rogue states," to an array of anti-state political struggles around the world, and to validate geopolitical opportunism (assistance to oppressive regimes in exchange for strategic support, especially military basing rights, and gaining an economic foothold, particularly in relation to energy resources), and global militarism (missile defense, weaponization of space).

To focus is to shed light responsibly on what is the most appropriate means of response to the specific challenge of megaterrorism. Most forms of "terrorism," for example, should be sharply distinguished from the phenomenon of megaterrorism. Furthermore, respect for sovereign rights and deference to the constraints regulating the use of force associated with international law should be affirmed, with departures as deemed necessary being scrupulously justified by the US government as exceptions that are both shown to be reasonable and as minimal as possible. That is, because the normal template governing state action has seemingly been overwhelmed by the eruption of megaterrorism, it becomes more important than ever to exhibit respect for the old structures of authority to the considerable extent that they retain relevance, at least until a more responsive comprehensive framework can be devised and becomes operational.

Aspects of this problem of focus preceded September 11, being highlighted by a number of developments that could not be accommodated within the standard operating procedures of a statist world order. As discussed earlier, the advent of nuclear weapons was problematic because it rendered obsolete conflict resolution by large-scale combat. Along somewhat different lines, a sharp normative trend subversive of state sovereignty resulted from the practice and ideology of "humanitarian intervention" in the 1990s, climaxing in the debate over the NATO War in Kosovo. The protection of international human rights was growing more salient as an ingredient of world order, causing a growing tension between the newer claims of humanitarian diplomacy and older ideas of territorial sovereignty and respect for the legal prohibition against intervention in the internal affairs of states. Satisfying the newer humanitarian claims was exerting serious strains on the guidelines embedded in the UN Charter as drafted and adopted in 1945, a time when deference to sovereign rights was so fundamental as to be taken for granted. Particularly at issue was the extent to which the world community's deference to the territorial supremacy of a state was now conditioned upon its show of respect for the basic human rights of its own citizens. Asian countries, especially, were suspicious of this drift of post-colonial, post-cold war humanitarian diplomacy, criticizing it on a few occasions for being selectively ineffectual (guilty of double standards) and much more often as seeking to put into operation a new doctrine enabling the rich and powerful states of the North to intervene in the poor and weak states of the South. These objecting countries, led by China, indicated their substantive acceptance of the normative architecture of international human rights, but refused to accept the international enforcement of human rights standards even by the UN, and were deeply opposed to validating self-serving mandates acquired by "coalitions of the willing" or issued by regional actors that were little different from regional security alliances.

In these regards, the Kosovo undertaking by NATO was resented, and opposed, and every effort was made by this group of countries in the South to prevent such practice from achieving the status of a precedent that could be invoked in the future. Even the intervening countries realized that their military action was on thin ice, and they were careful not to affirm their action as a model for the future.

The problems of adjustment were also felt within the UN itself. To what extent should the charter be modified by interpretations that took account of the evolution of international society, particularly the growing interdependence of states and markets, as well as the dramatic transnational rise of human rights and environmental consciousness? In light of these developments, the earlier restriction on UN authority written into the charter in Article 2(7) seemed awkwardly outdated to these new interventionists. Secretary General Kofi Annan stirred controversy a few years back when he insisted against the background of the Balkan Wars that the UN could not stand by while ethnic cleansing and other forms of humanitarian catastrophe were taking place within sovereign states. The Secretary General's statement was understood as a controversial endorsement on principle of humanitarian intervention, and a silent softening of the UN Charter inhibition against intervening in internal matters.

Again, there was a need for focus, not a generalized departure from the assurance that weaker states would not be targeted for intervention by stronger states, relying on the pretext of human rights. The most persuasive approach was a reasoned narrow breach of positive law under the factual and ethical pressures of humanitarian urgency taking the forms of "ethnic cleansing," genocide, and the onset of mass famine and disease. Such an approach should not pretend that existing law extends so far as to validate these initiatives, but rather contend that a moral and practical set of imperatives endow such action with legitimacy.[10] The further response here would be to fashion a political consensus among states to extend the law to cover as precisely as possible this domain of legitimacy so as to overcome the unwholesome gap between legality and legitimacy. The danger of legitimacy as a source of validation is that it seems to authorize violations of inconvenient restraints of international law, thereby diminishing the authority of law on an ad hoc basis, which could be understood as the empowerment of the strong, the only states with the capabilities to assert and act on such interventionary claims. To avoid this impression of realism disguised as normative imperative, it is important to justify each interventionary claim that invokes questions of legitimacy because of the unacceptability of existing law on a principled and fully articulated basis. It is then highly desirable to incorporate into law those claims successfully legitimated, thereby closing a potentially nihilistic gap between legitimacy and legality. As desirable as it might be to close such a gap, it may be impossible to the extent that there remains absent a political consensus among the great majority of states. In such a circumstance, there is no satisfactory alternative to acknowledging and living with the gap.

Overall, the argument for focus stresses the importance of a disciplined means/end relationship, clarity of purpose, necessity, and justification for departure from norms, as well as responsible effort to achieve the reconciliation of legitimacy and legality at the earliest possible time. If reconciliation is not achieved, then the template is not only being superseded, but the paradigm of restraint is likely to become deeply compromised, if not altogether abandoned. Such a normative maelstrom is almost certain to produce chaos and non-democratic forms of political order, a revival and rehabilitation of war talk, and a reliance on militarist approaches to the resolution of political conflicts. On all of these grounds, the overall response to September 11 that has been enunciated and managed by the George W. Bush White House seems deeply flawed. The loss of focus has virtually precluded reasoned discourse on an effective, adaptive response to megaterrorism, and this loss has actually shifted the locus of discussion and action to other diversionary issues that pose high risks of their own (such as the propriety of recourse to war against Iraq).

Limits

Since the birth of modern world order at the Peace of Westphalia in 1648, the outer boundaries of permissible behavior in world politics have been constantly modified by the assertion of reasoned and effective claims to take action in defense of vital interests by leading states. This process of lawmaking by powerful states has always been controversial, as it blurs the distinction between law and power, and relies on the subjective interpretation by the actors themselves as to what is reasonable and necessary. This experiential process of lawmaking has been influentially theorized in relation to international law by Michael Reisman under the rubric of "incidents jurisprudence"—that is, international incidents providing the concrete occasions for stretching existing international law to meet new challenges by reasonable behavior whether covered by prior legal rules or not.[11] Jurgen Habermas has impressively identified reasoned discourse as the indispensable feature of political democracy, which in this global setting of primitive institutionalization can be understood as argument among international actors about the permissible limits of international behavior by sovereign states in circumstances where the pre-existing and accepted limits seem unresponsive to pressures on valid security and national interests.

When the claim to stretch the limits of law is accepted by the wider international community (or at least not seriously and directly challenged) and seems generally congruent with our ethical consciousness, then it tends to become a precedent that others similarly challenged may rely upon in similar circumstances. This process of international lawmaking, while imprecise and susceptible to manipulation by more influential states, at least allows reasonable claims for adaptation to be accommodated to some degree at the global level without confronting governments with the stark choice of violating existing law or finding their reasonable needs, often seen as related to political survival, frustrated by legalistic constraints that are not adapting to changing circumstances. Changes in military technology exert particular pressure on the constraints of law on war, either providing new means of destruction or posing new dangers.

To the extent that states accept an obligation to justify claims to act in a manner that would seem to be unauthorized behavior, there ensues a discussion of proper limits by concerned governments under constantly altering circumstances that cannot be handled, as in domestic politics, by reliance on legislative and judicial responses to provide policy closure. In world politics there is no government to determine the comparative merits of contested claims by governments and other international actors and very little institutionalization of any kind is available; what little exists is almost entirely voluntary. When radical challenges to the established order occur, the lawmaking role of dominant or hegemonic states is unavoidable, and the quality of their leadership, as beneficial or not for the community of states treated as a whole, is tested in instructive ways.

From time to time this generalized problem of relocating the limits of permissible action takes on world historical significance, as when the atomic bombs were dropped by the US on Japanese cities in 1945. It is a virtual certainty, for instance, that if the atomic bombs had been developed by Germany and dropped on British or American cities, this weaponry would have been criminalized in 1945, assuming that the Allies had still managed to win the war; but given the outcome of World War II, the delegitimation of the weaponry has remained muted and non-authoritative to this day. The main struggle to achieve nuclear disarmament has long been waged only at the margins of civil society. The failure to produce a persuasive justification for the atomic attacks has haunted the world ever since Hiroshima, perhaps most memorably expressed by Albert Einstein's important comment that the atomic bomb "has changed everything except our way of thinking." Despite many attempts to do so, there has never been a reasoned explanation of reliance on nuclear weaponry that has been widely accepted by non-nuclear states. The World Court some years ago finally tried to address the question of the legality of nuclear weapons, at the behest of a General Assembly call for a clarifying advisory opinion, and came up with a series of responses by World Court judges that depart dramatically from the existing geopolitical practice: a slender majority found that a generalized stigma of illegality pertained to nuclear weaponry, possibly subject to the single exception of a permissible use in the face of ultimate survival claims of sovereign states. In addition, the World Court declared unanimously that nuclear weapons states were subject to an imperative legal duty to pursue nuclear disarmament in good faith.[12]

This was the most authoritative inquiry to date into legal limits, and it has been ignored by governments, and especially by nuclear weapons states. An unacknowledged normative crisis exists because the geopolitical claims relating to weaponry of mass destruction cannot be reconciled with prevailing international law discourses, whether the latter are treated as matters of legality (existing positive law) or legitimacy (reformulated limits that take account of moral and security pressures). This crisis was obscured during the cold war due to the bipolar confrontation of two nuclear superpowers, which gave a certain coherence and semblance of balance to the doctrine of deterrence, a mode of catastrophic threat that was supposedly neutralized as a result of its mutuality, meaning that it could not be rationally carried out.[13] Since the collapse of the Soviet Union, the continued reliance on nuclear weaponry seems less defensible than ever, and stretches to the breaking point the idea of reasoned limits or even the less sturdy reliance on rational coherence.[14]

My contention is that the September 11 attacks posed a similar challenge to that initiated by the use of atomic weapons, but with a different impact on the structure of world politics. With respect to nuclear weapons, the hegemonic states, and their acolytes, are the power-wielders that reject appropriate limits on their authority and capabilities. In relation to September 11, the main center of geopolitics was the targeted victim of attack, and the question of limits pertains to the victim's response—what it is reasonable and effective to do in defense against megaterrorist attacks and threats, given an absence of a territorial base of accountability and the impossibility of a negotiated resolution of the conflict (extermination of the enemy or the persistence of war seem to be the most plausible scenarios, although it is possible to imagine some sort of withering away of the threat to the point that it is almost forgotten). Also, September 11 reinforces the essential structural challenge of globalization, namely, the relevance of information and networking to the exercise of power, establishing the need to incorporate non-state actors into the procedures and institutions of world order.

The US government has augmented its hegemonic role in the aftermath of the attacks, seeking to provide justification for uses of force and other action "outside the box"[15] of prior norms of law and morality. Despite some over-generalized rhetoric, its efforts seemed to provide legitimate extensions of legality in relation to the Afghanistan phase and with respect to mobilizing global support for cooperative efforts to weaken al-Qaeda by disrupting its dispersed cells of militants and its financial and diplomatic sources of support. But the response has proceeded far beyond the reasonable necessities of the situation, including worrisome indications of a doctrinal shift in the direction of greater reliance on nuclear weaponry unhinged both from informal traditions of non-use, and altogether disregarding the relevance of international legal guidelines.

In these crucial respects, the US government has not identified reasonable limits that would govern its response to September 11, and has failed to fulfill its responsibilities as a hegemonic lawmaker under circumstances where it seems necessary to act beyond the limits of international law in order to protect threatened fundamental national interests. Such limits could have been clearly specified, thereby creating a basis for incorporating the challenge of megaterrorism, as historically associated with al-Qaeda, into an evolving international law bearing on global security. As it is, the American-led response appears, especially to those assessing the response from detached perspectives, as neither legal, nor legitimate, nor prudent. As a result, the normative crisis earlier posed by nuclearism, and later in different ways by globalization, climate change, and ethnic cleansing, is deepened and extended in dangerous ways by this failure to justify adequately and delimit acceptably the US response.

This set of circumstances is aggravated, as has been argued, by the further perception that the United States has used the September 11 attacks as a cover for energy geopolitics and the acceleration of its empire-building project, especially its military enactment via automated battlefield dominance and the militarization of space. Such a wider set of objectives, which implicitly denies the sovereign rights of all normal states, represents an undertaking that substitutes a unilateral mode of geopolitics for the preexisting mode of mutual respect and cooperation, and throws the very idea of shared limits on discretion to use international force into doubt. As earlier suggested, if the state system reacts to this exhibition of American global ambitions in its characteristic fashion, the most probable scenario is a new cycle of costly and risky geopolitical rivalry that arises from a coalition of states (and possibly joined by a variety of transnational social forces) resolved to resist American empire-building. Besides generating an expensive arms race, with attendant risks of war, this resumption of statist geopolitics diverts attention from the challenge of responding to non-territorial geopolitics that are empowering a range of economic, political, and criminal networks to operate beyond the regulatory reach of sovereign states.

Alternatives and Recommendations

The most profound challenge confronting humanity is to devise alternatives to war as the foundation of global and human security. As matters now stand, even political forces generally sensitive to the restraints of international law and morality are locked within the confines of the war system when confronted by fundamental security threats of the severity of those associated with megaterrorism. This decentralized system of states tends to absolutize the survival and well-being of the part, while giving only shallow attention to the interests, well-being, and sustainability of the whole. Such a self-help dynamic underpinned by violence and evolving technologies of destruction tends to empower the militarily powerful and rich, and to punish the weak and poor. It is a system driven by power and wealth, whether the focus is on empire-building with weapons or by the control of markets.

International institutions set up to soften the edges of world politics tend to be confined by limited mandates, by budgetary and geopolitical constraints, and if at all effective are likely to become instruments of the policies and ideas of leading states and of economic configurations of power. The results have not been pretty: frequent warfare, many incidents of ethnic cleansing and genocide, catastrophic risks of environmental collapse, massive poverty, a disregard of future generations. Even a commitment to address the most incendiary grievances and renounce empire-building ambitions would still leave world order at the tender mercies of fate, vulnerable to an eventual nuclear or biological war, susceptible to continuing bloodshed and oppressive rule, mass impoverishment, and constantly at risk of economic and ecological unraveling.

Human destiny is not so circumscribed. Liberating surprises are always concealed by "the realities" of the present. Humane aspirations are being pursued by individuals and groups all over the world. These aspirations center upon a reliance on nonviolent politics of change and resistance, on dedication to human rights, including the alleviation of economic deprivation, on a belief in the feasibility of disarmament and demilitarization, on a commitment to regional and global democracy, and on the belief that humane global governance is necessary and possible. The ethos of global civil society is increasingly guided by what might be called "utopian realism," the political understanding that the only realistic way to provide the peoples of the world and their descendants with a viable future is by institutionalizing power and authority within frameworks of law and governance that now appear situated beyond horizons of attainability. Looking beyond these horizons in the spirit of engagement is the only "realistic" escape from geopolitical despair!

Tolstoy asks in the Second Epilogue to *War and Peace* why historians consistently fail to explain or predict major developments in human experience. His illuminating and fascinating response centers on the idea that historians look at surfaces and personages, while ignoring the unseen forces that move people, producing seismic tremors that completely undermine our expectations about what is possible and likely. Social scientists and political commentators continue to work in the dark, however complicated and technical their way of interpreting the world may appear to the uninitiated. Not one of these highly touted experts predicted the end of the cold war, the release of Nelson Mandela, the religious resurgence, the potency of networks, the recourse to megaterrorism, or politics of popular resistance resting on suicide as a systematic weapon. Our rational capacities are not sufficient to inform us reliably about what is going to happen for better and worse, and why, at the core of human affairs.

Let us take heart from our failures as well as our successes, thereby further confirming that the best and worst of futures are both possible, and our struggle to make the best happen and avoid the worst is likely to be decisive. It may be well to be instructed by two recent happenings, rich with implication: the wasted excess effort to prevent Y2K disasters from disabling computer breakdowns around the world, surely in retrospect a mouse that roared; and then, the opposite lack of anticipation of the megaterrorism that facilitated the tragedy of September 11 and created the political space to provide cover for geopolitical overreach in the American response. Too much attentiveness to risk, as well as too little, can bring humanity to its knees, which suggests both the use and abuse of knowledge.

The only way forward is to trust our moral and political intuitions, and have the humility and prudence to test their relevance through dialogue, debate, experience, and nonviolent struggle. This is not a rejection of reason and knowledge, but it is a questioning of the ability to achieve change by scientific inquiry or to agreed-upon ends. Science and rationality, as well as spirituality, offer valuable help in gaining understanding, and above all, in cutting the ground out from under the dogmas of reassurance that commend the established order, whether emanating from religious or secular sources, asserting unconditional claims that a truth is being served and any resistance to what the power-wielders propose is evil. Such a mentality makes killing and dying fully justified, even an occasion of glory. In the end only a rejection of all fundamentalisms[16] will enable humanity to grope toward a safer, fairer, and more sustainable and hopeful future than now seems in the offing.

NOTES

INTRODUCTION

1 The Tobin Tax is a proposal made more than 25 years ago by James Tobin, a Nobel laureate in economics, suggesting that a small tax be levied on all transnational currency transactions. The revenues derived from this tax could be used to support a variety of global public goods, including UN activities. Such a proposal has long been advocated by peace groups favoring a more independent United Nations.

2 See, for example, Michael Scott Doran, "Somebody Else's Civil War: Ideology, Rage, and the Assault on America," in James F. Hoge, Jr. and Gideon Rose, eds., *How Did This Happen? Terrorism and the New War* (New York, NY: Council on Foreign Relations, 2001) 31–52.

3 The early debate focused on whether recourse to war was justified. For representative views on both sides, see pro-war voices in Strobe Talbott and Nayan Chanda, eds., *The Age of Terror: America and the World After September 11* (New York: Basic Books, 2001) and anti-war views in Kamla Basin, Smitu Kothari, and Bindia Thapar, eds., *Voices of Sanity: Reaching Out for Peace* (Delhi, India: Lokayan & Rainbow Publishers, 2001).

4 "Booknotes," C-Span interview with Bernard Lewis, 30 December 2001; Fouad Ajami, "The Sentry's Solitude," *Foreign Affairs* 80.6 (November/December 2001): 12.

5 Daniel Pipes, "Welcome to the War on Terror," *Jerusalem Post,* 2 January 2002.

CHAPTER I: WINNING AND LOSING THE WAR AGAINST GLOBAL TERROR

1 For an example of the anti-war voices, see "Prominent Americans' Statement: We Won't Deny Our Consciences," *The Guardian,* 6 June 2002.

2 For instance, compare Ariel Sharon, "The War Forward in the Middle East," *New York Times,* 9 June 2002: 4, 15, with Henry Siegman, "Sharon rewrites the peace script: Resolution 242 reinterpreted," *International Herald Tribune,* 12 June 2002.

3 There is also some ambiguity as to what groups should be treated as extremist; for instance, it is a gross over-simplification to treat Hezbollah as a terrorist organization, overlooking its primary role as a resistance movement in Lebanon and as a community-based Islamic civic organization with a changing political agenda, which includes prospects of an eventual acceptance of Israel's legitimacy and America's regional role.

4 For thorough review see the comprehensive study prepared and released 6

August 2002 by Global Policy Forum and several other respected NGOs, "Iraq Sanctions: Humanitarian Implications and Options for the Future." Also see Falk, "Iraq, the United States, and International Law: Beyond the Sanctions," in Tareq Ismail, ed., *The Iraqi Question in World Politics*, forthcoming 2003.

5 See my *Predatory Globalization: A Critique* (Cambridge, UK: Polity, 1999).

6 See Alan B. Krueger and Jitka Maleckova, "Education, Poverty, Political Violence and Terrorism: Is There a Causal Connection?" unpublished paper dated May 2002.

7 Tariq Ali, *The Clash of Fundamentalisms: Crusades, Jihads and Modernity* (London, UK: Verso, 2002) 256.

8 Again, see my *Predatory Globalization* for discussion of these pre-September 11 trends.

9 Eliot A. Cohen, "A Tale of Two Secretaries," *Foreign Affairs* 81.3 (May 2002): 33–46, at 46.

CHAPTER 2: DIMENSIONS OF MEGATERRORISM

1 Quoted in Peter Bergen, *Holy War, Inc.: Inside the Secret World of Osama bin Laden* (New York: Free Press, 2001) 19.

2 See the online transcript at www.terrorism.com/terrorism/BinLadenTranscript.

3 See Bernard Lewis, "The Revolt of Islam," *The New Yorker*, 19 November 2002: 50–63, at 63; see also his "What Went Wrong?" *The Atlantic*, January 2002: 43–45.

4 Bernard Lewis, "Did You Say 'American Imperialism,'" *National Review*, 17 December 2001: 26–29, at 29.

5 Bernard Lewis, 30 December 2001 C-Span interview.

6 David Barsamian, Interview with Edward Said, *The Progressive*, November 2001: 41–44.

7 Mark Juergensmeyer, *Terror in the Mind of God: The Global Rise of Religious Violence* (Berkeley, CA: University of California Press, 2001) 217.

8 Eric Rouleau, "Politics in the Name of the Prophet," undated ms. from 2001.

9 Such an outcome in the Gulf Crisis is hinted at in the memoirs of Perez de Cueller, who was Secretary General of the United Nations at the time. See his *Pilgrimage for Peace: A Secretary-General's Memoir* (New York: St. Martin's Press, 1997).

10 Walter Laqueur, *The New Terrorism* (New York: Oxford University Press, 1999) 7.

11 As reported in the *New York Times*, 28 January 2002.

CHAPTER 3: APPRAISING THE AFGHANISTAN WAR

1 For an assessment of post-war Afghanistan, see Amin Saikal, "Afghanistan After the Loya Jurga," *Survival* 44.3 (2002): 47–56. *Survival* is the quarterly of the International Institute of Strategic Studies in London.

2 See Michael Ignatieff, "How to Keep Afghanistan from Falling Apart: The Case for a Committed American Imperialism," *NY Times Magazine*, 28 July 2002: 26–31, 54.

3 Rumsfeld quoted in the *Los Angeles Times*, 16 January 2002: A6.

4 Murray Campbell, "Afghan civilian toll notably high," *Globe and Mail*, 19 January 2002: A11; see also special report "The War Crimes of Afghanistan," by Babak Dehganpisheh, John Barry, and Roy Gutman; "The Death Convoy of Afghanistan," *Newsweek*, 26 August 2002: 22–30.

5 10 October 2001; Peter Singer moderated the forum, and James Turner Johnson, Gideon Rose, and I participated.

6 On the gruesome realities of Taliban Afghanistan see the excellent summary article of Pankaj Mishra, "The Afghan Tragedy," *NY Review of Books*, 17 January 2002: 43–49, esp. 43–44.

7 For an assessment along these lines see "Helping Afghanistan: More than Money," *The Economist*, 26 January–1 February 2002: 10.

CHAPTER 4: THE US GOVERNMENT'S WORLD-ORDER ARGUMENT

1 See Noam Chomsky, *9/11* (New York, NY: Seven Stories Press, 2002).

2 For discussion of the US approach to defining terrorism see Bruce Hoffman, *Inside Terrorism* (New York: Columbia University Press, 1998) 14–44.

CHAPTER 5: WRECKING WORLD ORDER

1 For evaluation of this trend see Falk, "Reviving the 1990s Trends Toward Transnational Justice: Innovations and Institutions," *Journal of Human Development* 3.2 (2002): 167–190

2 For the classic account of "international society" see Hedley Bull, *The Anarchic Society: A Study of Order in World Politics* (London: Macmillan, 2nd ed., 1995); see also along the same lines Robert Jackson, *The Global Covenant: Human Conduct in a World of States* (New York: Oxford University Press, 2000).

3 See the Independent International Commission on Kosovo's report: *Conflict, Response, Lessons Learned*, (Oxford, UK: Oxford University Press, 2001).

4 See Alan Cullison and Andrew Higgins, "Inside al-Qaeda's Afghan Turmoil," *Wall Street Journal*, 2 August 2002: A1, 10.

5 For a recent influential rendering of this perspective, see Robert D. Kaplan, *Warrior Politics: Why Leadership Demands a Pagan Ethos* (New York, NY: Random House, 2002) esp. 52–77; it is hardly surprising that Henry Kissinger, the arch-Machiavellian of our time, should sing the praises of Kaplan's book on its back cover.

6 See here Anthony Clark Arend & Robert J. Beck, *International Law and the Use of Force: Beyond the UN Paradigm* (New York: Routledge, 1993); A. Mark Weisbrud, *Use of Force: The Practice of States since World War II* (University Park, PA: Pennsylvania State University Press, 1997).

7 See John Ikenberry, *Beyond Victory: Institutions, Strategic Restraint, and the Rebuilding of Order after Major Wars* (Princeton: Princeton University Press, 2001).

8 See positions represented in *Voices of Sanity* (see Introduction note 3) and Chomsky's *9/11* (Chapter 4 note 1).

9 "Decoding the Chatter," *Time*, 3 June 2002: 34–36.

10 For a generally positive account of the American approach to the Afghanistan War see Michael E. O'Hanlon, "A Flawed Masterpiece," *Foreign Affairs* 81.3:47–63. O'Hanlon ends his appraisal with this glowing and somewhat exaggerated conclusion: "... the situation in Afghanistan has improved enormously since October 7—and so has American security. The Afghan resistance, the Bush administration, its international coalition partners, the U.S. armed forces, and the CIA have accomplished what will likely be remembered as one of the greater military successes of the twenty-first century."

11 See Robert W. Tucker, *The Just War: A Study in Contemporary American Doctrine* (Westport, CT: Greenwood Press, 1960; reissued in 1978).

CHAPTER 6: CHALLENGING THE NEW PATRIOTISM

1 See Charles Duelfer, "Military action, carefully planned to further our political goals, is necessary," *Los Angeles Times*, 11 August 2002: M1, 2.

CHAPTER 7: THE ECLIPSE OF HUMAN RIGHTS

1 "Is the Human Rights Era Ending?" *New York Times*, 5 February 2002.

2 On various dimensions of this trend see Martha Minow, *Between Vengeance and Forgiveness: Facing History after Genocide and Mass Violence* (Boston, MA: Beacon Press, 1998); Geoffrey Robertson, *Crimes Against Humanity: The Struggle for Global Justice* (New York, NY: The New Press, 1999); Priscilla B. Hayner, *Unspeakable Truths: Confronting State Terror and Atrocity* (New York, NY: Routledge, 2001).

3 See Nicholas Wheeler, *Saving Strangers: Humanitarian Intervention in International Society* (Oxford: Oxford University Press, 2000); Linda Melvern, *A People Betrayed: The Role of the West in Rwanda's Genocide* (London: Zed, 2000); or for a more sympathetic view of the West's response, see Michael Barnett, *Eyewitness to a Genocide: The United Nations and Rwanda* (Ithaca, NY: Cornell University Press, 2002).

4 See "The Princeton Principles on Universal Jurisdiction," (Program in Law and Public Affairs, Woodrow Wilson School, Princeton University, 2001) 1–67.

5 For depiction see Falk, "The First Normative Global Revolution," in Mehdi Mozaffari, ed., *Globalizations and Civilizations* (London: Routledge/Taylor & Francis, 2002) 51–76.

6 See Richard Rosecrance, *The Rise of the Virtual State: Wealth and Power in the Coming Century* (New York: Basic Books, 1999).

7 For one account of these efforts see William M. Arkin, "Dressed—and

Equipped—to Kill," *Los Angeles Times*, 4 August 2002: M1, 6.

8 See Ken Booth, "Human Wrongs and International Relations," International Affairs 71.1 (1995): 103–126; also, Tim Dunne & Nicholas J. Wheeler, eds., *Human Rights in Global Politics* (Cambridge, UK: Cambridge University Press, 1999).

9 Conservative commentators view this drift toward the rule of law in Europe and as a foundation of foreign policy as an expression of geopolitical weakness rather than as a sign of political maturation. See Robert Kagan, "Power and Weakness: Why the United States and Europe see the world differently," *Policy Review* 113 (June/July 2002): 3–28.

10 For account see William Orme, "Dispute May End U.S. Role in Bosnia," *Los Angeles Times*, 1 July 2002: A1, 4

11 See the important article, Edwin Dobb, "Should John Walker Lindh Go Free?" *Harper's Magazine*, May 2002: 31–41.

12 The pressures to abandon civil rights are being strongly articulated in the media. See, e.g., Douglas W. Kmiec, "This Is War, and Military Justice Is Appropriate," *Los Angeles Times*, 14 June 2002: B15; National Review Editors, "No Ordinary Crime: The Case of José Padilla," *National Review*, 15 July 2002. See also Jonathan Turley, "Camps for Citizens: Ashcroft's Hellish Vision," *Los Angeles Times*, 14 August 2002: B11.

13 See Amin Saikal's *Survival* article (Chapter 3 note 1).

CHAPTER 8: FACING THE FUTURE

1 For a useful demonstration of these requirements written shortly before September 11, see Charles W. Kegley, Jr. and Gregory A. Raymond, *Exorcising the Ghost of Westphalia: Building World Order in the New Millennium* (Upper Saddle River, NJ: Prentice Hall, 2002); also Falk, *Law in an Emerging Global Village: A Post-Westphalian Perspective* (Ardsley, NY: Transnational, 1998).

2 For a useful exaggeration of this observation see Gore Vidal, *Perpetual War for Perpetual Peace* (New York: Thunder Mouth's Press/Nation Books, 2002).

3 For an assessment of these phenomena, see the *Global Society Yearbook*, (Oxford: Oxford University Press, 2002).

4 For an excellent overview of the globalization debate, including reform prospects, see Robin Broad, ed., *Global Backlash: Citizen Initiatives for a Just World Economy* (Lanham, MD: Rowman & Littlefield, 2002).

5 This dynamic has been exhaustively analyzed by Manel Castels in his three volume *The Information Age: Economy, Society, and Culture* (New York: Basic Books, 1996–98).

6 David Johnston, Don Van Natta Jr., and Judith Miller, "Qaeda's New Links Increase Threats from Global Sites," *New York Times*, 16 June 2002: 1, 10; Bob Drogin, Josh Meyer, and Eric Lichtblau, "Al-Qaeda Gathering Strength in Pakistan," *Los Angeles Times* 16 June 2002: A1, 6.

7 A position eloquently argued years ago by Jonathan Schell in *The Fate of the Earth* (New York: Knopf, 1982).

8 For the overall relevance of peace settlements see G. John Ikenberry, *After Victory: Institutions, Strategic Restraint, and the Rebuilding of Order after Major Wars* (Princeton, NJ: Princeton University Press, 2001).

9 I have tried to explore this theme in *Law in an Emerging Global Village: A Post-Westphalian Perspective* (Ardsley, NY: Transnational Publishers, 1998).

10 For one attempt in this direction see the Final Report of the Independent World Commission on Kosovo, 2000.

11 See W. Michael Reisman and Andrew R. Willard, eds., *Incidents Jurisprudence: The Law that Counts in World Politics* (Princeton, NJ: Princeton University Press, 1988); for the fuller exposition of this perspective see the work of Myres S. McDougal, for instance, *Studies in World Public Order* (New Haven, CT: Yale University Press, 1961).

12 Advisory Opinion on the Legality of Nuclear Weapons, International Court of Justice, 1996.

13 For exploration of these issues in a cold-war setting, see Robert Jay Lifton and Richard Falk, *Indefensible Weapons: The Political and Psychological Case Against Nuclearism* (New York, Basic Books, updated edition, 1989).

14 For sharp critiques under these circumstances see Francis A. Boyle, *The Criminality of Nuclear Deterrence: Could the US War on Terrorism Go Nuclear?* (Atlanta, GA: Clarity Press, 2002); Helen Caldicott, *The New Nuclear Danger: George W. Bush's Military-Industrial Complex* (New York: The New Press, 2002).

15 See David Kennedy's article on thinking outside the box: "When Thinking Repeats: Thinking Against the Box, *Journal of International Law and Politics* 32.2 (2000): 335–500. Although in the setting of international-law scholarship, this bears directly on efforts to adjust policy and action to the innovative realities of a drastic political change.

16 This viewpoint underlies Tariq Ali's important book, *Clash of Fundamentalisms* (London, UK: Verso, 2002); it is a position with strong resemblances to George Soros' advocacy of Karl Popper's open society anti-perfectionist worldview. See George Soros, *On Globalization* (New York: Public Affairs, 2002), especially the final chapter, "Toward a Global Open Society." See also my *Religion and Global Governance* (New York: Palgrave, 2001).

INDEX

A

Afghanistan, xix, xx, xxii, xxv, xxvii,
1,4, 7, 9–10, 12, 14–15, 30, 37,
39, 44–48, 59–70, 73, 79–80,
91–92, 99, 101–107, 109–110,
113–115, 118, 120, 123–126,
131, 164, 168–170, 177–178,
180, 186
war against, xxii,1, 4, 7, 12, 14–15,
30, 62–64, 67, 73, 99, 101,
103, 106, 114, 120, 124, 177
arms race, 5
Africa, 91, 95, 130, 154–156, 162
Ajami, Fouad, xxiv–xxv
Ali, Tariq, 31
American Civil War, 136
Annan, Secretary General Kofi, 182
anthrax, 27, 40, 141
Arabian Peninsula, xxi, 44
Arafat, Yasir, 20, 22, 113
Argentina, 28
Ashcroft, Attorney General John,
133
Asia, 28, 111, 130, 148, 158, 181
Augustine, St., 70
axis of evil, 30, 33, 54, 109–110,
122, 132, 144
Ayatollah Khomeini, 110, 151

B

Baghdad, xiv, 144
Balkans, 38, 153–156, 162, 182
Balkan wars, xiv, 153–156, 182
Barak, Ehud, 20
Belgium, 157
Belgrade, xv–xvi
bin Laden, Osama, xx, xxi,

xxvi–xxvii, 3–4, 6–7, 13–14, 16,
26, 39, 42–49, 54–56, 59–60, 62,
64–67, 92, 95, 99–100, 102, 108,
115, 121, 131, 140, 143, 161, 168
bio-war, 52–53, 102, 188
Booth, Ken, 166
Bosnia, xiv–xv, 89, 140, 149,
155–156, 165
Brazil, 29
Bush, President George W., xxii,
xxvi, 3,4, 7, 22, 30, 33, 40, 41,
50, 57, 65–67, 70, 73–75, 106,
108–109, 112–113, 116,
119–120, 125, 130–132, 137,
144, 158, 161, 183
Bush, Sr., President George, xii, 42, 50

C

Camp David II, 20
Carter, President Jimmy, xix,
155–156
Central America, 125, 158
Central Intelligence Agency (CIA),
xi, xx, 96
Chechnya, 162
Cheney, Vice President Dick, 103
China, xiv, xv,4, 32–33, 47, 87, 112,
148, 152, 158, 162, 174, 181
Chile, 156–157
Chomsky, Noam, 74, 155
Clinton, President Bill, xiii, xxv, 20,
50, 52, 152–153, 158
Cohen, Eliot, 32
cold war, xi–xiv, xvii, xviv, xxvi, 4–5,
27, 32, 36, 42, 70, 87, 96, 108,
114, 121, 137, 139, 147, 153,
171, 181, 186, 189
Colombia, 59, 80

Commonwealth Club, 125
Conetta, Carl, 68
containment, 55, 178
counterterrorism, xxv, xxvi, 6, 12,
  16, 43, 67, 77, 100, 106–107,
  109, 132, 170
Crime Against Humanity, 43, 77,
  95, 99, 118, 131, 153, 159
Crime Against the Peace, 133
Cuba, xx, 34, 92, 96, 106, 116, 148,
  149
  Fidel Castro, 149
  missile crisis, 106

D

Declaration of Independence,
  146–147
Defense Posture Statement, 5
Department of Defense, 37, 68, 76,
  138
  Defense Secretary Donald
    Rumsfield, 68, 103
Dergam, Raghida, 57
Duelfer, Charles, 144
Durban Conference on Racism, 159

E

Egypt, 113, 166
Einstein, Albert, 185
ethnic cleansing, 90, 153, 155, 182,
  187–188
Europe, 21, 24, 28, 33, 49, 76,
  84–85, 104, 111, 123–124, 129,
  135, 144–145, 152, 154,
  162–163, 174–175, 177
  European Court of Human
    Rights, 175
  European Parliament, 28, 175
  European Union, 21, 28, 175

F

Federal Bureau of Investigation
  (FBI), 75, 103
  Director Robert Mueller, 103
Friedman, Thomas, 25

G

General Assembly, 74, 120, 185
Geneva Conventions, xiii, xviii, 35,
  85, 114, 115, 116–118, 145
Geneva Protocols, 85
Genocide, 43–44, 95, 140, 153,
  154–156, 168, 182, 188
Germany, 26, 27, 80, 133, 179, 185
Giuliani, Mayor Rudy, 45
globalization, xiii, xxvi–xxvii, 4, 6–7,
  13, 17, 25, 27–29, 32–33, 36–37,
  40, 42, 65, 78, 81, 83, 88, 89–90,
  95, 108, 115, 129–130, 135, 137,
  143, 145–146, 159–161, 170,
  173–175, 177, 186–187
global warming, 174, 177
Gore, Vice President Al, 101
Great Britain, 50, 111, 132,
  156–157, 185
  House of Lords, 157
Great Depression, 136
Great Terror War, xxv, xxvi–xxvii,
  1–2, 7, 11, 16–17, 27, 29, 37, 38,
  51, 54, 57, 62, 73, 77, 81, 112,
  137, 143, 156
Grotius, Hugo, 83–84, 93
Ground Zero, 131, 159
Guantanamo Bay, xxvi, 35, 118,
  145, 164
  Camp X–Ray, 35, 118, 164
Gulf War, xii–xv, 42, 47–48, 51, 73,
  88–89, 110, 127, 137, 140

H

Habermas, Jurgen, 184
Hague, the, 85, 87

Peace Conferences, 85
Hamas, 142
Hezbollah, 142
human rights, xii, xiv, xv, 25, 27–29,
    31, 35–37, 58, 60, 62, 64, 66, 70,
    82–83, 85, 88–90, 105, 107,
    114–117, 119, 125, 135,
    146–157, 159–166, 168–170,
    172, 175, 181–182
Huntington, Samuel, 42
Hussein, Saddam, xiv, 24, 30, 51,
    110, 115, 125, 132, 144, 157, 174

I

Ignatieff, Michael, 147, 160
International Monetary Fund (IMF),
    28
India, 47, 55, 59, 61–62, 98,
    105–108, 111–113, 122, 142,
    162, 164
Indonesia, 59
International Committee of the Red
    Cross, xxvi
International Court of Justice, 6, 85
    Advisory Opinions, 6
International Covenant on Civil and
    Political Rights, 165
International Covenant on
    Economic, Social, and Cultural
    Rights, 165
International Criminal Court (ICC),
    87, 117, 149, 158, 165, 174
    Anti–Personnel Landmines Treaty,
    27
    Rome Treaty, 27
Immigration and Naturalization
    Service (INS), 167
intifada, 21
Iran, xviii, xx–xxii, 3,5, 20, 22–23,
    25, 34, 51, 106, 110, 132, 144, 151
    Iranian revolution, xviii, 151
    President Mohammed Khatami,
    23, 25

Iraq, xiii, xiv, xx, xxii, xxvii, 3, 5, 7,
    11–12, 18–20, 30, 33–34, 48–51,
    56, 60, 62, 83, 88, 93, 100, 110,
    122, 125–127, 132–133, 140,
    144, 149, 163, 183
Islam, xiv, xv, xx–xxiii, xxv, 3, 6,
    19–21, 23–25, 29, 34, 44–46, 49,
    55–58, 62, 64–65, 100, 105–106,
    129, 142, 151, 160–161, 163
Israel, xii, xiii, xviii, xxi, 19–24, 34,
    44, 48, 50, 55, 57, 76, 80, 91, 98,
    106–107, 109, 111–112, 114,
    142, 144, 146, 149, 164
    Six Day War, xviii, 114
Italy, 26
    Rome, 158

J

Jaish-I-Mohammed, 142
Japan, 1–2, 26, 33, 53, 60, 133,
    158, 171, 179, 185
    Hiroshima, 5, 185
al-Jazeera, 106
Jerusalem, 20, 22
jihad, xxv, 44, 46, 54–55, 95, 103,
    142
Jordan, 113
Juergensmeyer, Mark, 49
just-war doctrine, xxiv, 17, 66,
    69–71, 82–83, 85, 93–94,
    122–126, 178–179

K

Kabul, 169
Karzai, Hamid, 66
Kashmir, 108, 162, 164
Kenya, 7, 79
    1998 American embassy bombing,
    7, 79
King, Jr., Martin Luther, 173
Kissinger, Henry, 157, 174
Korea, 69, 139

Kosovo, xv–xvi, xxvii, 32, 50, 69,
    89–91, 140, 153, 156, 165, 81
    War, xv, 69, 181
    Independent International
      Commission on Kosovo, xvi, 90
Kuwait, xiii, 49–51, 88–89, 93
Kurds, xiv

L

Laqueur, Walter, 52
Latin America, 154
Lebanon, xviii, 80, 91
    Beirut, xviii
Lewis, Bernard, xxiv, 48–49, 100
Libya, xx, 34, 79
Lincoln, President Abraham, 146
Lindh, John Walker, 133–134, 164,
    167–168

M

Mandela, President Nelson, 189
megaterrorism, xvii, xxiv, xxvii, 3–4,
    7–19, 21, 30, 34–35, 38–60,
    62–63, 66–68, 70, 79–81, 83, 95,
    99, 104, 106, 117, 121–122, 128,
    132, 134, 140, 143, 154, 161,
    163–166, 168–170, 173, 176,
    178, 180–181, 183, 186–189
militarization of space, 19, 32, 83,
    89, 180, 187
Milosevic, Slobodan, 156, 165, 174
Moussaoui, Zacarias, 168–169
mujahedeen, xiv
Musharraf, General Pervez, 62, 111
McCarthy, Eugene and
    McCarthyism, xi, 171

N

NAFTA, 28
non-governmental organizations
    (NGOs), 150, 152
nationalism, 3, 33, 130, 134–135,

138, 142
National Review, 48
Native Americans, 136
NATO, xv– xvi, 32, 50, 90–91,
    155–156, 181
New York Times, 41
Nicaragua, xviii, 86–87, 96
    Contras, xviv
Nixon, President Richard, 172
North Korea, xx, 5, 34, 110, 132,
    144, 149
Northern Alliance, 63, 65, 105, 133,
    168
Northern Ireland (Good Friday
    Agreement), 45
Nuremburg obligation, 87, 133

O

occupied territories (Palestinian), xiii,
    xviii, 19, 34, 48, 56, 113–114,
    164
oil, xiii, xxvi, 13, 17, 24–25, 45, 48,
    50, 80, 83, 113, 114
Oklahoma City terrorist attack, 26,
    38
    Timothy McVeigh, 26
Oslo Peace Process, 20, 45
Omar, Mullah Mohammed, 7, 92
Operation Enduring Freedom, xxvi, 68
Operation Infinite Justice, xxvi, 108

P

Padilla, Jose, 164, 167
Pakistan, 14, 16, 61–62, 65,
    104–107, 111–114, 122, 158,
    178
Palestine, xii, xiii, xviii–xviv, xxi,
    19–24, 34, 45, 48, 56, 100, 106,
    108, 112–114, 142, 146, 164
patriotism, 2–3, 34, 129, 131–147,
    167, 173
Pearl Harbor, 1–2, 53, 60, 102

Philippines, the, 16, 59
Pinochet, General Augusto,
156–157, 165, 174
Pinsky, Robert, 129
Pipes, Daniel, xxv
pollution, 177
prisoners of war (POWs), 35, 116, 179
Project on Defense Alternatives
(Cambridge, MA), 68

Q

al-Qaeda, xxi–xxvii, 1,4, 6–19, 26,
30–31, 33, 35–38, 40, 42–44, 49,
51–52, 54–56, 58–62, 65–68, 71,
73, 75, 77–80, 82, 91–92, 94,
99–106, 108, 110–111, 113,
115–118, 120–122, 124–126,
131–132, 138, 140, 142,
144–145, 147, 151, 160, 164,
166, 168, 173, 177–179,
186–187

R

Reagan, President Ronald, xviii, xviv,
xx, 79, 132, 137
Reagan Doctrine, xviv, 121
Reisman, Michael, 184
Revolutionary War, 147
rogue states, xix, 6, 30, 67, 78, 88,
109, 111–112, 114, 149, 180
Roosevelt, President Franklin
Delano, 1
Rose, Sir Michael, 132
Rouleau, Eric, 49
Rushdie, Salman, 57
Russia (see also Soviet Union), xv, 4,
21, 33, 46, 55–56, 112, 162, 173
Rwanda, xv, 87, 155–156

S

Said, Edward W., 49
Saigon, xvi

Saudi Arabia, xx, xxi, 3,7, 42, 56,
101
1996 Khobar Towers bombing
(Dhahran), 7, 42
School of the Americas, 96
Serbia, xiv, xvi, 50, 91, 155–156
Senate Foreign Relations Committee,
133
sharia, 65
Sharon, Ariel, 21–22, 34, 106, 109,
112, 157, 174
smart bombs, 89
Somalia, 16, 47, 88, 135, 140, 155
South Africa, 36, 121, 152, 154
Soviet Union, xiv, xviv, xx, 36, 47,
64, 103, 132–133, 137, 140, 154,
186
Spain, 39, 60, 156
Srebrenica, xiv, 155
State of the Union Address, 109, 132
Sudan, xxv, 34, 79, 91
Switzerland, 158
Syria, 34

T

Taba, 20
Taliban, xxii, xxvi, 7, 9, 14, 30,
35–36, 44, 46, 59, 62, 64–67, 70,
73, 80, 91–95, 101, 105–106,
109, 115, 116–118, 120–121,
125, 131, 133, 145, 167, 169,
179
Tanzania, 7, 79
1998 American Embassy
bombing, 7, 79
terrorism and terrorists (see also
megaterrorism), xvii–xxviii, 1–15,
18–19, 21, 24, 26–33, 35–73,
73–75, 77–83, 91–114, 117–134,
136, 138, 140–149, 152,
154–157, 159–161, 163–171,
173, 175–181, 183, 186–189
definitions, xviii, xviv, 7–8, 12,

52–53, 75–77
"freedom fighters," xviv, 96, 121
in French Revolution, xviv, 76
global terrorism, xxii–xxviii, 2, 6,
    10–11, 18, 27, 29, 39, 44, 54,
    66, 81, 91, 102, 105, 111,
    117–118, 137, 140, 156, 159
Palestinian, xiii, xviii, xviv
in self–determination struggles,
    xxiv, 45, 57, 77, 108, 122, 142
September 11 and, xi, xvii, xviv,
    xxi–xxiv, xxvi, xxviii, 1–8, 12–14,
    16–19, 21, 24, 28, 30–33,
    35–44, 47–51, 53–58, 59–61,
    63–67, 69, 73–75, 77–83,
    93–103, 105–108, 110–112,
    114, 118–134, 136, 138,
    140–149, 152, 154–157,
    159–161, 163, 166–171, 173,
    175–177, 179, 181, 183,
    186–187, 189
Thirty Years War, 84
Tibet, 162
Tobin Tax, xv
Tora Bora caves, 62, 104, 113
Turkey, 28, 149

U

unilateralism, 97, 110–111, 119,
    132
United Nations, xii–xvi, xviii,
    xxiv–xv, 6, 9–10, 12, 15–18,
    20–22, 24, 27–31, 50–51, 56,
    59–60, 64, 67, 71, 73–74, 82,
    86–87, 90–951 93–94, 96, 99,
    105, 109–111, 114, 119–124,
    126–127, 132, 135–137, 139,
    149–150, 153, 155–166, 165,
    171, 175, 177, 181–182
Ambassador Negroponte, 120
charter, xvii, xxiv, 10, 17, 71, 86,
    90, 93, 96, 111, 126, 155,
    171, 177, 181

Human Rights Commission, 64
resolutions about September 11,
    15, 17, 22, 119
Security Council, xv–xvi, 9, 15,
    22, 59, 74, 86–87, 90–91,
    119–123, 127, 139, 156
US Patriots Act, 167
US government, xi, xvii–xxvii, 1–5,
    7–8, 10–14, 16–22, 29, 30–32,
    34, 39, 48, 52–53, 54, 58–67,
    70–71, 73, 76–77, 80, 82–83, 86,
    88–89, 94, 96–100, 102–103,
    105, 107, 112, 114, 116–117,
    120–121, 125, 127, 133–135,
    141–142, 149, 152, 155, 158,
    161, 163–164, 166, 168,
    170–172, 175, 180, 183,
    186–187
Bush administration, xxii, xxvii, 3,
    7, 9, 11, 21, 63–64, 97, 102,
    107, 142, 163
Democratic Party, 133, 144–145
policy, xiv, xvii–xviii, xx, xxii–xxiii,
    2–3, 17, 20–21, 38, 57–59,
    63, 67, 76–77, 80, 83, 96,
    120, 125, 140, 147, 151–152,
    155, 166, 170–172
Republican Party, 145
Supreme Court, 2
war on terrorism, xxii, xxv–xxvii,
    1–2, 7, 11, 16–17, 27, 29, 54,
    57, 62, 73, 77, 81, 98, 109–110,
    112–113, 120, 156
White House, xiii, xxiv, 1, 3–4,
    13–14, 18, 22, 32, 48, 52, 54,
    70, 75, 97, 112–113, 133–134,
    141, 151, 158, 183
Universal Declaration of Human
Rights, 58, 150–151

V

Versailles Peace Treaty, 179
Vietnam syndrome, xii, xvi, 88, 103,

Vietnam War, xi–xiv, xxviii, 68–69,
    87–88, 127, 135, 139, 142, 151,
    172

W

Walzer, Michael, 69
War and Peace, 189
Washington consensus, xii, 28
Watergate, 172
weapons of mass destruction
    (WMD), xii, xiii, xx, xxvii, 4–6,
    20, 24, 32, 51, 52–54, 62–63, 68,
    87–89, 94, 102–103, 105,
    110–112, 123–124, 139, 144,
    171, 178, 102–103, 105, 111,
    123, 139, 144, 171, 178, 181,
    185–188
Westphalia, 83–84, 92–93, 176,
    178–180, 183
World Bank, 28, 31
World Court, 86, 123, 157, 185
    Advisory Opinion, 123
World Ecomomic Forum, 28
World Social Forum, 29
World Trade Center (WTC), 38–40,
    69, 130
World Trade Organization (WTO),
    28, 31
World War I, 85, 137
World War II, xi, 1, 69, 85, 132,
    137, 150, 159, 171, 179, 185

Y

Yemen, 7
    attack on USS Cole, 7, 42, 75
Y2K, 189
Yugoslavia, xiv, 87, 90, 153, 156